God of Justice and Mercy

A Theological Commentary on Judges

Isabelle M. Hamley

scm press

Published in 2021 by SCM Press
Editorial office
3rd Floor, Invicta House,
108–114 Golden Lane,
London EC1Y 0TG, UK
www.scmpress.co.uk

SCM Press is an imprint of Hymns Ancient & Modern Ltd
(a registered charity)

British Library Cataloguing in Publication data
A catalogue record for this book is available
from the British Library

978-0-334-06020-8

Typeset by Regent Typesetting

Contents

To Paul and Aelwen

Foreword

By Justin Welby, Archbishop of Canterbury

Who would ever choose to write a commentary on Judges? I was recently interviewed by a Christian journalist who asked me to reflect on some public events at the time. I started the reflection with the book of Judges. She looked astonished. 'Judges? We have been doing these interviews for years and nobody has ever chosen a text from Judges!'

Judges is notoriously the darkest place of the Old Testament. Few preachers venture there unless well armoured with proof texts or critical thinking, or simply extracting their favourite stories. Samson and Delilah may be a great tale, but a moment's close examination reveals a psychopath entrapped by stupidity and greed. We may ourselves meet people who, like Jael, we might (metaphorically) desire to pin to the ground with a tent peg, but we don't really think of it as an improving tale. The choir boys may relish the reading about the king so fat that the sword stuck into him disappeared, but the compilers of lectionaries tend to leave it out. And those are the jolly bits. Our hearts break at the sacrifice of his daughter by the foolish Jephthah and we recoil at the horrific rape and butchery of the concubine in the last three chapters. Even the compiler of Judges shares this view, exclaiming several times, 'There was no King in Israel in those days. Everyone did what was right in their own eyes.'

There are moments of far deeper lament in the Bible, moments when the presence of darkness is more willingly recognized; Lamentations and Job are good examples. But there is nowhere else that seems to bring us into such close contact with the harshest of reality and with a God who seems to inhabit this desert, this rock-strewn landscape of wild humans and hideous actions done with the intensest cruelty.

Yet Isabelle Hamley has produced a commentary that is riveting to read, exciting to think about and profoundly instructive for anyone who takes scripture seriously.

Which she does – I know that from working alongside her for almost four years. This commentary is very much centred on the meaning of the text and on the theological conundrums that it exposes and calls into clarity. Very quickly the reader discovers that this is not the collected myths of a far away people more than 3,000 years ago of whom we know little. It is a King Lear-like unpacking of the human character in relationship to God, amidst anarchy, cruelty and chaos. It is the stuff of our daily news and websites. It is human reality.

Isabelle combines a number of questions and unpacks not only what the text says but also what it chooses to leave out. She points to the increasing silence of women as they are shut out of an utterly dysfunctional society and become victims not agents – or so it is thought, wrongly. The development of the narrative is alive and shows a master refactor, a storyteller of genius whose work brings us face to face with God when the world is at its worst in terms of injustice.

She unpacks the mystery of the presence, the absence and the attitudes of God. We are drawn into seeing the tensions between law and grace, the Deuteronomic consequentialism of unfaithful actions leading to bad results, combined with the God who is moved by compassion for his wicked and wandering people.

Above all, she reveals the key role of Judges in demonstrating that God is to be trusted and is to be obeyed and what happens in a society that forgets the former and chooses to ignore the latter.

This book has had a profound impact on my thinking. I hope it brings Judges back to the mainstream of our preaching and teaching of scripture.

Introduction

The book of Judges is not the first place most people would go to when opening the Bible. Many preachers shy away from its stories of blood and gore, often dismissed as advocating war and violence, some even suggesting it should be banned from liturgical use. Heavily edited stories occasionally make their way into public worship, but overall, Judges has been spurned by worshippers and interpreters alike. A regaining of interest in recent years has seen feminist critics noting the high proportion of female characters and their increasingly abusive treatment. Yet Judges is still often shunned in the process of reading canonically and theologically. The paucity of interaction with Yahweh and the lack of narratorial, theological or ethical commentary have no doubt contributed to the fate of Judges in the Christian theological imagination, together with ongoing disputes around its historicity, composition and authorship. Nevertheless, many thematic threads in Judges resonate with timeless questions: the difficulty of finding socio-political systems that enable the flourishing of all; corruption of local and national leadership; the problematic nature of political and military power; ethnic, land-based and socio-economic tensions; war and armed conflict; the inability of violence to achieve lasting peace; abuses of power in private and public settings; child abuse; domestic abuse; sexual violence; scapegoating and refusal of accountability; individualism and the breakdown of social cohesion; moral and religious confusion. The list is not exhaustive but marks out Judges as deeply embedded in the realities of human life. Since the text is posited as a sacred text, part of the Jewish and Christian canons, it is crucial to ask: How does Judges speak of God, humanity and the relationship between them?

This book is an attempt to answer this question; the exploration will inevitably be limited and non-exhaustive, shaped by my cultural, philosophical and theological context, as commentaries always are. While I will pay close attention to the text and its literary construction to discern intended meaning, my readings will nevertheless be shaped by the questions that I ask, and readers will therefore find that writers from different times, places, genders and so on explore different aspects and come to different conclusions. Theology is something we do as a Church, and diverse voices are crucial in enabling all of us to discover more of the text than we would on our own. I will of course interact with a wide range of critics, but would encourage readers to read widely, comparatively and openly. I will focus very specifically on a theological interpretation of the text; I will not deal at length with matters of sources, dating, authorship and composition, unless they are crucial to a specific point of interpretation, not because these things do not matter but because they are not the focus of this particular volume and have been explored in great depth elsewhere. My starting point will be the text as received, as part of the Christian canon, redacted in its most common form.

Historical–critical considerations

Questions of Judges' place in the canon inevitably lead to questions of dating and positioning of texts with respect to one another, explored through historical–critical methods. These studies often dismiss parts of the book, such as chapters 19—21, as an appendix, historically fanciful and largely irrelevant (e.g. Boling, 1975; Soggin, 1981). Polzin (1980, p. 8) critiques the pervasiveness of the historical–critical method. While its proponents rightly argue that it stops us modernizing the text too quickly, the search for an original author and meaning itself reveals a central contemporary bias, the belief in objectivity and the superiority of historical–critical methods in yielding unbiased interpretation. Objectivity is impossible for human beings situated in and limited by time and place. However, texts are written by real people seeking to communicate. Speech-turned-text is a manifestation of the otherness of those who first uttered it. It may be fixed, it may be misinterpreted, it may prevent reciprocal exchanges. But it still remains a manifestation of another consciousness that must be respected and encountered as 'other', a consciousness embedded into a certain time and place, with its own rules of discourse and life. Recognizing this otherness is as important as recognizing our own. Given its various redactions, the biblical text bears the mark of multiple consciousnesses; but at some point, redactions finished, the text was deemed final and became part of a growing canonical collection. While successive viewpoints and theologies will have shaped the evolution of the text until its final form, Judges as *sacred text*, is found only in this final form, its final editor, consciously and unconsciously, shaping the overall intent and meaning. That the text is part of the canon adds a further layer to interpretation by implying some form of divine inspiration, which has profound implications for interpretation. The weight of being 'sacred' adds an enormous capacity for the text to be used for good or ill.

The textual history of Judges adds to the complexity, since there are two Septuagint (LXX) versions, Alexandrinus (A) and Vaticanus (B), with significant differences between them and LXX^{A} being much closer to the Masoretic Text (MT). The differences, however, have little theological impact. The Targum, Peshitta and Vulgate generally follow MT and most of the differences in LXX are either facilitations or regular errors (see the BHQ (Biblica Hebraica Quinta) critical apparatus for extensive study of these). As such, I will take MT as my base text and follow the linguistic and textual choices of BHQ.

Defining the base text in terms of linguistics is a starting point; the next question is what type of text it is, with the caveat that to define genre too tightly risks restricting vistas for interpretation. Is this an 'example' text, a warning, a model, a commentary? Genre is not easy to define across time and interpreters have long disagreed over Judges: is it a historical novel, built around 'exemplary figures from popular folklore', distanced from the historical real by humour and irony (Abadie,

2011, p. 13), similar to Bal's historiography (1988a, p. 17)? A tragedy recounting the fall of Israel as the central character (Heller, 2011, p. 8)? A realistic, gritty portrayal, between the stylized depiction of Joshua's success and the candid portrayal of David (Boling 1975, p. 29)? Or pure literary creation, with little link to actual 'history' (Brettler, 2002)? What is clear is that Judges exceeds its themes and cannot be contained in an easily defined category. It displays a collection of genres: conquest and political rule annals; paraenetic narrative; theological exposition; comedy; tragedy; epic narratives; historical records; political speech; riddles; poetry. Mythological and folk-tale elements lead some to term it fiction, but this ignores vast swathes of the book and the distance between ancient and modern concepts of history. Judges' setting in the Former Prophets places it within homiletic and paraenetic agendas: a persuasive work, to be read within a religious context, rather than purely historical or political. Paying attention to the multiplicity of genres avoids over-concentrating on the political affairs of men and overlooking Judges' depiction of the fullness of life. Despite its generic complexity, Judges exhibits the usual characteristics of Hebrew narrative: an omniscient, reliable narrator and restraint in narration. Specific characteristics include humour as a weapon of the oppressed, the pervasive use of irony, and intertextual references as the main vehicle for narratorial evaluation. Ambiguity and reticence are key to a narrative strategy that invites readers to ponder the text for themselves.

Regarding historicity, there are few extra-biblical sources about Israel in the latter half of the second millennium BC, making judgements difficult. The Menerptah stele refers to Israel as a people group, but not a geographical area, and the Armana letters depict Canaan as a territory divided into small city-states with turbulent and competitive relationships (Block, 1999, p. 27). The composition of Judges suggests an amalgam of material from different times drawn together by later editors. There is no reason to dismiss the possibility that Judges opens a window onto the time between conquest and monarchy, even if not 'history' in contemporary terms. It is well-established that the final form was arrived at much later, with different time frames mentioned as within the text itself (1.12; 18.30). Critics have tried to discern various editions by proposing the relevance of different readings: early in the monarchy for a Benjamin/Judah polemic, later in the monarchy for a Rehoboam/Jeroboam polemic, or around the time of Hezekiah if explaining the fall of the Northern Kingdom. However, all these are conjectures that reduce the meaning of the book rather than allow it to be read differently in different times. The question is whether there are key themes that have theological coherence, albeit with varying degrees of prominence and nuances depending on the time of reception.

Composition

Judges is not primarily organized chronologically, which strengthens the evaluation of its main aims as theological and homiletic rather than purely historical. It is organized in cycles, concentrating on key figures in different geographical areas. The final two stories bear time markers suggesting an early date, giving the impression of a return to the beginning, a pervasive turning away from Yahweh that affects all Israel at every moment. Generally, scholars agree on a three-part division, with introductory material that sets the overarching themes (1.1—3.6), followed by the main body of the book, organized in major and minor cycles, finishing with an epilogue (17—21). The prologue builds a framework for interpretation and expectations of a repeating behaviour cycle: sin-punishment-crying out-deliverance. General consensus is that Judges went through successive redactions, starting with separate stories of local heroes collected together in ways that transformed local hero stories into stories of national deliverers, whose plot reflected the prologue's cycle (Butler, 2009, pp. xlv–xlviii). The collection was then brought into the wider story of Israel as an account of the period between the Conquest and the monarchy. The dating of different stages and the overall number of redactions is widely disputed – at the apex of the David/Solomon monarchy, in the reign of Josiah, or in a post-exilic community (Wong, 2006, p. 199), with varied motives implied, whether disappointment with the monarchy, explaining the exile, or warning a fragile post-exilic community (García Bachmann, 2018, p. xlii). Diachronic readings shed little light on the canonical and theological meaning of the text: they tend to fragment it and dismiss elements considered appendiceal or later additions. While dates and sources were a primary focus of study for a long time, the wide variety of opinions, ever-increasing fragmentation of the text and dismissal of problematic elements risk making it impossible to consider the text's theology (however untidy), and sometimes a contemptuous tendency to categorize ancient writers as less skilled or intentional than contemporary ones.

Diachronic readings alert us to cultural conditioning – the culture and social lives of the late Bronze Age cannot be treated as identical to those of a post-exilic redactor. The text itself reminds us that it looks back on a former time through the lens of a new present: 'in those days ...' (19.1). Synchronic readings, in contrast, highlight overall thematic coherence and organization. Judges can then be read as a gradually worsening picture of tribes struggling to actualize the unified nation portrayed at the end of Joshua, and their increasing assimilation to the surrounding culture. As Israel becomes Canaanized, its identity and distinctiveness ebb away, and it becomes vulnerable internally and externally. A synchronic reading magnifies the issue of identity of the nation, played out in the individual lives of its people, reframed and understood by a later writer. The question is deeply theological, since Israel's identity is relationally given by Yahweh and derives from Yahweh's own character, epitomized by the twin drivers of justice and mercy.

While the idea of a worsening spiral undergirds most synchronic studies (Block, 1999; Butler, 2009; Klein, 1989; Schneider, 1999; Webb, 1987), all writers argue for deeper coherence through themes, specialized terminology and narrative modes. The many themes include a critique of leadership, identity, family and gender relations; conflict between tribes, the Israel/Yahweh relationship, and an exploration of justice, human and divine, and its relationship to mercy and compassion.

Why 'judges'?

Judges takes its name from an activity – although this activity is little mentioned and unclear in focus. In the wider Old Testament, the root *šfṭ* means to judge, execute judgement, govern, exercise leadership. The horizon of the term, whether applied restrictively to judicial matters or more widely to leadership and governance, focuses on what brings about justice in its various aspects (Schultz, 1997, pp. 213–20). The related word *mišpāt*, often translated as 'justice' and ubiquitous in the law, the prophets and wisdom literature, only occurs three times in Judges, once with a judicial meaning (4.5) and twice meaning way, manner (13.12 and 18.7); but the concept threads itself through the specific designation of the leaders. The title of the book therefore alludes to the link between leadership and justice, Yahweh as ultimate judge, and how divine and human justice relate. Individual leaders are not identified as judges: the *title* is only applied to Yahweh (11.27), though the prologue mentions Yahweh 'raising judges who delivered them'. Not all judges are said to deliver, and not all deliverers judge: Othniel and Tola both judge and deliver; Deborah, Jephthah, Jair, Ibzan, Elon and Abdon judge but do not deliver; Shamgar and Gideon deliver but do not judge; Samson is predicted to deliver, but the text never says he did, though he does judge; Abimelech and Barak do neither: Yahweh does both. Judging and delivering are strongly linked, but not co-terminous. The verbal form of judging, *šāfat*, is used of the activity of leaders – Othniel, Deborah, Jephthah, Samson, Tola, Jair, Ibzan, Elon and Abdon, yet only Deborah exercises her role in a judicial position and the word is absent from 17—21. The questionable character of those said to 'judge' Israel further adds to the confusion. They may be epic heroes who lead through charisma, but they consistently fail to address the enemy within: idolatry, spiritual decay and injustice.

To 'judge' is to exercise some form of leadership, with a focus on justice, hence deliverance, and including peace-time governance. The term is applied beyond Judges to Eli and Samuel (1 Sam. 4.18; 7.6); Samuel is included in a list of judges alongside Gideon, Barak and Jephthah in 1 Samuel 12.11. Judgeship is not inherited, but rooted in Yahweh's response to Israel's oppression. Furthermore, Othniel, Jephthah and Samson receive the gift of the 'Spirit of Yahweh' as they go into various battles, a gift specifically linked to personal empowerment. Judges therefore emerge as figures from a specific time in Israel's history, when the nation had not fully coalesced into a political state or settled within defined borders and political and military leadership went hand in hand. The text gives a window onto this unsettled period, with leaders who are far from perfect but reflect the fact that Yahweh works with Israel in grace. As such, Judges works within the bigger story of Scripture as one chapter, told retrospectively, during which Israel rejects Yahweh as king, worships other gods and loses its distinctiveness. This sets the scene for the failure of the monarchy and the Exile. The failure of human saviours in Judges is part of the pattern that lays the foundation for the coming of Jesus as true saviour and king, who undermines human notions of power and redefines the divine–human relationship. Judges draws on previous covenantal history and assumes what has come before – the conquest of Joshua, the Exodus, the legal material – explicitly and through intertextual parallels. Judges and its events rarely figure in the rest of Scripture. 1 Samuel 12 treats Yahweh raising deliverers as paradigmatic of his grace and source of hope for the present. Psalms 78 and 106 use the settlement period within a wider recounting of Israel's history to stress a consistent pattern of rebellion, sin, divine anger, punishment and deliverance. Psalm 83 draws on Yahweh's intervention to deliver Israel in Judges as a basis for appealing to Yahweh in the present. Hosea refers to the evil of Gibeah (Judg. 19) as typical of that historical period (Hos. 9.9; 10.9). The period of the Judges is treated as paradigmatic of Israel's sin and Yahweh's deliverance. The New Testament only mentions Judges in Hebrews 11.32, the list of 'heroes of faith'. The overall argument of this chapter is to bring out the weakness or powerlessness of human beings, and God nevertheless working with and through them to achieve his purposes. Gideon, Barak, Samson and Jephthah are no more perfect than Abraham (who did not act justly with Hagar, Sarah and Ishmael), Moses (who murdered an Egyptian) or David (adulterer and murderer). These men are not included because they were heroes and perfect followers, but precisely because they were not. Whatever faith they had was enough and Yahweh worked with them. The canon encourages a balanced appraisal of leaders, recognizing their flaws yet not writing them off, since Yahweh himself has not. The ability to hang on to the good and cast the story under the sign of grace is deeply counter-cultural for today. Yet Scripture itself gives a theological direction for interpretation that demands that we hold grace and justice firmly together.

Themes in Judges

The most salient aspect of interpretation over the centuries has been the tendency to focus the story through the lens of politics and the affairs of men, which occludes the reality of women's lives despite their prominence in the narrative, and prevents a discussion of ethical and moral norms of behaviour for gender relations. This tendency also clouds over the many themes interwoven in individual stories and fails to attend to the narrator's careful portrayal of the interaction between the personal and the political, the public and the private.

Becoming Israel

As Israel tries to settle the land and move towards living in peace, what it means to be Israel comes into sharp focus socially, politically and religiously. In Sinai, Israel was given an identity as Yahweh's people, with laws to shape their life together. Judges explores the liminal state between moving towards the Promised Land and having moved in: Israel and the Canaanites are still largely cohabiting; territory is gained and lost; Israel's composition is fluid, with porous boundaries not entirely shaped by ethnicity. Whether Israel will remain distinct or merge with Canaan is an ever-present question. This concern shows itself in the frequent use of the word 'Israel', multiple pan-Israelite expressions, naming of the tribes and differentiating Israel from the people of the land. Conflict between the tribes is part of working out how they should relate and what holds them together, with tension between blind loyalty to the in-group and faithfulness to the covenant as an organizing principle. Judges chronicles a nation's struggle to self-define (and *self*-defining is part of the problem). It is a historical commentary on the difficult birth of a nation, with its constant reconfiguration of boundaries, complex negotiation of shared values, and ambivalence about religious and cultural allegiance. That Israel does not disappear at this point is consistently attributed to Yahweh's deliverance: Israel is a work of grace. Judges is therefore a theological and political interpretation of who Israel is and gives a window onto a messy reality that far exceeds a neat theological narrative. Keeping these two arcs in mind is essential in being faithful to the text and the historical realities that gave birth to it, but are transformed and theologized through it.

Struggles to define Israel's identity go hand-in-hand with a struggle with the identity of the Other, whether the people of the land or Israelites who depart from emerging cultural norms. The boundary between insider and outsider is not always clear, despite attempts at sharp differentiation between self and other. Sharp differentiation makes it easier to fight for the land, but harder to understand why intermingling is so attractive. Israel is faced with the questions of any immigrant group: can they thrive and be themselves without either annihilating or assimilating with the other? While the narrative often seems binary, completely erasing the perspective of the other, the counter-narrative of the inclusion of the stranger, present in Joshua, continues in Judges and challenges easy recourse to the idea that 'Israel' has impenetrable boundaries. Israel and the Canaanites take turns in Judges being the oppressed and the oppressors, Yahweh does not consistently side with Israel, and the narrator emphasizes that being the people of Yahweh is not primarily about ethnicity but about belonging to a covenant large enough to accommodate others who wish to enter. Israel and the Canaanites are both self and other, capable of both good and evil. Ultimately the question is how Israel can form a constructive distinctive identity, one built on Yahweh's gift, rather than over and against an excluded 'other'.

Leadership

Judges opens and closes with leadership questions: 'Who is going to go first?' (1.1 and 20.18). In between, the narrator explores many configurations of leadership: how leaders get to office, their relationship with Yahweh, their character and motivations, their relative power before and after battle, and their strengths and frailties. The prologue offers a paradigm for competent, godly leadership in Joshua and Caleb, while the epilogue reverses the image, with disorganized, nameless leadership, without clear mandate, taking Israel to self-destruction. Judges does not favour one configuration of power as 'the' way to lead a nation; instead, it explores the pitfalls of leadership and the ever-present threat of abuses of power, so that what matters is not whether Israel has a judge or a king, but what kind of judge or king they have, and what the people's expectations are. It is the character of leaders and those they lead that exercises the narrator, though some configurations of power, like Canaanite kingship, are portrayed as inherently prone to abuse.

Critics focusing on politics often argue that Judges is a pro-monarchic polemic in its depiction of a lawless Israel when 'there was no king' and, furthermore, anti-Saulide and pro-Davidic (Amit, 1999; Brettler, 2002; Butler, 2009; Frolov, 2012; O'Connell, 1995). Frolov (2012, p. 322) argues that the Gibeah affair would have been less likely to occur under a king, would have been dealt with swiftly if it had, and a Gibeonite rebellion would have been quashed easily by a professional army. The record of Israelite kingship hardly reinforces his case, since sexual violence, abuse, idolatry, rebellions and civil war occur with alarming regularity in Samuel and Kings. Furthermore, kingship hardly gets a good press in Judges, consistently associated as it is with oppressive Canaanite practices. Arguing that Judges is unswervingly pro-monarchic fails to attend to the text, and to the likelihood of an exilic/postexilic redaction, which would inevitably consider the failure of the monarchy. Judges' approach to leadership is cautious about the elevation of leaders, keen to limit their power, and emphasizes the need for nation and leader to be equally committed to Yahweh as overall king and the covenant as their organizing principle: whenever they depart from covenantal life, no matter what political configuration they espouse, disaster awaits.

Covenant and the life of faith

A theme conspicuous in its paucity is that of Israel's spirituality and participation in organized religion. While the narrator points to the nation's idolatry, there is no response of repentance and judges fail to address moral decay and even lead the nation further away from covenantal life. Public worship is reduced to pragmatic acts to appease Yahweh in times of national crisis. The prologue's covenantal background sharpens the absence of covenantal living in the rest of the book. Increasingly, religion becomes a matter of individual choice, often linked to quasi-magical beliefs and treating Yahweh as a tribal god that the people attempt to bribe and manipulate. The regular repetition of 'Israel did evil in the eyes of Yahweh' underlies this state of affairs. 'Evil' is not reduced to a spiritual category or idolatry; instead, Judges chronicles the pervasive breakdown of all social structures (nation, clan, tribe, and family) as the people move away from Yahweh. Just as covenant and salvation shape the whole of life, so does sin, and no area remains untouched. Hence the conjunction of public and private, of politic and domestic life, is crucial to the theology of Judges. As the people lose their focus on Yahweh and allegiance to the covenant, the entire nation suffers, starting with its most vulnerable members.

Violence

Judges is a violent book. It displays war violence, sexual and family violence, verbal and psychological violence. Defining violence with respect to biblical texts is not straightforward, given the lack of an equivalent conceptual word. Reeder (2012, p. 5) argues that in Scripture, legitimate or legal violence is not strictly speaking considered violence; violence is the purview of the unrighteous, usually associated with oppression, injustice and wickedness. Hence Hebrew words for violence do not cover actions prescribed by law in dealing with sinful behaviour. The words that most closely match our current understanding of violence include *ḥāmās* (Gen. 6.11, 13; 49.5; Ex. 23.1; Deut. 19.6; Judg. 9.24; Ps. 11.5; Prov. 10.6; Isa. 53.9; 59.6), *pārîṣ* (Ps. 17.4; Ezek. 18.10) and *šōd* (Prov. 21.7; 24.2; Isa. 16.4; 22.4; 60.18; Jer. 48.3; Amos 5.9), none of which cover legally sanctioned violence. *Ḥāmās*, the most common, almost always describes 'an action perpetrated with a disproportionate share of power' (Lynch, 2020, p. 254), linking violence to injustice. Injustice and wrongful violence are then symbolically pitted against rightful force for the sake of justice. This is clear in Judges' repeated attacks on cities as the symbol of Canaan. The cities represent higher power, better technology, a more comfortable lifestyle, and are characterized by unjust kings reigning in them. Key cities are targeted, with no account of systematic attacks on small villages. Judges' violence symbolizes the importance of justice, and Yahweh's rooting out of unjust communities. Judges is written largely from the perspective of the underdog fighting a more powerful enemy that threatens its very life, a feature that can on the one hand risk condoning or exalting violent action, yet on the other should preclude its easy appropriation by later, powerful readers (though it has not).

Judges itself problematizes what is legitimate or illegitimate violence. While it largely shows violence as part of a struggle between a smaller, oppressed nation and a stronger enemy, it also exposes acts of particular barbarity by Israel against enemies and against Israel's own people. As the story progresses, a space opens for questioning violence as a whole, and the links between legitimized violence and other forms of violence. Violence and war are symptoms of the deeper fragmentation of Israel's identity and its increasingly destructive individualism.

In addition, in the context of the canon, the type of violence seen in Judges and Joshua is not portrayed as paradigmatic, or prescribed for all times. God's relationship to violence is multifaceted and complex, and includes deep lament at human violence and at the necessity of divine intervention; time and again, Yahweh is said to refrain from violence in response to human actions, and divine pathos is foregrounded, suggesting that Yahweh makes himself vulnerable in relation to human beings, and ultimately takes the consequences of violence on himself, in a motif that culminates in the Gospels.

Gender

Feminist critics have noted the preponderance of female characters in Judges, in particular named characters (Klein, 1993, pp. 24–26). Women often play the role expected of them, creating relationships between men, offering doorways in and out of conflict, yet they are not mere narrative foils. Women at the beginning are epitomized by Achsah and Deborah: confident, moving into public spaces, initiating dialogue, living in a patriarchal culture but working within it with agency and power of their own. As covenantal life breaks down, domestic relationships worsen, women disappear from public spaces and lose speech and names. Women are neither silent nor nameless as a rule in Judges: they *gradually* slip into silence and namelessness, as their precarious status in a patriarchal world makes them more vulnerable. To move away from the covenant exposes the most vulnerable members of society to abuse first. Women embody the reality and consequences of Israel's spiritual, moral and social deterioration. Yet despite their prominence, women have often been erased in the work of commentators because of a consistent focus on political and historical matters.

While the context of Judges is inevitably a deeply patriarchal society, and limits the reality and imagination of characters, narrator, writers and editors, this does not mean that the narrator accepts the ambient culture or condones its abuses, even less that Scripture as a whole condones or prescribes such culture. In Judges, the narrative itself undermines underlying principles of patriarchy, particularly in relation to hegemonic masculinity. Biblical culture(s) is therefore neither uniform nor consistent – like any culture. Clear aspects of patriarchy, different forms of patriarchy, and counter-currents to patriarchy therefore overlap into a complex and fluid picture that resists easy appropriation. The narrator's attention to gender relations, however, opens up the possibility that patriarchy and its consequences may be questioned, with a searing critique of hegemonic masculinity epitomized by the warrior-type, whose war ethic eventually leads Israel to turn on itself, victimize women, and massacre its own people.

God of justice and mercy

Yahweh often only has a walk-on part in Judges, appearing seldom and consulted infrequently, though his shadow shapes the entire story, his portrayal caught between narrator and character perspectives. The narrator portrays Yahweh as orchestrating events behind the scenes, deeply involved in human history yet rarely recognized by a people who have not been formed in the ways of the Lord. Yahweh speaks to his people and makes his will known through general covenantal principles and specific directions regarding battle, in prophets and messengers and responding to prayer and enquiries. He musters the natural world in displays of transcendence, yet chooses to work in partnership with human beings so that there is a constant interplay between divine and human will. Human unwillingness to work with Yahweh is met with divine pathos, manifested in anger, pain and compassion. Yahweh works with human beings as they are, sharing in the pain caused by brokenness and sin. This acceptance of the reality of the human predicament leads to a relationship built equally on justice and grace. Yahweh holds his people responsible, but has compassion for their weakness and pain. The pattern of Yahweh's involvement in Israel is one of dogged determination to preserve the nation while still granting them the freedom to walk away. When they do, the divine presence fades and Israel is left to the mercy of their enemies, until Yahweh's own mercy prompts him to rescue them even when Israel does not ask for it. Covenant and election by grace underlie and shape every story.

The portrayal of Yahweh is focalized sharply through the cyclical nature of Judges. Because the cycle is based on notions of sin/consequences on the one hand and crying out/deliverance on the other, the nature of Yahweh is explored primarily through justice and mercy. The word 'evil', rather than 'sin', describes Israel's choices, and works itself out in its spiritual, social and political life. While 'evil' is first represented as worshipping other gods, what is at stake is not simply a cultic matter, but how the whole of life is oriented. To follow other gods means to follow the socio-economic and cultural models derived from a different set of values and leads to injustice, abuses of power, sexual violence, child sacrifice and widespread violence. By contrast, Israel was to embody a different kingdom, where the people are called to mirror Yahweh's care for widows, orphans and strangers as paradigmatic of vulnerability (Ex. 22.21–24; Lev. 19.34; 25.35; Deut. 10.18; 14.28–29; 24.17–18; 26.12; 27.19; 31.12); the land is cherished but not hoarded, and economic justice prevents increasing inequality (Lev. 25); hard work is balanced with appropriate rest, and greed and productivity do not drive everything; leaders do not abuse power, amass wealth or extend territory (Deut. 17.14–20); justice is dispensed fairly, and revenge and justice are clearly differentiated, with a stronger drive for restoration than punishment (Lynch, 2020, p. 171). A nation that embodied the character of Yahweh in these ways would be blessed and function as a priestly nation that could become a blessing to other nations and invite them in (e.g. Isa. 56). Such a vision is idealistic, but gave Israel a horizon of being as they started life in the Promised Land. The gap between vision and reality yawns wide in Judges, depicting the practical consequences of giving up on the vision; however, through Yahweh's patience and mercy, Judges explores the art of the possible, rather than the ideal.

In its focus on justice and mercy, Judges is set in a Deuteronomic horizon shaped by laws of action and consequences, as well as in continuity with the Exodus. In Egypt, Israel was oppressed and exploited, bodies and minds held captive, under threat of annihilation. Yahweh is moved by compassion to respond to his people's groans and crying out (Ex. 1.23) and acts in justice and liberation: defeating the oppressor, and leading the people into new life. The pattern of justice and liberation is echoed powerfully throughout the cycles of Judges. It is Yahweh's compassion and justice that create the possibility for new life, yet this new life needs to be shaped by compassion and justice so that it does not lapse into new forms of oppression.

Compassion undermines a mechanical relationship of action-consequences, and sets up a deeply challenging basis for relationships, based on freedom and love rather than merit or achievement; socially, compassion as an organizing principle yields very different forms of community, which value justice yet do not fall into harshness. Compassion takes injustice seriously, validates pain and hurt, yet ensures the welfare of all human beings. As Brueggemann (2018, p. 88) points out, compassion was a forbidden quality in the age of empires – Pharaoh's or Canaanite – as the very nature of compassion prevents the injustice and inequality that makes empires possible. Hence the covenantal vision includes laws to prevent the growth of inequality and amassing privilege at the expense of others, at individual, national, and international levels. This vision of Israel is rooted in Yahweh's own nature: 'a merciful and gracious God, patient, great in love and faithfulness, who shows goodness into the thousandth generation, who forgives misdeeds, transgressions and sins, but does not let the guilty remain unpunished' (Ex. 34.6–7).

In this study, Judges will emerge as a complex literary work, one that builds theology through narrative and invites readers to think for themselves, through ambiguity, irony and the problematizing of first impressions. Interpreters often try and resolve ambiguities, to define the exact meaning or intention of a text. Yet storytelling in Judges uses ambiguity and uncertainty as a pedagogical tool to invite readers into making moral judgements and examine their own assumptions, like the parables of Jesus. Lingering questions with multiple possible answers, therefore, are not necessarily a theological problem, but rather a theological method that takes readers seriously as moral agents and, in prophetic fashion, asks them to learn to discern where and how Yahweh is at work so that they can be formed into the ways of the Lord.

1

Setting the Scene (1.1—3.6)

Chapters 1.1—3.6 introduce key themes and set up expectations of patterns of behaviour and leadership to follow. This prologue is a different type of text to the main stories, more reflective, with a stronger narratorial presence, designed to set the book within its historical, theological and spiritual framework. It recounts similar events in chapters 1 and 2, with a focus on history and politics in 1, and on theology and ethics in 2. Right from the outset, questions of leadership and covenantal faithfulness take centre stage. The introduction diagnoses the problem that will recur throughout: Israel moved away from Yahweh.

1: Historical overview

1.1–10: Judah first

Judges opens by setting the story in its wider context. 'After the death of Joshua' is more than a temporal marker: it announces a paradigm shift in Israel's history. Until now they were strangers in the land, seeking to establish themselves, their leader a military man focused on conquest. Now they are called to become dwellers in the land. Judges forms the transition from nomadic refugees to an agrarian society with some budding urban centres. The attendant search for suitable governance underlies the importance of the question, 'Who will go first/lead?' (1.1) The mention of Joshua sets up both continuity and discontinuity. As the book of Joshua culminates in the renewal of the covenant at Shechem, we expect Judges to open onto the same triumphal sense of national unity, covenant faithfulness, and readiness to possess the land. The picture already shows cracks. The book of Joshua had opened with 'after the death of Moses', followed by Yahweh designating a new leader, Joshua, nurtured into leadership by Moses (Deut. 34.9), with clear instructions about covenantal faithfulness. Judges similarly opens with the death of the old leader, yet no one obviously formed into leadership, the people unsure how to organize themselves, and no mention of the covenant. Did Joshua not plan for succession? Why did Yahweh not intervene? One could argue that the instructions about the land and how to live in it, given to Moses and Joshua, were sufficient. Canonically, the people were given the law and a shape for living in the Torah. Judges marks a new chapter in learning how to walk with Yahweh, not relying on constant, ongoing revelation in times of crisis but learning to live well in more settled times – a task which the people of God find almost impossible throughout the Hebrew Scriptures, and beyond.

Judges chronicles the birth of a nation, the liminal stage of starting out with no institutions, no systems, whether political or religious, and negotiating how the different kinship groups relate. Israel's question is instructive; they ask who should lead, a tactical question, but not how they should proceed, or whether they should wage war. It is unclear whether the question is a mark of deference for Yahweh as commander-in-chief, or a hint of what is to come: the people treating Yahweh as a tribal god to ensure victory and prosperity. Implicitly, it suggests that Israel will act as a whole, following the leadership of Judah; however, this unity never materialises and the exchange with Yahweh gives way to a tribe-by-tribe account. The question refers to the 'Canaanites', a term used as a generic marker for all the inhabitants of the land in their various tribes and city-states, in a geographic area covering most of Palestine west of the Jordan, modern Lebanon and Southern Syria. Yahweh responds: 'I have given the land into his hand.' The tense is perfect (*qatal*), hence this has already been done, in contrast to passages that promise that Yahweh *will* give the enemy into

Israel's hand. Yahweh has already promised, and acted. Israel needs to make the promise a reality. Yahweh's response places the emphasis on the land, rather than the Canaanites. Israel focuses on war and battle, Yahweh on life in the land. Israel's identity is shaped around ethical and practical ways of living that interweave the land and its people. The land is a key theological concept here, in continuity with what has come before (the promise to Abraham, the Exodus, the conquest), and what will come later (the cataclysmic impact of the loss of the land and return to it), and will be eventually reshaped in the New Testament into a community of faith. Israel's ethical behaviour is repeatedly said to impact the land in Exodus–Deuteronomy (Num. 35.33–34; Lev. 18.25–30; Deut. 21.23; 24.4) and later by the Prophets (e.g. Isa. 24.5; Jer. 2.7; 16.18; Ezek. 36.18). The book of Joshua explores how much of the land the people will conquer; Judges, by contrast, concentrates on why the people haven't possessed the land that Yahweh had already given into their hand.

While the book opened on Israel as a whole, we immediately move to a more tribal, local focus, with Judah and Simeon. Critics are divided on their alliance: have they deviated from Yahweh's command for Judah to lead (Beldman, 2020, p. 60), or is it healthy cooperation (García Bachmann, 2018, p. 4)? Instances of cooperation lead to good outcomes in these early chapters (Oeste 2011, p. 298), with victory in the story of Deborah and Barak, though critics are keen to see their cooperation as a negative attribute. The text here bears no overt judgement and simply records a positive outcome. The tribes continue the strategy set in Joshua of attacking the main centre of city-states to destabilize a region.

1.5–7 is the first of three vignettes in chapter 1 that focus on individuals(Adoni-Bezek, Achsah and the man from Luz) and the conquest of major cities (Jerusalem, Hebron, just south of Debir, and Bethel). Each is theologically significant and links to themes of justice, fairness, and mercy, and all three have echoes in the closing chapters through place (Jerusalem and Bethel), focus on women, mutilation and questions of appropriate justice.

Adoni-Bezek is a Canaanite overlord; Judges will consistently explore leadership not only within Israel, but in contrasting pen pictures of enemy leaders, inviting readers to ponder whether Israel is truly distinctive. The introduction of enemy leaders, however sketchy, serves to portray them as people; they are not just generic, faceless Canaanites. Against the specific instructions of holy war, Judah does not execute Adoni-Bezek, but mutilates him and holds him captive. Cutting off thumbs and big toes was particularly humiliating as opposable thumbs are a key mark of humanity, while big toes enable erect walking. The practice de-humanizes the enemy, marking them out as a lesser 'other'. Adoni-Bezek had set this as his personal practice, reducing enemies to the status of dogs under his table. The laws of Deuteronomy did not permit Israel to dehumanize their enemies in this way; instead, they were to be put to death. Israel chooses Canaanite practices over those of the covenant. Adoni-Bezek articulates his fate theologically: just deserts for what he has done as a cruel leader, which he attributes to God. His god would not have been Yahweh. Israel following the practice implies that they choose another god's approach to justice. They are already behaving like the people of the land.

Jerusalem reappears in 1.10, out of sequence with previous verses. Ambiguity around when and whether Jerusalem is taken persists throughout Judges: it is still called 'Jebus', its pre-conquest name, in chapter 19. The equivocation around Jerusalem is symbolic of Israel's relationship to the land as a whole. There is no definitive conquest, but a constant struggle to establish themselves. The language used in 10.11 is that of *ḥērem*, the ban/extermination. *Ḥerēm* is the most complete form of war in the Hebrew Bible, mostly directed against foreigners. It always involves killing humans and the complete destruction of booty. *Ḥerēm* comes with a prohibition against profiting from war, is rooted in direct divine command, and is normally supervised by religious leaders. The fight then extends from city to country. Twice the Canaanites are referred to as those who 'live in' the hill country or Hebron. It is Israel that is supposed to live in the land post-Joshua, but they are still newcomers seeking to establish themselves. The entire book explores the struggle to settle, the ambiguity of who are the residents and who the aliens, and what it means to possess a land given to them as an *inheritance*. Joshua 13.1 recognized that much of the land still remained to be possessed, and Judges graphically chronicles the reality of a partial, painful and slow settlement.

1.11–21: Judah's successes and incipient failure

The next section keeps the focus on Judah, with another short vignette of war and leadership. Caleb, who was not an official leader but had been granted land in Joshua 14 in recognition of his faithfulness, features as a clearly influential man seeking to encourage the men to battle by offering his daughter Achsah as a reward. The story is repeated almost word for word from Joshua 15.13–19, which shows that Judges is not organized chronologically to strictly follow from Joshua but rather explores its own motifs around the conquest and settlement. The trio of characters set up an important theme: the porousness of Israel's ethnic and identity boundaries. All three protagonists are Kenizzites, yet they lead for Judah; Caleb and Achsah are the first named individuals to receive land for Judah. The Kenizzites were a people who had chosen to follow Yahweh and were therefore integrated into the covenant (starting out as the 'people of the land' in Genesis 15.19, to become models of covenant faithfulness in Joshua 14). Therefore, the first representatives of Israel that we meet are not ethnically Israelite. Yet they shape a paradigmatic story of successful conquest and healthy family structures to enable settlement. The story establishes a counterpoint to *ḥērem* and extermination of the Canaanites. Foreigners can be integrated into the covenant people as they choose to serve Yahweh. They do not forgo their ethnic identity – Caleb, Achsah and Othniel are still called Kenizzites – but ethnicity is secondary to covenant belonging. The high praise for Caleb's faith in Joshua 14 forms part of the wider scriptural theme of the inclusion of the Gentiles in the community of faith, a story that will only develop fully in the NT, but whose seeds are scattered throughout the Old (Melchizedek, Jethro, Rahab, Ruth ...).

It is unclear why the men needed additional motivation to fight, given this was already part of an overall military campaign; it contrasts with the question in 1.1: who goes first now will be a contest between men for courage, status and, possibly, lust. The practice is not unusual: giving and taking women in war was a traditional way of sealing alliances between clans and tribes and cementing kinship networks, feeding into the theme of households and the health of families. While Achsah had no apparent choice, the story shows a system of interrelated households, with clear positioning of status and rights, something that will gradually ebb away in Israel. While Achsah is the object of men's bargaining, she quickly becomes a subject in her own right, in a story where women are safe, secure and negotiate for themselves. Achsah decides on what her own value should be and requests it. She asks her husband to negotiate (1.14); the phrase, 'as she came to him', suggests consummation of the marriage and Achsah using sexuality as a way to achieve her goals. Many translators struggling with the idea of a woman initiating this sequence of events reverse the sentence to say that Othniel persuaded her to do the asking (Klein, 1993, p. 57). MT has no such scruples. Achsah travels alone across country, a dangerous enterprise, to meet her father. She contrasts sharply with another woman, who will also travel to her father, in Judges 19, yet meet a very different fate. The interaction with her father is respectful and affectionate, presuming a deeper relationship. Her father's question, 'What is with you?', sounds terse, but likely expresses surprise and concern that she had travelled alone. Unusually, Achsah uses the imperative talking to her father (Schneider, 1999, p. 15) and presents her request as self-evident. She reminds her father of what he has done to her, 'set me in the land of the Negev'. She does not say 'set us', or ask for something for her and her husband. She simply assumes she can ask for property. The frequent translation of 1.15 as 'give me a present' is a poor choice; what she actually asks for is a 'blessing'. Not a dowry, a blessing, as sons get when leaving home, and daughters may get when there are no sons (Num. 27.1–11), though there is no mention of whether Achsah has siblings. She asks for water, essential for life and an agrarian lifestyle. Achsah considers herself as responsible as her husband for the flourishing of her household.

The story is an important marker, at the very beginning, of what healthy households look like. Achsah behaves in ways acceptable within her (patriarchal) culture, using the power she has despite overall limitations. She is bold and creative, qualities often depicted as desirable and attractive in women in the Hebrew Bible (Klein, 2003, pp. 18–20). Power is *negotiated* between different groups, between men and women, husband and wife, father and daughter (Niditch, 2008, p. 41). The picture that emerges is of positive household and gender relations, a picture that will serve as yardstick against which to plot the later degeneration of social structures. Here, structures are clear, power negotiated, children respect parents and parents bless children. Some argue that this is depicted as a model marriage and Achsah as a model woman. 'Model' is not quite the right word. What it depicts is a configuration of relationships (within a specific context with its own limitations) promoting peace, safety and prosperity. This configuration can then work as a paradigm to assess different configurations of relationships for the fruit that they bear. In Judges, we see the failure of blessing by Jephthah towards his daughter, and the failure of both father and husband towards the woman of chapter 19.

1.16 moves the focus onto another liminal group that flits in and out of Israel's life, the Kenites, who fight with Judah but settle 'with the people'. While many translations emend the text to read 'with the Amalekites', following Moore and Budde (Webb, 2012, p. 106), there is no textual reason to do so, as both MT and LXX have 'with the people'. Hence the status of the Kenites is unclear, as are their overall loyalties – a motif that reappears in the story of Jael. Once again, the boundaries of 'Israel' are porous, not defined purely on ethnic grounds. Judah fulfils its responsibilities by taking Hormah and carrying out *ḥērem*. So far, they have been worthy leaders. The comment, 'Yahweh was with them' reflects their success, yet also problematizes what is to come. If Yahweh was with them, why couldn't they take the lowlands as well as the hill country? The explanation blames iron chariots, more useful in the plains than in the hills. Yet chariots are not an insurmountable obstacle, as the story of Deborah will show. This creates questions right at the outset: is this Judah's fault? Is Yahweh's power limited? Did Yahweh only want to give the hill country? Clearly, divine presence only confers *potential* for success (Bowman, 1995, p. 36); it is up to human beings to actualize it, through faithful covenantal partnership. A pattern now starts of retelling partial, difficult settlement of the land. Benjamin also fails to drive out the inhabitants of the land, but this time the narrator points out that they simply *did not*, rather than *could not*, drive them out. Benjamin simply can't be bothered to follow Yahweh's orders, settling with the people. Israel is just one of many in the land, which will set the background for most of the other stories. The picture of Israel which emerges is not of a unified whole with Yahwism as their organizing principle, but multiple tribal settlements in the midst of largely Canaanite areas.

1.22–36: Conquest annals

The rest of chapter 1 chronicles the tribes' incomplete attempt at settling the land. A short vignette zooms in on the house of Joseph (Ephraim and Manasseh). As before, the narrator emphasizes Yahweh's presence, which should have led to easy victory; instead, they send spies and make a covenant. The episode echoes Joshua 2 and 6 and the taking of Jericho. In Jericho, the spies' lives were threatened, hence the need to enlist local help. Here, spies find a random local outside the city and ask for information that would have been obvious – city gates are not hard to find! In Jericho, Rahab volunteered testimony to Yahweh's saving acts, asked for mercy (Josh. 2.8–13) and was incorporated into the covenantal community. Here, the man from Luz does not testify, is not incorporated into the covenant but offered a separate, parallel covenant and founds another city with the Hittites, who will remain antagonists of Israel. Joseph has made a covenant with the people of the land, a forbidden practice (Ex. 23.32; 34.15; Deut. 7.2). Israel itself sows the seeds of its later struggles. 1.24 has one of only two mentions in Judges of *ḥesed* (loving-kindness). Here, in a forbidden covenant, and in the story of Abimelech, *ḥesed* is withheld from the household of Gideon. Israel does not testify to Yahweh's loving-kindness for them, but chooses to love the wrong people and withhold love from those they should care for.

Chapter 1 resembles Assyrian descriptions of military campaigns, with a geographic rather than chronological logic (Block, 1999, p. 80). Assyrian documents, however, usually celebrate the victors, whereas the account here is more balanced, acknowledging as much failure as victory. The leitmotif 'Yahweh's presence was with them' gradually disappears. Manasseh not only does not drive the people out, but makes them perform forced labour (*mas*), which suggests that the problem was not military strength, but willingness. Forced labour is distinguished from slavery (*'bd*), as an Ancient Near East practice specifically distinguishing between victors and defeated nations (Klingbeil, 1997, p. 993). It is tragically ironic that so soon after having been slaves in Egypt, the Hebrews are forcing others into service. As Israel becomes more Canaanized, they will in turn be forced into compulsory labour. Deuteronomy 20.11 does make provision for the people of the land to choose to surrender to Israel, in which case they will not be exterminated or driven out but agree to forced labour as part of a settlement. There is no indication that this applies here. The rest of the chapter repeats the failure to drive out inhabitants. The narrator subtly signals the unsettled status of Israel: in 1.21 the Jebusites have 'lived among the Benjaminites'; in 1.27 the Canaanites 'continue to live in that land'; in 1.29, 30 'the Canaanites lived among them'; in 1.31, 33 it is the Israelites who live among the Canaanites, and by 1.34–35 Dan completely fails to occupy the coast, setting the scene for their move north in chapter 18. The chapter is therefore organized as is the book as a whole, starting with the best, finishing with the worst – an implicit conclusion that instead of Israel forming a new, distinctive, covenantal community, they are being shaped by the people of the land and leave Yahweh and covenant behind.

2.1—3.6: A spiritual assessment

Chapter 2 ushers in a different mood, with an analysis of Israel's spiritual condition. The renewed reference to the death of Joshua in 2.6 indicates that it does not follow chronologically from chapter 1. This reference problematizes what has come so far, suggesting that apostasy started very early, possibly even before the death of Joshua. The chapter as a whole hinges around the question in 2.2, 'What is it you have done?' The NRSV translates this as an exclamation, 'See what you have done!' However, the particle *māh* is rendered better as an interrogative, yielding a question that haunts the rest of the book, whose final story asks a similar question, 'How has such evil happened?' (20.3).

2.1–5: An angelic visit

Chapter 2 opens with one of three confrontations between Yahweh and Israel. The first comes via a messenger/angel; the second by a prophet, as a preface to the story of Gideon (6.7–10); and the third by Yahweh himself, ahead of the story of Jephthah (10.10–16). All three mark Israel's abandonment of covenant living. The messenger's identity is not defined; what matters is the message. A similar messenger will appear again (to Gideon, to Samson's parents), revealing a little more of himself each time. The word is frequently translated 'angel' but it is ambiguous and human beings are often initially unclear about the status of the messenger. The messenger casts the entire story of Judges as one of breakdown in covenant. Israel is reminded that Yahweh had taken the initiative in rescuing them from slavery and has promised everlasting faithfulness. The messenger reminds Israel of the story they are part of, a story they had committed themselves to, which they appear to have forgotten or turned away from. The Torah had set out multiple ways for the people to nurture their knowledge of and belonging to the story, with festivals, rituals, Levitical instruction, and the shaping of family life. Few of these appear in Judges, and at times are presented as deeply perverted, such as with the Levites of 17—19. Yahweh had promised never to break the covenant, but the people broke it from their side. The breach is exposed, together with its consequences. As the people withdraw from the covenant, Yahweh's presence does not go with them in battle and he no longer gives them victory. However, Yahweh sending a messenger shows that he still seeks to mend the relationship and reaches out even though they have walked away. Yahweh's message starts with his faithfulness to Israel, then reminds them of their obligations. Mercy and deliverance come first, the people's response second. The messenger reiterates two key commands. The first, not to make covenants with the people of the land (Ex. 34.12, 15; 23.32–33; Deut. 7.2), has been broken by the house of Joseph. Instead of inviting the nations to join the covenant, they formed a parallel covenant without Yahweh. The second command, to tear down their altars, is unlikely to have been carried out, since Israel is described as cohabiting with the inhabitants of the land. The story of Gideon will bear this out and Jephthah's story graphically illustrates the perils of syncretism. The twin commands not to make covenants and to tear down altars presuppose a degree of cohabitation rather than total extermination. The messenger's rebuke does not mention *ḥērem* at all but is couched in terms of covenantal faithfulness through Israel remaining distinctive. This poses an ethical question: is it possible to frame identity in ways that do not seek to either assimilate or annihilate the other? Do foreigners brought into the covenant lose their identity, or do they broaden their identity while forgoing negative cultural practices? The text presupposes that not everything in a culture is good and that not all cultures and forms of belonging in the world are equal. Framing the covenant in terms of justice and flourishing for all people is essential to a discussion of Yahweh's instructions.

The people weep in Bochim, just as they will weep in Bethel in 21.2–3. The focus of the weeping is unclear: is it sorrow for sin? Repentance? Fear of consequences? An attempt to assuage Yahweh? The focus and nature of the sacrifice in 2.5 is equally unclear, as are the intentions and feelings around it. The people seem adrift, without a solid system to help them understand how their relationships with Yahweh should proceed. Instead, they use ritual as a substitute for repentance and change, or to manipulate Yahweh in a mechanistic style. The tension surrounding the nature of the relationship resonates throughout the Old Testament: is it mechanistic, with obedience leading to blessing, disobedience to curse? Or is there freedom on both sides that allows for both grace and withdrawal?

2.6–15: Failure to walk in the ways of Joshua

A flashback to the death of Joshua reminds readers of the commitment the people had made, and the hope embodied in the renewal of the covenant at Shechem (Josh. 24). There, Joshua challenged the people to choose between Yahweh and the gods of the land (24.25). The people answered with wholehearted commitment (24.16–18), reinforced twice (24.19–28): a united people, working together under a covenant they all chose to make their own, ready to become the people of Yahweh in a new land. 2.6 recounts Joshua sending the people away. The future could have held peace and prosperity, cooperation and a common vision. But as Judges progresses, the united people divide, refuse to cooperate, and fragment into an individualistic nation whose gatherings at Mizpah and Bethel in chapter 21 will lead not to covenant renewal but to internecine war. Here in 2.6, they all go to their 'inheritance' (*naḥalā*), a word that stresses that this land is a gift, undeserved, directly related to Yahweh's promise. Their task is living the covenantal life as they take possession of the land. The repetition of the phrase in 21.15 will, in contrast, mention tribes and clans and be qualified by the comment that each Israelite did what was right in their own eyes, marking the downward spiral of Israel's fragmentation and abandonment of the covenant. The covenant is primarily a covenant with Yahweh; its horizontal dimensions derive from a vertical relationship with Yahweh, not a social contract between Israelites. Both dimensions will fail as they reject Yahweh and turn against one another.

2.7 reinforces the picture of Joshua as ideal leader, who led the people into faithfulness and whose contemporaries owned faith for themselves. Yet one wonders why, if Joshua was such a great leader, faith and faithfulness disintegrated so quickly. 2.10 stresses the problem of passing faith from one generation to the next, a persistent theological theme in Deuteronomy and beyond, as each new generation must choose faith for themselves, not just knowing the story, but finding their place within it. The importance of memory, family and community practices that nurture faith are the responsibility of parents and elders, and the sins of parents consistently affect their children; however, children often struggle to follow Yahweh for themselves, even when their parents do, as with Samson, Eli's sons (1 Sam. 2), or Samuel's sons (1 Sam. 8.1–3). 2.10 uses the idiom 'did not know the Lord or what he had done'; 'knowing' is about much more than cognitive information. To 'know the Lord' is to live a covenantal relationship involving the whole person, emotions and actions (Deut. 6.5). Deuteronomy 6 focuses on the practices and shapes of life needed for a people to learn to love the Lord and form a distinctive identity out of memory and current practice. But in Judges 2.10, a 'new generation' introduces a fracture with the past, which kick-starts cycles of apostasy. This suggests that there is an experiential component to faith. When a new generation has not experienced Yahweh and his saving acts, they struggle. The conundrum that then faces Israel, and the Church, is how to enable a new generation to move from head knowledge to some form of experiential knowledge, combining both.

2.11–23: The cycle

The next section of the introduction foreshadows the structure of the rest of Judges, sets expectations and defines the theological framework within which to interpret Judges as a whole. Traditionally, the pattern has been dubbed the 'Deuteronomistic cycle', exemplifying the correlation between sin and punishment, between Israel's actions and God's response, which yields a recurring pattern of sin-punishment-repentance-deliverance. However, close examination of the cycle, in the introduction and as it develops, belies a simplistic mechanical relationship. Repentance is never mentioned explicitly. The people 'cry out' and God responds, not to their repentance, recognition of sin or intention to change, but to their primal cry of suffering, which makes Yahweh's response one of grace and mercy.

2.11–12 sets out the basic problem: the people did 'evil in the eyes of Yahweh', a common biblical phrase for doing wrong in an ethical and moral sense. The phrase harks back to the stark choice offered Israel in Deuteronomy 30.15, between 'life and the good (*ha tôb*), and death and the evil (*ha ra'*)', a choice echoed in the covenant renewal ceremony of Joshua 24. Deuteronomy 30 sets the notion of 'evil' into a wider context than idolatry; to turn away from Yahweh is to turn away from life, from all that is good, and from the covenantal configuration of community that sought justice and flourishing. The emphasis on turning to other gods draws a sharp contrast with the earnest promises in Joshua 24.16, 'far be it from us to forsake the Lord to serve other gods'. The same word, *'āzab*, is used in Joshua 24.16 and Judges 1.12 for forsaking/abandoning Yahweh, highlighting the fickleness of human beings and pointing to divine pathos. The relationship with Yahweh is exclusive, and worship of other gods is spiritually and ethically incompatible with Yahwism, a claim that did not sit easily within the culture of the time. Surrounding cultures, whether Egypt or Canaan, were polytheistic, with tribal gods in different incarnations in different places (Webb, 2012, p. 142) and exciting, sometimes erotic, rituals (Block, 1999, p. 129). Between Egypt and the Promised Land stands the divine revelation at Sinai, with its emphasis on monotheism and sharp ethical demands. Looking at Egypt and Canaan, the people make their own choices towards what is right in their own eyes, rather than follow what has been revealed as right in the eyes of Yahweh. The motif 'they did evil in the eyes of Yahweh' punctuates Judges (2.11; 3.7, 12; 4.1; 6.1; 10.6; 13.1) until the concluding chapters (17—21) when it morphs into 'every man did what was right in his own eyes'. The temptation to judge for oneself, to see what is good and evil through human eyes rather than follow what has been given by God, goes back to the paradigmatic story of the garden of Eden (Gen 2.1–7), when the serpent says to the woman 'when you eat of it your *eyes* will be opened and you will be like God, knowing good and evil'. The woman then '*saw* that the tree was good for food ... and their *eyes* were opened'. Every generation re-enacts the sin of wanting to judge good and evil for itself through what it sees, regardless of God's, or older generations', instructions. The consequences of inhabiting the world in this way are graphically depicted in Judges. The further the people get from covenant living, the more the social fabric of the nation disintegrates, with injustice, oppression and horror becoming everyday occurrences. The notion of seeing goes deeper still, striking right at the heart of faith. Centuries later, the writer of the letter to the Hebrews will say, 'Faith is the assurance of things hoped for, the conviction of things not seen.' The problem with the people here, is that they are unduly swayed by what they see – a pattern that will culminate in Samson. What they see is the nations around them, their practices, their exciting religions and their ways of linking gods and natural phenomena. It was easier to reduce the world, and God, to what could be seen, felt and touched, than to rely on the testimony of generations past or practise a radically different way of living not modelled before them. To embrace and perform their identity as the people of God was a step of faith, of embracing the unseen; this theoretical identity constantly came into tension with the reality of the world they lived in, one that pulled them towards the identity of surrounding nations.

The language of rivalry and exclusivism in 2.11–12 then makes sense: the choice between Yahweh and the Baals is not a choice between morally and ethically equivalent options, it is a choice between truth and lies, between a God who exists and one invented by human minds. The social and ethical consequences of Israel's choices as exemplified later in the book seem to justify the rigidity of Yahweh's demand for unswerving allegiance in these opening chapters. To call the people to faithfulness calls them to flourishing and fullness of life. The other way, as Deuteronomy predicted, lies only death. Hence 2.14–15 concentrates on divine anger and divine withdrawal.

As Israel withdraws from the covenant, they become no more than they are in the world: a small nation in a hostile land, surrounded by enemies more powerful than them. 2.15, however, introduces a key element: 'they were in great distress'. This is the pivot into the second part of the cycle, 'the Lord raised up judges who delivered them'. The people are not said to cry out, even less to repent or change. Yahweh's action responds purely to the pain of the people. Yahweh acts completely freely, in grace and mercy, opening a window onto the narrator's theology of God. God is free, merciful and loving. God is also just and responds to sin, but this response is slowed, tempered and eventually overcome by love and mercy, as the recurrent formula states: 'The Lord is merciful and gracious, slow to anger and abounding in steadfast love' first occurs as part of the revelation of Yahweh at Sinai (Ex. 34.6–7; Num. 14.18; Neh. 9.17; Ps. 86.5, 15; 103.8; 145.8). Aspects of the formula recur in many parts of the OT (e.g. Deut. 5.10; Neh. 9.17; Is. 55.7; Jer. 32.18; Ps. 130.7) and find themselves echoed in the NT, particularly in the letters of Paul and his emphasis on the superabundance of grace over sin (e.g. Rom. 5.20–21; Eph. 1.7–8).

2.16 introduces the figure of the judge (*šōpēṭ*) and their two main characteristics: they are raised up by Yahweh and they deliver Israel. Neither the manner of the raising or the delivering is specified, and the ensuing narratives will display a range of options. The initiative is Yahweh's, and the single focus of the judge is deliverance, though 2.17, 'they did not listen even to their judges', suggests that they would have had functions beyond deliverance from physical enemies, as spiritual leaders. 2.17 therefore sets up the cycle: it does not matter what Yahweh does and what the judge does, they keep going back to their evil ways. Evidence for repentance or a change of behaviour is scant; 2.17 suggests there is none, while 2.19 speaks of relapse into even worse behaviour. The character of Yahweh is further exemplified in 2.18, as he is 'moved to pity by their groaning', making it clear that Yahweh's saving action is rooted in his love and mercy rather than in Israel's repentance. The 'groaning' is an inchoate response to pain. The verb translated 'moved to pity', *niḥām*, in the *Nifal*, is more usually translated as changing one's mind or being sorry. However translated, the source of Yahweh's change and move towards deliverance is the suffering of his people, therefore an expression of compassion. The focus of Yahweh's action on deliverance from oppression recalls the God of the Exodus, moved to pity by Israel's plight in Egypt. There is an implicit idea of justice here, as Brueggemann (1994, p. 84) argues: 'The characteristic statement shows that the formula speaks of Yahweh as a source of political power who will liberate from another, lesser political power that oppresses.' The very raising of judges and the attendant deliverance gives Israel a chance to repent and change *in response to* Yahweh's gracious action; the fact that they don't is a graphic judgement on the state of Israel. The judges therefore bring judgement by their very presence and the way they expose the underlying, persistent problem. The judges themselves are presented positively here, as offering the possibility of change; the stories will show them increasingly becoming part of the problem. 2.19 sets up the theme of a deteriorating spiral, with each generation being worse than the one before. The people's choice to break the covenant frees Yahweh from his obligations, hence he will not drive out the nations from before Israel anymore (2.20–21); yet Yahweh takes the initiative to invite his people back into the covenant through his liberative action. The covenant as contract may have been broken, but the covenant as promise still stands (Webb, 2012, p. 147), a promise only fully fulfilled in Jesus. The picture of a deteriorating cycle showcases another attribute of Yahweh, also drawn from the revelation at Sinai (Ex. 34.6–7): 'slow to anger and abounding in love'. Grace does not seem to be working out well, yet Yahweh extends grace and the offer of relationship repeatedly, though the effort appears doomed.

Modern audiences may not consider the withdrawal of divine presence, with its attendant loss of military back-up and inevitable oppression by foreign nations, part of a merciful pattern. However, the very attribute of Yahweh that leads him to rescue them from oppression is also the attribute that prompts him to act when sin abounds in Israel – justice. Exodus 34.6–7 links those two attributes tightly, 'forgiving iniquity and transgression and sin, yet by no means clearing the guilty'. A god who rescues Israel from oppression is a god who acts against all oppression. Israel's mistake is often to treat Yahweh as a tribal god who will be on their side no matter what. Even Joshua had to be taught that this was not the case. In Joshua 5.13–15, Joshua meets the supernatural 'commander of the Lord's armies'. Joshua tries to ascertain which side he is on, the Israelites' or the enemies'. The response cuts to the heart of the problem: 'Neither; but as commander of the army of the Lord I have now come.' Yahweh does not take sides, he stays on the side of justice. Human attempts to co-opt, coax or manipulate him are doomed to fail. Joshua understood this, but the following generations did not. When Judges 3.2 explains that nations were left in the land so that new generations could be taught war, this is part of the picture. It is not skills or courage they need to learn, but rather that Yahweh does not take sides, that it is Yahweh who brings victory rather than their own actions. This theme will be explored at length in the story of Gideon in chapters 6—8. The idea in 2.21—3.2 that Yahweh may no longer drive out the nations is potentially a death sentence for the small, vulnerable group of tribes that is seeking a home in the land. Their survival is entirely predicated on Yahweh's grace.

War in the Hebrew Bible

Here it is helpful to explore briefly how war is portrayed in the Hebrew Bible. War is an omnipresent reality, never far off in narrative and codified in the legal corpus. It is not presented in monolithic ways, either historically or ethically. It ranges from small feuds and raids to organized military conflict between nations; there are conflicts which escalate from small groups to entire nations, wars of conquest, and internecine wars. Judges itself is varied in its depictions: a war assassin with Ehud, followed by organized conflict; the story of Abimelech as a critique of unbridled aggression; self-defence with Gideon; Jephthah's negotiations as an attempt to articulate just war; the immoral attack on Laish in 18; and anarchic internecine conflict in 20—21. The rest of the biblical corpus is equally varied, with many wars depicted as expedient and greedy, prompted by exploitative rulers who want to maintain and extend their rule. Niditch's extensive study of war in the Hebrew Bible (1993) argues that despite different types of conflicts, war is not presented in unambiguous, positive ways. She states that 'killing and placing oneself in the position of being killed requires considerable self-justification, rationalization, psychological and social sanction' (p. 20), a fact reflected in rituals marking the exit from war that address guilt and ambivalence. This is particularly marked in Judges 20—21 as the nation struggles with civil war (which inflicts even higher moral injury), tries to justify its actions and struggles to use rituals such as the exchange of women in marriage as a doorway out of war. The instability of Israel's identity, with a constantly shifting array of tribes struggling to define themselves over and against other nations, is an added factor likely to precipitate war. The more sure and stable a group is, 'the less likely they are to be warlike, and the less rigid and totalistic their war ideologies are likely to be' (Niditch, 1993, p. 21). Once again, this is exemplified well in the troubled times of Judges, particularly in the conquest of Laish in chapter 18. The people of Laish are repeatedly portrayed as safe, secure and peaceful, over and against amoral, warlike Dan, a tribe struggling to establish itself within the land. Judges is psychologically and sociologically astute in its portrayal of human dynamics. Yet war is not presented in altogether negative terms; it often leads to an increase in stability for a time, partly by increasing group solidarity for those who unite against enemies (Niditch, 1993, pp. 13–25) or by addressing the source of the instability; Judges illustrates both dynamics, with Israel appearing more united at times of war, though those tribes that choose not to participate are treated increasingly harshly, and with wars often leading to 'rest in the land'. Exceptions to the rest formula are worth noting: the self-serving, oppressive reign of Abimelech; the self-centred judgeship of Samson; the crusade of the Danites; and the civil war of the end. War is problematized in canonical perspective.

One of the most problematic practices, looking back from the twenty-first century, is that of *ḥerēm*. While there is not enough space here for a full consideration, it is worth noting the following features. *Ḥerēm* is the most complete form of war in the Hebrew Bible; it is mostly directed against foreigners, though in certain specific circumstances – an entire town led into apostasy (Deut. 13.12–18) – it can be applied to Israelites deemed to have departed from their identity as Israelites and become indistinguishable from 'the nations'. It always involves killing humans and usually the complete destruction of booty (hence a prohibition against profiting from war), it is rooted in direct divine command and is normally supervised by religious leaders. There seems to be no space for mercy. However, the Hebrew Bible is rarely monolithic or unambiguous. The nations are offered a get-out clause in Deuteronomy 20.10; there are numerous examples of foreigners brought into the covenant; texts concerning *ḥerēm* in the legal corpus are not entirely clear (e.g. Deut. 7.2 seems to counsel complete destruction, but then goes on to forbid intermarriage, which would not be possible if all had been killed, and then focuses mostly on the destruction of religious sites). The emphasis of the ritual also seems to shift in different texts between its symbol as a sacrifice of enemies to Yahweh (enemies as worthy sacrifices) and a symbol of God's justice on sinful others (who are then dehumanized) (Niditch, 1993, pp. 28–77).

The ambiguity of the biblical witness to the practice is a helpful reminder of the complex feelings that attend war and the reality of moral injury. The impact of moral injury rises to tragedy in Judges as Jephthah blurs war and peace, becoming unable to evaluate the immorality of his own violent actions. War carries a heavy psychological toll, and texts about the destruction of enemies show attempts to justify and rationalize actions taken in war through religious, ethical and pragmatic means.[1] Boling (1975, p. 29), in line with most commentators, argues that a strong contrast is formed between Joshua and

1 For a fuller theological exploration of *ḥerēm*, see Niditch, 1993; Stern, 1991; Hoffman, 1999. For an exploration of moral injury and Scripture, see Kelle, 2020.

Judges, which problematizes *ḥerēm* in the latter. In Joshua it is consistently accompanied by seeking Yahweh and an exploration of violations of *ḥerēm*. In Judges the people go far beyond their orders and do not follow the pattern of *ḥerēm*. The end of the introduction suggests that Yahweh is purposefully withdrawing from expansionist wars.

3.1–6: The nations that remain

Chapter 3.1–6 concludes the prologue with additional reflections on the nations left in the land, and introduces an additional element of Israel's disobedience: intermarriage. The testing motif is repeated, with the expectation that Israel will fail, unlike the beginning of Joshua with its expectation of obedience. Why use war as a test? Was there no other way for Israel to come to experience/know Yahweh? Or is it that as Yahweh's presence withdraws, and as the people fail to drive out the nations, those that are left will inevitably test Israel's commitment to Yahweh? Either way, the parenthetical statement of verse 2 establishes that the benefit of the test is not for Yahweh (as if Yahweh needed to know whether Israel was going to be faithful) but for Israel, so that it could learn the same truths about itself and about Yahweh as previous generations. The list of remaining nations (3.5) mirrors that found in Deuteronomy 7.1. Only the Girgashites are missing, and the Canaanites come first in the list, not connected with the conjunction *vav*, which suggests that 'Canaanites' functions as a generic name and the others as subgroups.

3.5–6 reflects on the complete failure of Israelites to follow Yahweh's covenantal instructions. Even though intermarriage is banned, an insistent canonical counter-narrative exemplifies positive mixed marriages that bring non-Israelites within the covenant, such as with Ruth and Rahab, both of whom appear in the genealogy of Jesus (Matt. 1.5), showing that this arc of inclusion is central to the story of Scripture. Intermarriage has an effect beyond tempting the people into apostasy; it creates new networks of loyalty, and the possibility of divided loyalties. It affects the household, which functioned as the basic unit of society in an agrarian culture, with economic and social ramifications. Furthermore, Fewell (1995, p. 140) perceptively points out that marriage impacts women differentially. While non-Israelite girls are brought in to share the land of Israelite men, Israelite girls would be given to the 'other', which would dispossess them from their ancestral land, in sharp contrast to Achsah's assertion of her inheritance rights. To speak about intermarriage therefore is not just to speak about ethnic purity, but about questions of power, control and justice, with particular consequences on gender relations.

Reflections

The double introduction sets out key themes in the book, many of which connect to the question, who is Israel? What does it mean to be the people of God? How do actions embody identity? What is the right relationship between actions and consequences? Are the people of God defined by ethnicity? How is their identity shaped and transmitted down generations? Chapter 1 explores the question on a political and social plane, 2.1—3.6 on a more theological plane, but they both illustrate how Israel struggles to know who it is, and how to enact its identity in a new context. This identity is problematized through the relationship with the 'people of the land'. The rights of locals to inhabit the land are never acknowledged (though of course, 'rights' are a modern concept), but when others invade Israel, then Israel considers its own rights against what they conceptualize as oppression. The notion of right here is implicit and only ever applied to the self. A battle of 'rights to the land' occurs later in Jephthah's exchange with the Amorite king. To consider the rights of locals would have hampered Israel's efforts not just to settle the land but to survive altogether, especially as a whole group. For an agrarian people, land equals life. If they had no right to Canaan, having left a land of death (Egypt), Israel would have no future. The ethical dilemma facing the people at the time, and in recounting their story retrospectively, is how they could justify their right to land, hence their right to life. The identity of Israel is further challenged as the cycle goes on and they break the covenant, supposed to be the organizing centre of their identity, and the nations around them are used as agents of Yahweh's justice (Block, 1999, p. 82). Right from the start a complex picture emerges, showing Israel's struggle with understanding its vocation in the world.

The cycle, the lens through which the rest of Judges must be read, establishes its fundamental theology, one that holds justice and mercy closely together. Justice, because the problem with idolatry is not so much the worship of other gods but the worldview and lifestyle that comes with them. As García Bachmann points out, it is the 'socio-economic, political, and cultural model derived from following the Baals and Astartes' that Judges denounces (2018, p. 23). The consequences become increasingly obvious as Judges progresses: child sacrifice, massacre of peaceful people, perversion of justice, accumulation of land, sexual violence and gross misuse of power by leaders. Yet mercy spills over as Yahweh keeps responding to Israel's need, as he had in the wilderness, revealing a theology not of sin and punishment but of 'election and grace' (Greenspahn, 1986, p. 394). Brueggemann (1994, p. 75) helpfully sees the cycle as one formula with distinct halves in tension with each other. The first half of the formula, doing evil and punishment, is intensely theological and covenantal, focused on exclusive loyalty to Yahweh. It is also deeply political; it can be used to advocate for a specific social order, and easily abused. Yahweh's anger focuses on the wrong order of society and rejection of the right order (Brueggemann, 1994, p. 77). This first half is largely retributive, and echoed in Proverbs, Wisdom, Psalms and the prophets. The deed–punishment sequence paints a predictable world. It can be used to promote covenantal living, but equally to justify the dominance of certain groups by arguing that their privileged position derives from Yahweh's blessing. The first part of the formula on its own makes no space for grace, relationship, or the freedom of either Yahweh or the human person. Yahweh's anger is directed towards the possibility and reality of oppression. As Israel yields to syncretism, negative social configurations are actualized. Politics and theology walk hand in hand, and theology makes possible a different kind of political thinking based on the paradigmatic story of Yahweh's actions in the Exodus as a God who liberates from oppression. The second part of the formula, in contrast, is based on the people's need and Yahweh's loving and gracious response, a formula we see clearly in texts of lament in the Exodus and texts based on the Exodus tradition. This tradition will be powerfully built on in the ministry of Jesus, as people cry out to him in need and he responds. The mechanistic world of the first half of the formula fails, giving birth to an existential cry of pain that rises up to Yahweh, who responds. It is the failure of the deed–consequence model to produce flourishing that prompts the suspension of that order through grace. The second half of the formula breaks through the brokenness but yields a world that is not safe anymore; Yahweh cannot be used or manipulated and acts in complete freedom. Human beings are then invited to partner in that freedom, and see a world transformed by grace. This issue is therefore deeply political. A political and social system whose primary organizing principle is grace rather than retribution will be shaped in radically different ways. The formula as a whole, with its inherent tension, functions as a prophetic call for Israel: 'The use of the entire formula summons Israel to shift from one life-world to another, with its alternative theological, epistemological, and political claims' (Brueggemann, 1994, p. 88).

2

Othniel and Ehud (3.7–5.31)

Now that theological and social themes have been established, the curtain rises on the stories of individual judges, the so-called 'main cycles'. The style of writing changes, with a more immediate narration that focuses on key characters. The cycles are all set against the prologue's framework, and elements that follow or diverge from it are key to interpreting individual stories. Each story is unique, told in a unique way. Some are very short, some much longer: length is not in itself determinative of significance. Instead of focusing on all Israel, most stories zoom in on a sub-set of tribes and generalize their story as 'Israel'. Hence each story offers a dual-lens character study. One, the judge and the people within the narrative; the other, Israel as the main character, seen through a series of representative members. Both perspectives feed into the construction of a national narrative of identity for Israel as an emerging nation.

3.7–11: Othniel, a model judge?

The first story, Othniel's, is short and paradigmatic, picking up all elements of the framework: Israel did evil in the eyes of Yahweh, forgot Yahweh, worshipped foreign gods, the anger of the Lord was kindled, Yahweh sold Israel into the hands of enemies to serve them, Israel cried out, Yahweh raised up a deliverer. New elements are added and will reappear at various points in the stories of other judges: length of oppression, sending of the Spirit, war and deliverance, judging Israel, rest for the land, death of the judge.

First, the people are said to forget (*šākaḥ*) Yahweh, a strong term for disregarding, not considering (Block, 1999, p. 151), characteristics of Deuteronomic warnings. Remembering Yahweh is about identity-forming and relationships; forgetting Yahweh tears apart the identity of the people of God. As forecast in the prologue, the people 'do evil in the eyes of the Lord'. The formula will introduce the story of all the major judges (those whose stories are longest): Othniel (3.7), Gideon (6.10), and 'continued to do evil' for Ehud (3.12), Deborah (4.1), Jephthah (10.6) and Samson (13.1). One may add Abimelech to the list, with a similar but not identical statement at the end of Gideon's tale (8.33–34). Evil is defined as worship of foreign gods, the consequence of which is serving foreign earthly lords (3.8). The word for 'serve' (*'ābar*) is the word used for slavery in Egypt, not merely the 'forced labour' of Judges 1, and marks a reversal of the Exodus. Throughout the journey in the wilderness, the people rebelled and sometimes longed to go back to Egypt rather than face the uncertainty and potential of the desert. Judges continues the theme of the people choosing paths that lead back to slavery rather than forward into Yahweh's freedom.

The oppressor, Cushan-Rishataim from Aram, is not listed as part of the people left in the land, but comes from abroad to attack Israel, hinting at national rather than localized oppression (Oeste, 2011, p. 301). Aram is far away and represents a powerful people group with a world-class ruler (Block, 1999, p. 152), whose reputation precedes him. His name, 'Cushan of double-wickedness', may have been given by terrified people, or an intentional choice to inspire fear. This is the first of many pen pictures of enemy leaders that contrast them as oppressors, with judges raised by Yahweh as deliverers (Webb, 2012, p. 160), a picture that will gradually blur as Israel's leaders take on more and more characteristics from surrounding leaders. But here, with Othniel, we are dealing with paradigmatic leadership in Israel. Othniel, introduced in Judges 1, links back to Caleb and the Joshua generation that had stayed faithful, and therefore serves as pivot between the two books. The prologue had ended with Israelites marrying foreigners. The main cycle opens with Othniel, whom we know has married a woman who, despite being of foreign descent, has like him been incorporated into the covenant. It is highly telling that the paradigmatic judge is not himself of 'pure' Israelite ethnicity. He is paradigmatic because of his faithfulness to the covenant. His story also shines a retrospective light onto the command not to marry foreigners – it is not their ethnicity that is the problem, but their loyalties.

3.9 is the first instance of Israel 'crying out' (*zā'aq*) to Yahweh (in the prologue, Israel 'groaned'). The term is not normally used to indicate repentance, which is usually mentioned separately and explicitly (Beldman, 2020, p. 139). Some scholars (Chisholm, 2013, p. 170, Frolov and Stetckevich, 2019, pp. 129–39) argue that repentance is implicit, but this relies on reading Deuteronomistic theology into a text that does not make this clear. Chisholm points out that the people cry out to Yahweh, hence it at least constitutes a recognition of Yahweh's power and a turning towards him; however, the 'crying out' is not always addressed to Yahweh and sometimes fails to materialize (as in Samson's story), yet Yahweh still acts in deliverance. 1 Samuel 12.10–11 will recount the period of the Judges with a reference to turning back to Yahweh and confessing sin. In Judges itself, however, it happens only once, and there are doubts as to whether the confession is genuine or instrumental (Judg. 10.10). Here lies the tension highlighted by Brueggemann (1994, p. 75) between the two parts of the framework. In Samuel there is heavy reliance on the first part as a way to encourage a set social order. Judges itself keeps a better balance between the two parts, and the 'crying out' motif is not linked to repentance but harks back to the Exodus and Yahweh's response to Israel's need.

Yahweh then raises a 'deliverer' (*môšî'a*). Not a 'judge', as in the framework. No leader is called judge, they are only said to judge Israel, as an activity. The deliverers may have been expected to do more, lead Israel into repentance and righteousness and foster justice. Instead, the text focuses almost exclusively on them as military leaders or local warlords, giving little indication that they sought to be spiritual leaders.

The stress on deliverance is a strong link to Yahweh's liberating action and the Exodus paradigm, normally associated with a call to transformed living in response to Yahweh. 3.10 expands on Yahweh's action with the sending of the Spirit. The gift of the Spirit, as throughout Scripture, equips the recipient with the skills and attributes needed to accomplish the task set before them. The coming of the Spirit in battle is often described as urgent and overwhelming, underlining the fact that it is Yahweh who grants the victory rather than human skill or courage. The Spirit of Yahweh operates much more widely than this in the Old Testament (as indeed in the New Testament). It is the agency through which God works in creation, gives life, cares, equips for service, seals the covenant and bestows prophetic gifts. Here, as with most judges apart from Samson, it is unclear exactly what the Spirit does; rather, we are told about the results (the fruit) – deliverance. The first person in Judges to receive the Spirit is not an ethnic Israelite, once again a nod to the strong interwoven narrative of the inclusion of Gentiles into the covenant that will bloom in its fullness in the narratives of the Acts of the Apostles, where the seal of the Spirit on the Gentiles is the undeniable sign of their inclusion into the Church. In Judges, deliverance is the focus, and nothing detracts from it.

There are no details of what happens to the foreign ruler; later deliverers (Ehud, Barak, Gideon, Jephthah) will be concerned with the fate of foreign rulers in ways that, more often than not, bring out their own character flaws (Schneider, 1999, p. 42). Here the clipped narrative is a tribute to Othniel's faithfulness. There is no delight in military exploits and violence, nor is there an account of Othniel's accruing of property and descendants. Othniel's legacy is summed up in deliverance and peace. 'The land had rest' formula concludes individual stories in the first half of the book (apart from Shamgar's). It is not just the people that have rest, but 'the land'. Human beings are always part of a wider, cosmic reality that Yahweh is concerned with. This theme is woven through all the stories of the OT, as human beings are first introduced as part of a much wider ecosystem in Genesis, and when things go wrong with human beings, the natural order is also disrupted (Gen. 3); they are held responsible for life (Gen. 9.1–7), and the fate of Israel is intimately tied to that of the land, so that Israel's behaviour has a direct impact on the health of the land, the land reacts to sin (Lev. 18.25–28; 19.29; 20.22; 26.14–45; Num. 35.33–34; Deut. 4.5, 14; 6.3; 7.13; 11.11–17; 16.20; 19.10; 21.23; 24.4; 25.15; 29.27), and laws are given to frame relationship to the land (Lev. 19.9, 23; 23.10, 22, 39; 25; 26.4–6; 27.30; Num. 15.19). The NT will pick up the theme, albeit in more muted tones, with pictures of cosmic struggle and renewal (Rom. 8.18–38) or the reconciliation of the entire cosmos (Col. 1.15–20).

The notice of Othniel's death concludes this short window into a model judge; his story will serve as a paradigm against which other judges can be evaluated. It is not accidental that the model judge comes out of Judah, foreshadowing David. Othniel is not presented as perfect; he is a model because of faithfulness to his calling and, pointing away from himself, to Yahweh's deliverance. Increasingly, each story will have less of Yahweh and more of the judge themselves. The structure as a whole will gradually break down, with fewer and fewer elements of the framework present.

3.12–30: Ehud, or the James Bond of Judges

3.12–14: Here we go again

The 'model' cycle of Othniel gives way to a new cycle of sin and deliverance. The 'doing evil' formula is prefaced by the Hebrew *wayosipû*, often translated 'they again did evil'. A better translation would be 'they continued to do evil', since there was never any indication of change. 'Continue to' highlights that the stories build on one another cumulatively, as indicated in the prologue, and reinforces the idea that Yahweh responds primarily out of grace (Greenspahn, 1986, p. 94). Now Yahweh does not sell Israel to their enemies by withdrawing, but actively strengthens their enemies or sides with them. Other elements of the framework are intensified, with a longer period of bondage and Israel's sin mentioned twice in 3.12. The 'strengthening' of the enemy appears elsewhere in the OT, as Yahweh works for justice through the existing attributes of human beings, in an example of double causality (e.g. Deut. 2.30–33; Josh. 11.20). The best known example is that of Pharaoh (Ex. 4.21; 7.3, 13; 9.12, 35; 10.1, 20; 14.8) whose heart Yahweh hardens (same Hebrew verb, *ḥāzaq* in the *Piel*). In both cases, evil intent is already present, and Yahweh strengthens what is already there, or enables it to come to fruition. Human and divine action combine to fulfil Yahweh's purposes. In Judges 3.12 the narrative is focalized through the eyes of Israel, with no glimpse of the enemy perspective. One wonders whether the God who acts in mercy and kindness towards Israel extended mercy to foreigners too, and how. The text is not really interested in this question. There are other parts of the canon, however, that hint at the possibility (and reality) of Yahweh's dealings with those outside Israel, such as Melchizedek (Gen. 14.18–20) or the story of Jonah and Nineveh. Focalization through Israel enables an intensely human, emotional and psychologically astute perspective to emerge; conversely, it often limits that perspective to what Israel could see, imagine or be interested in. Hence the counter-narrative of the inclusion of the stranger woven through the narrator's perspective. It is a challenge that Israel struggles with, and hence only comes through in patches and glimpses.

Israel's enemy here is Moab. They were not listed in the people left in the land, as with Cushan-Rishataim. It is unclear whether it is significant that it is Moab, or whether the nation acts as a cipher for any foreign power. There was a long history of antagonism between Israel and Moab. They were relatives of Israel through Lot. The daughters of Lot become pregnant from their father; the first names her child Ben-Ammi (son of my people), the second, Moab (from the father), a brazen and unabashed acknowledgement of incest. Israel is forbidden to encroach on Moabite territory (Deut. 2.8–9). Moab is particularly reviled in Deuteronomy, with an absolute prohibition on admitting Moabites to the assembly of Yahweh, or to ever seek their welfare or prosperity (Deut. 23.3–6). The portrayal of Moab as evil and unclean is clear in the story of Ehud and Eglon, the king caricatured as fat and stupid and the story redolent with scatological humour and questionable sexual innuendoes. This fits the general portrayal of Moab and its provenance, suggesting that the use of Moab is more pointed than a simple generic enemy. Moab's genealogical proximity to Israel makes it more threatening, hence a fiercer demarcation of self and other. All this sharpens the contrast with the book of Ruth, next in the canon, where Ruth the Moabite proves herself faithful to Israel and is included into the covenant, finding her place as ancestor to David and in Jesus' genealogy. Once again, the canon subtly undermines a narrow Israelite perspective.

3.15–23: Grace breaks through

Finally, Israel cries out to Yahweh. Surprisingly, it took 18 years. The 18 years may reflect the length of punishment, or how slow the people were in realizing their predicament and in crying out to Yahweh. The cry is the defining moment moving from the logic of action-consequence to that of need-mercy. The story draws the reader into a complex ethical picture, portraying Israel as guilty yet inviting sympathy for their pain. Readers are drawn into asking, What is justice? What is the right thing to do? What kind of world is enabled with either course of action? A deliverer is raised, but there is no mention of the Spirit of Yahweh and no indication of whether his choice of a covert assassination rather than leading troops in battle was sanctioned by Yahweh. The deliverer's identity links the story to the wider arc of relationship between Judah and Benjamin, prefiguring the David/Saul contrast. Ehud was an unexpected deliverer from a small tribe, from the clan of Gera, who will insult David in 2 Samuel 16.5, begging further canonical questions of representation. In addition, Ehud is left-handed, a recurring pattern for Benjaminites yet something considered abnormal at the time. The idiom in Hebrew is unclear, translating as 'bound in the right hand'; as the Benjaminites are later said to have a force of 700 left-handed fighters (Judg. 20.16), it is unlikely they would all be naturally left-handed, and more likely that Benjamin trained warriors to be ambidextrous through binding their right hand, leading some scholars to argue that Ehud was the closest thing to a professional soldier in Israel (Christianson, 2003, p. 61; Halpern, 1992, p. 41; Park, 2015, p. 701). The depiction is laden with irony, as Benjamin means 'son of the right hand'. The valorizing of the right over the left appears recurrently, particularly in ritual contexts (Ex. 29.20; Lev. 7.32–33, 8.25–26, 8.23, 9.21, 14.14, 17; Num. 18.18; Eccles. 10.2).The use of the left hand therefore increases the subtext of uncleanness and scatological humour, as the left hand is usually associated with lower bodily functions, thereby unclean, an unlikely source of strength and deliverance. A secondary pattern, the unexpected hero, is emerging: first, Othniel the Kenizzite, then Ehud the left-handed Benjaminite. It is a frequent trope in stories of hope and encouragement for oppressed people, making it possible to imagine that deliverance may occur. The unexpectedness of the deliverer serves two other purposes. One is to enhance that it is Yahweh who gives the victory. Second, it also serves the biblical pattern of bringing those who are disregarded into positions of leadership, thereby challenging entrenched privilege, and widening Israel's social imagination. Throughout the Hebrew Scriptures, Israel will struggle as a small nation surrounded by more powerful ones and be tempted to play the power game of having worthy, strong leaders. Yet the story consistently shows that military strength is not reliable or conducive to long-lasting peace. The pattern powerfully moves into the NT with the birth of a messiah from Nazareth in a borrowed room, away from palaces, and gathering a group of unexpected disciples around him who will go on to shape the early Church. A consistent undermining of cultural notions of worth and power shapes the bigger biblical narrative and redefines the meaning of power and strength, including the meaning and practice of divine power. Ehud's name underscores irony, as it could be taken to mean 'Where is majesty/glory?' Indeed, one of the messages of the story is that glory is not found in expected places, and a gap is created between the characters' expectations (that Eglon is esteemed as king, while Ehud is a shamed member of an oppressed group bringing tribute to his conqueror) and the readers, who already know that Ehud is Yahweh's chosen deliverer.

3.16 then shows Ehud preparing. He has a clear plan, structured around deception. Ehud's sword is small and strapped to his inner thigh – a detail that would have brought laughter to listeners for its sexual innuendo. It is also double-edged, meaning it can be used with either hand. Ehud plans carefully, yet much is left to chance. He assumes that he will only be searched on one side. He may have a plan for being left alone with the king, but that is not revealed. There is no mention of an escape plan, hence it could easily be a suicide mission – or, as it turns out, a James Bond-like feat of luck and prowess. Ehud's plan hinges on the Israelites' choice that he should take their tribute to the king, adding a further layer of irony as the instrument of oppression (tribute) is used to overturn the oppressor. Symbolically, it reinforces the idea that oppression always sows the seeds of its own reversal. A tribute symbolized a nation's subjection and the means of keeping them oppressed by draining their best resources. The specific words used here for giving a tribute (*qārāb* in *hiph* + *minḥâ*) are normally only used in cultic or ritual contexts (Amit, 1989, p. 110). The allusion feeds into a portrayal of Eglon, whose name means 'fattened calf', as a sacrificial beast. The detail that Eglon was 'very fat' reinforces the picture since this word for fat, *bārî*, is often used for good quality animals ready for sacrifice. Eglon's corpulence (and that of his warriors later) highlights the contrast between the well-fed oppressors and Israel's oppression. It also adds to the comic portrayal of the enemy leader as object of ridicule, laughter being one of the only weapons of the oppressed. The audience takes place – and nothing happens, leaving readers wondering.

Ehud turns round in 3.19. The mention of the idols (*pəsîlîm*) at Gilgal is significant, symbolically and narratively. *Pəsîlîm* is always pejorative, referring to pagan idols (Beldman, 2020, p. 79). They may be a simple geographical marker, possibly the passage between Israel and Moab. However, Gilgal was the place where Joshua had set up 12 memorial stones (Josh. 4.2) and where the first Passover was celebrated in the Promised

Land (Josh. 5.10). Now it is a place known for its idols. Symbolically, it points to the undoing of Joshua's achievements. Narratively, the idols may give the pretext Ehud needs to go back to the king, pretending to have a message from the gods, an oracle. He returns, and no one disputes his story, he is not searched thoroughly, and is allowed to be alone with the king. It is a typical underdog portrait of oppressors as fools, but it also highlights the sheer arrogance of the powerful, who cannot imagine that they may be challenged by those they despise, or barely even see. Their complacency and blindness to the pain they cause is brought into sharp relief. Ehud, in contrast, has emerged from the grassroots, bearing the weight of his people's cry of despair.

Ehud tells the king he has a secret word/thing/message for him. The Hebrew *dĕbar* can mean word/message, but also thing/object/experience, and heightens irony, as the king may expect an oracle, or perhaps an additional gift, or a political report, but Ehud's 'thing' is the sword hidden up his thigh and the death it will bring. Eglon rashly sends his attendants out. It is unclear whether they move to a different part of the palace, or of the throne room; it is unlikely to be an 'upper' room if it is cooler – heat rises – and more likely a private raised area at the back of the throne room. What matters is that they are alone, enabling Ehud's plan to unfold. Readers are aghast at the foolishness of the king. Reader sympathy lies with Ehud at this point, as the tale is presented in a David and Goliath manner. Yet it may be worth pausing for a moment and considering the overall trajectory of Judges, when Israel's leaders mirror the kings of the nations. Do they deserve the same treatment? Is this justice? Does the end justify the means? Ehud initially addresses the king with respect, 'O king'. Once alone, he drops the honorific. The king's status is diminishing. Ehud's is increasing, as he now claims his message/word/thing is 'from God' (not Yahweh). There is no record of Yahweh ever speaking to Ehud, so it may be a ruse. Yet at a deeper level, as Ehud is God's deliverer, his sword may be from God for the king.

Ehud kills the king. One may wonder whether the assassination was wise, necessary, or even useful in the sequence of events.

The narrative gives no indication either way, leaving readers to ponder the morality of Ehud's actions. The scene is redolent with grim humour. The death of the king is utterly undignified. He does not die as a warrior, or stabbed in the heart, but is penetrated by the sword from the warrior's thigh, a rather crude innuendo, designed to effeminate the enemy as often seen in ancient war tales, enhancing humiliation and shame. Eglon is further lampooned for his girth as the 'two-mouthed' sword is swallowed in his belly, and his excrement seeps out. The picture fits the stereotype of Moab as unclean and reverses expectations – it is the king who is unclean, not Ehud the left-hander. There is also a grim, symbolic justice in the depiction of Eglon's fatness turned against him; he had wrongfully taken the fat of the land for himself, depriving others.

Ehud sneaks out unseen, though the sparseness of the narration has led to much conjecture about the physical layout of the palace and the exact means of escape (A backdoor? The front door? The latrine chute?). The details are withdrawn so that the readers concentrate less on Ehud's feat and more on the comic scene about to unfold, as the combination of closed door and smell of offal leads the servants to think that the king was relieving himself. They wait until they are 'ashamed' – a wink from the narrator who knows it is the king who has been shamed. Where they would expect to fall to the ground before the king, it is the king who has fallen. Eglon's physical characteristics have enabled Ehud's escape by creating the servant's delay. Their reaction, however, could not have been foreseen, suggesting Yahweh's hand in the providential concatenation of circumstances.

3.26–30: Delivering Israel

Ehud makes his escape, taking advantage of the servants' delay. Once again, the enigmatic idols at Gilgal are mentioned. Ehud cuts a lonesome figure; he alone carried out the assassination, with no accomplices, taking no one into his confidence. He does not tell the people what he has done, and his actions remain shrouded in mystery – we never know whether they were rooted in a 'word/thing/message' from God, or, indeed, which god. Ehud summons the people to battle. The death of a king would send the country and its elite in disarray, making it easier to act, though it may also spur revenge. Ehud the Benjaminite summons the Ephraimites in 3.27, though tribal identities are immediately collapsed into 'the Israelites', with Ehud at their head. For the first time since 3.15, Yahweh is mentioned by name. Ehud had used 'god' (*'ĕlohîm*) to speak to foreigners, but now uses 'Yahweh' to speak to Israel. For the first time, Ehud makes a theological statement, attributing victory to Yahweh. He tells the troops that 'Yahweh has given *your* enemies the Moabites into *your* hand', completely removing himself from taking any glory, much like Othniel before, and unlike leaders to come. The battle concludes swiftly as the Moabite army is lured into a bottleneck area by the fords of the Jordan, a tactic that would have served the smaller, untrained army (Amit, 1989, p. 119). 3.29 is a typical battle tally, recognizing the valour of the enemy, thereby enhancing the Israel's victory.

Ehud's individual violence toward Eglon leads to the corporate violence of Israel against Moab. The overall event is placed under the sign of deliverance, and leads to rest for the land for 80 years (3.30), hence it seems justified and 'just'. The long period of peace should enable Israel to consolidate its hold on the land and make progress on covenantal living.

Assessing Ehud

The apparent rightness and theological justification for Ehud's actions may – and possibly should – leave readers feeling slightly uncomfortable. Ehud's wit, daring and cunning make him a natural hero, while his terse speech and skill with a sword set him up as a masculine symbol, a man of few words who lets his sword do the talking. Readers are easily drawn into a traditional tale of a dark handsome hero who fights the odds against comical, foolish oppressors.

It would be easy to forget Yahweh's role in the excitement of the story. Yet the story is a model example of double causality.

The attack is carefully planned by Ehud, yet there are so many coincidental elements that success can only be attributed to divine providence in conjunction with human skill. However, double causality does not imply Yahweh's approval of human tactics. After all, Yahweh had also used Eglon's hard heart. As Judges progresses, readers increasingly ask themselves whether Yahweh works *with* human beings or *in spite of* them. Ehud is Yahweh's deliverer, but never takes counsel with Yahweh, does not receive the Spirit, and Yahweh is absent from the assassination account. At no point is there any suggestion that the assassination contributed to victory.

We may also question the dark, unpleasant humour. On the one hand, it serves to assert the self of an oppressed people against the crushing hand of the oppressor. Yet in the Hebrew Bible there constantly lurks the warning against a reversal of the polarity of oppression. Israel is consistently told to care for the stranger, because they were once strangers themselves (Ex. 22.21), and to remember they were once slaves. The underlying message is that being oppressed does not justify any action, in particular once a new order is established. Here, from the vantage position of a much later historical time, the nation looks back and laughs at Moab, othering that nation just as they once were othered. It may satisfy a logic of sin-punishment, but there is little that suggests the possibility of the completely different order of things evoked by the crying out-deliverance formula. Israel is always only one short step away from being assimilated to the people of the land, whether by force or through their own actions.

As such, critics disagree on assessing Ehud's morality. The text itself is ambiguous, with some positive clues, neutral clues and ominous omissions. Yet this is the nature of the text, and its power: instead of telling readers what to think, it invites them to wrestle with it and ask themselves questions both about the characters and their actions, and also about their own reactions to the narrative. Each episode can be looked at on its own, and in this particular case the reader can conclude that Ehud is a 'good' judge. Setting him within the trajectory of the book as a whole problematizes his legacy: he is set into a deteriorating spiral; he does not address moral and spiritual degeneracy; underlying questions in Judges about the nature of justice, and its interweaving with mercy, prompt uneasy reflections. Equally, Ehud is a deeply human character. It is difficult to tell what is from God and what is not; he may have mixed motives, and a mixed character, yet this is no barrier to Yahweh working with him, and to the flourishing of Israel. Judges does not paint an ideal land with ideal choices or ideal leaders; nor does it paint a simple binary world of good and bad. It portrays the complexity of humanity, the difficulty of making ethical judgements, and the inevitably compromised nature of political actions in a less-than-perfect world. Yet for all the ambiguity, one fact is certain: Israel cried out to Yahweh, and Yahweh delivered.

3.31: Shamgar

The next judge is dispatched in one verse. We know hardly anything about Shamgar, save his name and unclear filiation. The name is not based on the usual triliteral roots of Hebrew, but appears to be Hurrian (Block, 1999, p. 31). The filiation 'son of Anath' is equally intriguing, because Anath was a Canaanite goddess, which implies either non-Yahwist parents or the possibility of a non-Yahwist deliverer (Beldman, 2020, p. 80). Shamgar therefore comes as another unexpected deliverer whose origins are unclear at best, and the entire focus is on his actions against the Philistines, a new enemy. He uses an ox-goad, a typical tool of a farmer, which suggests guerrilla warfare rather than organized combat. There is no clue about his motivation, and the only framework element is 'he delivered Israel', almost an afterthought. Just like Ehud, he is not said to judge Israel. Yahweh is not mentioned at all, yet Shamgar's inclusion suggests an implied framework to understand the need for a deliverer, the action of Yahweh, and the result, once again, deliverance.

4—5: Deborah and Jael

Chapters 4 and 5 tell a longer tale, twice over, organized around two sets of protagonists; the initiators of action are two women, Deborah and Jael, who are in many ways opposites; the other two are Barak and Jabin, the men. Scholars have long agreed that the two versions of the story do not date back to the same time, because chapter 5 uses more archaic language, with many unusual words of unclear meanings. The two stories have different perspectives and emphases yet are complementary and articulated together within the wider framework: the first element of the frame, doing evil, appears in 4.1, while the final element, 'the land had rest', concludes both chapters in 5.31. The positioning of the framework elements suggests that the final editors meant for the prose and the poetry to be read sequentially as one story. Narratively, this makes sense: the 'facts' are recounted, followed by a character recounting events in song, as in the songs of Moses and Miriam in Exodus 15. While diachronic readings are helpful in unearthing layers of text and historical information and exploring some differences between the two accounts, here I will consider the text as received, as the theological meaning of the text within the canon is shaped by the final editor(s)' decision to introduce the song where it comes. The retelling of an event by its participants gives crucial clues about theological thinking and framing; placing the narrator's point of view side-by-side with that of the characters illuminates narratorial perspective and judgement. The divergences between the two accounts will be explored as a technique to create meaning, rather than explained through source differentiation.

4: The prose account

4.1–3: The framework

The advent of a new judge is placed straight after Ehud, missing out Shamgar, which may reflect the geographic limitation of each judge's sphere of influence. Ehud had called Ephraim to battle, and this story opens in the hill country of Ephraim (4.5). The framework, absent from Shamgar's story, resumes here, with continued evil in Israel. 'After Ehud died' may suggest that Israel had turned back to Yahweh, or at least desisted from some of their practices in his lifetime, in which case they resumed doing evil. Either way, it shows Ehud's failure to bring lasting and significant change. The deliverers bring socio-political deliverance but they do not address the root problem. The cyclical elements create a sense of futility about the great military feats described, and the value of the judges. Will this one do better? King Jabin of Hazor is introduced as the source of the oppression, king not just of one city-state, but of Canaan, though Canaan was never a single political entity (Butler, 2009, p. 89). The description magnifies his power and fearsomeness and enhances the Israelites' victory. Another king, Jabin of Hazor, had been thoroughly defeated in Joshua 11, and Hazor destroyed and not rebuilt until the time of Solomon (Beldman, 2020, p. 82). 'Jabin of Hazor' may be a dynastic name given to a descendant who has resumed his rule with the help of Canaanite allies. Symbolically, it shows the fragility of the initial conquest, the tenuousness of political power, and the undoing of Joshua's achievements in Judges. Focus quickly shifts from the king to his chief general, Sisera. In Joshua, kings fought their own battles; here, Jabin is conspicuously absent. Israel cries out to Yahweh without any indication of repentance. There is no record of Yahweh's response. The detail about iron chariots echoes Judah's inability to take the plains in 1.19, and symbolizes the oppressors' technological advantage, a technologically advanced iron age society versus a primitive agrarian one. The discrepancy enhances the epic feel, the magnitude of the victory, and, by default, Yahweh's role in it. It also aligns reader sympathies with Israel and justifies the level of violence inflicted on the enemy – a questionable strategy. The detail is also significant as it is presented as the perceived cause of oppression. The people see no link between their own actions, divine withdrawal and their present situation.

4.4–10: Raising a deliverer

The typical framework beginning takes an unexpected turn, as the raising of a deliverer takes a new shape. 4.4 introduces Deborah as 'a woman-prophetess, wife of Lappidoth, judging Israel'. Her gender is clear from the double feminine form woman-prophetess (*'iššâ nəbî'â*), though it is unclear whether this is special emphasis on her gender or a standard way to indicate a woman's occupation (see García Bachmann, 2018, for uses of the woman-X construction). Other female prophets include Miriam (Ex. 15.20), Huldah (2 Kings 22.14), Noadiah (Neh. 6.14), Anna (Luke 2.36) and the four daughters of Philip the evangelist (Acts 21.8–9). Other female prophets are usually introduced as 'the prophetess', with the definite article and no 'woman' (García Bachmann, 2018, p. 27), though Judges also has the only instance of a 'man-prophet' in the Deuteronomistic History (6.8), suggesting a strong intentional parallel between the two accounts of prophetic intervention. Here, prophets are still respected, listened to and known by name. There is no surprise or condemnation by the narrator about Deborah's gender, rather he gives a matter-of-fact description, as with all the other main characters, though she was also an unexpected leader.

Several features of the introductory sentence enhance Deborah's uniqueness. As a prophet, Deborah functions as a spokesperson from Yahweh, speaking up to leaders, and composing verse that is remembered. She differs from other judges in that she is already well-established and recognized as a spiritual leader. While the Spirit of Yahweh is not mentioned, prophets in the OT are usually under the influence of the Spirit (Num. 11.17, 25; 1 Sam. 10.6, 10; Hos. 9.7; Joel 2.28–29), while prophecy is specifically mentioned as a gift of the Spirit in the NT (1 Cor. 12.7–11). The family link, wife of Lappidoth, has caused some controversy among interpreters, disputing whether this is a typical association of a woman with her closest male relative, establishing Deborah's social belonging via the kinship structure, or whether, because of the unusual feminine form of the name, it is an epithet describing her fierceness. There is no obvious reason to doubt that Deborah was married, particularly since she describes herself as a mother in Israel in the song. Being married and a mother would have strengthened her credibility. The text, however, remains ambiguous, simultaneously open to both meanings. The description of her 'judging' is interesting. No named male leader is called 'a judge'; instead, the recurring description is 'he judged' (*šāpat* in the *qal* imperfect), an active verb describing action (10.2, 3; 12.7, 8, 9, 11, 13, 14, 15.20, 16.31). Here, in Deborah's case, we do not have 'she judged' but 'she', followed by the participle, which most translators and commentators choose to render as a verbal form: she was judging. This is certainly possible; however, the verb is in the *qal* participle female singular, and the masculine equivalent is always translated as a noun form, a judge. Hence it would be logical to translate, 'she was a judge in Israel', and the only reason not to do so is, presumably, a judgement on her suitability because of her gender, something not present in the text. This would make Deborah the only named character to be described as a judge instead of judging, an interesting fact in view of her dual involvement in spiritual and political leadership. 4.5 expands on the nature of her ministry, which appears to have a judicial component, giving judgements under her tree. Trees are often associated with pagan places of worship; the figure of Deborah the prophetess cuts a strong contrast, with justice, as a central Yahwist concept, being dispensed under her tree, located between Ramah and Bethel, two significant places in Israel, and fairly central, accessible to the entire nation. Parallels for her role include Moses, to whom the people came for judgement (Ex. 18.13), and Samuel, also a judge, arbiter and someone who appointed leaders (1 Sam. 7.15–16). Both parallels suggest a positive framing for Deborah.

After a lengthy introduction, Deborah summons Barak, whose role is more passive. Deborah is identified as a judge, but not as a 'deliverer'. Instead, she makes deliverance Barak's role (Barak is never said to judge Israel). Every story departs from the framework pattern somehow; here the function of judge and deliverer is split between two people who nevertheless work together. Many critics have interpreted this split as a problem, a failure in Barak, or insisted that Deborah is not a judge, Barak is; there is, however, a different possibility. Given Judges' focus on leadership, its styles and pitfalls, a story of shared leadership is not out of place – and echoes the successful cooperation of Judah and Simeon in 1.3. The man she summons is introduced briefly, by name, father, place and tribe, a secondary character in comparison to Deborah. He represents a new tribe, Naphtali, followed by Zebulun in the next verse. He is from Kadesh, a Levitical city, though not a Levite himself. Deborah clearly has enough authority to summon him. Her instructions in 4.6–7 follow the conventions of prophetic speech, a charge in the first person in Yahweh's name; the formula is typical of pre-battle oracles, with mention of summoning troops, drawing out the enemy and Yahweh giving them 'into your hand'. Yahweh is acting as commander-in-chief, setting the terms of the battle and defining tactics. This is much closer to the holy wars of Joshua than the actions of Ehud.

4.8 unveils the words Barak is famous for. Interpreters disagree on the meaning and legitimacy of Barak's reluctance, many seeing irony in a man refusing to lead while a woman acts decisively (Amit, 1999; Block, 1999; Butler, 2009; Chisholm, 2013; Soggin, 1981), even though Barak's equivocation is not very different from that of Moses or Gideon. The text itself gives no indication that Barak was a first choice of leader, displaced by Deborah. It is Deborah who is treated as the principal character and called a judge. The exchange between them fits the pattern of a protested call narrative. Barak's words echo Moses' words to Yahweh in Exodus; some argue that Barak transfers confidence from Yahweh to Deborah. This is unfair: Deborah has been speaking as the mouthpiece of Yahweh, in the first person. Barak's response conflates Yahweh and Deborah. She becomes an embodiment of the presence of Yahweh. Barak's response shows willingness to recognize leadership in others, awareness that the presence of Yahweh is indispensable; Barak may not trust his own listening to God but wants a prophet's guidance. Whether it is to listen to God or to ensure victory is unclear.

There is no overt condemnation; the oracle was clearly given for Barak, but there is no reason why Deborah should not be involved. Except that she is a woman and traditionally women do not go to war. Barak could be a forward-thinking man who does not mind breaking with convention to ensure the true leader of Israel is seen to be Deborah, regardless of gender. Or he could be scared and a coward, wanting to be able to attribute failure to a woman's bad counsel. Or he could genuinely want to work collaboratively and recognizes that what is needed is a combination of skills he does not possess on his own, but they have as a team. Hence Barak could be an excellent leader, who does what is right regardless of personal cost, or he could be a failure ... The text itself is ambiguous.

Deborah's answer in 4.9 comes where an assurance of divine presence would appear in a call narrative, with the prophet functioning as Yahweh's alter ego. Deborah's warning that a woman will claim the victory is ambiguous. Is it a simple prophetic statement? A shrewd observation of a patriarchal society? Laying out the consequences of Barak's choice so that he is fully informed? Or a condemnation? Scholars (often male) have usually interpreted her words as punishment for Barak's unwillingness, shaming him as less than a proper man (see Schneider, 1999, p. 70). In the light of the wider exploration of leadership, however, Barak comes across as acknowledging both Yahweh and Deborah's leadership, and more concerned about divine presence than about glory or honour for himself – the fault of the next three leaders. Deborah does not say she herself will get the glory, though readers may assume she will, but points to the other woman who will complete the story. Both Barak and Deborah point away from themselves, making space for Yahweh to be acknowledged as the true leader of Israel. In the light of the prologue's statement that Israel would be tested, and learn war, is this a test for Barak? A traditional, patriarchal, warlike culture would expect him (along with many commentators) to lead strongly and seek glory. Yet what Yahweh wants to teach his people in Judges, which is particularly obvious in 6—9, is that it is not strength or skill that matter, but his presence. Barak is asking for Deborah's presence as human representative of Yahweh ... Underneath the surface of the text lie some complex representations of self and gendered other, for the characters, for the cultures that frame the narrative, and for successive readers. Barak is not hostage to specific ideas of masculinity; instead, in today's psychological analysis, he comes across as secure in his expression of self, showing appropriate self-differentiation, and hence does not need to enter into the type of bargaining that diminishes the other (woman) in order to secure his own position. He is therefore much less hampered by his own frailty than his successors. Deborah is equally secure and generous; she understands the limitations and constraints of the surrounding culture, yet transcends them as leader, and offers Barak the chance to be shielded from the negative impact of patriarchy on men. The theological drive of Judges, on leadership and the right way to conduct war, suggests a more positive explanation of the story than is often given, though ambiguity remains, and answers often mould themselves to the culture of the interpreter. Furthermore, while in patriarchal terms Barak may bring shame on himself, cultural notions of shame are undermined within the canon, with the Christ-event redefining the notion of what is shameful. The text itself offers the possibility of questioning prevailing cultural norms. To assume that Barak, as male, was supposed to be the main leader and Deborah, as female, wasn't supposed to be on the battlefield, is to yield to the prevalent culture in a text that consistently speaks out against yielding to culture. The story of Deborah subverts the expectations of a patriarchal culture; women, traditionally seen as 'weak', unexpectedly show their strength – just as Ehud deconstructed Eglon's concept of the people he oppressed. Barak then summons and leads the troops, as is his role as commander, and Deborah follows. Both characters understand their role, and respect each other's skills, in a positive example of joint leadership.

4.11–16: Battle report

4.11 introduces Jael, an apparently disconnected aside, though every detail matters in terse Hebrew narrative. The Kenites appear again. They had remained somewhat separate (cf. 1.16), but one of them, Heber, had separated from his original group and pitched his tent near a Hebrew holy site. Tribal and ethnic boundaries are porous and shifting; characters do not live where expected, which sets up a pattern of displacement and intermingling rather than a neat delineation of identity. This suggests that Judges reflects the messiness of real life, rather than merely a later ideological shaping of national identity. We then move to the narrative's turning point, when Sisera hears about Barak and summons his own overwhelming forces. Sisera calls *all* his chariots in a show of strength. As prophet, Deborah communicates the timing for the battle and assures the troops of Yahweh's presence with them. The battle is instigated by Yahweh, the ultimate commander and deliverer, whose presence renders 'all the chariots' irrelevant. Deborah tells Barak when to move, and he obeys. There is complete trust between them. He does not question her spiritual judgement, she does not question his military leadership, and events proceed apparently as they were meant to.

The battle report is brief, focusing on divine action, as usual in holy war reports. The narrator ironically reprises the picture of Sisera 'and all his chariots', now merely toys in Yahweh's mighty hand. The strength Sisera had trusted in is irrelevant, and he leaves his chariot to flee on foot, now equal to the Israelite soldiers. Sisera abandons his troops, against warrior expectations, though Barak does not notice and goes the opposite way, pursuing the army, a more logical strategic decision. The narrator yet again ironically stresses that '*all* the army fell', no one was left – well, except the runaway general.

4.17–24: Complete victory

Barak courageously follows the army, while Sisera ironically flees the other way, towards the tent of a woman whose people are allied with his and therefore perfectly safe. Expectation is set for the unexpected (or a really boring end to the story). Readers had half-expected Deborah to reappear at this point, but it will be an external, marginal character who will bring about symbolic victory through slaying the enemy commander. Sisera trusts his political position and his strength as a man. There is a political alliance with Heber and he relies on it. The Kenites once had Mosaic connections, had allied with Judah, and now have an alliance of peace with Jabin. They occupy a liminal place, belonging fully to neither group, their loyalties not entirely predictable. Sisera does not consider the nuances of the situation, or ethnic and political boundaries as porous or unstable. He does not see Jael as dangerous because she is a woman, whose loyalties he assumes will match her husband's, as expected in a patriarchal culture. He does not expect a woman to think and act for herself. The dynamics are like those in Ehud's tale: an overconfident leader underestimates those whom he considers 'other', and this 'other' exploits the underlying assumptions of fealty. Jael is doubly other, through gender and ethnicity, hence even less visible on Sisera's map of power. In both texts the leader is lured into false security, attacked with brutality in a private place, with sexual overtones. Both stories show the futility of trusting in military and political power, and underline the ironic blindness of the privileged, who fail to see the potential and power of those they oppress or disregard. The invisibility of the underprivileged becomes their weapon in a complete reversal of power dynamics.

Sisera makes straight for Jael's tent, presumably because it would be the least likely place for a warrior to be, hence a safe hiding hole. The biblical corpus shows multiple instances of women having their own tents as part of a nomadic household (Gen. 18.6; 24.67; 31.31–36). Jael comes out to meet him, a normal act of welcome for a visitor, though one would have expected her husband to take the lead. Jael feels safe enough to come out and address the enemy general. As Judges progresses, it will become increasingly dangerous for women to move out of domestic spaces, as with Jephthah's daughter (11.34–40), the Levite's concubine (19.1–30) and the daughters of Shiloh (21.15–24). Jael's tent, as a female space, symbolized safety and domesticity; the traditional dichotomy of public/domestic and its attendant meaning is subverted and used against Sisera. In further chapters, the public/private boundary will blur as domestic spaces gradually become unsafe, not just for the men who trespass within them, but for the women who are supposed to be safe there (e.g. Samson's wife, burnt in her house; the concubine, dismembered in her house). The story of Jael and Deborah still marks a high in the social organization of Israel and treatment of women. Jael's motives are unclear, but her position would have been precarious at best. The ubiquity of rape as a weapon of war loomed in the background. Turning away the Canaanite general would put her at risk of violence; leading him to her tent would risk unwanted sexual advances. Sisera was clearly fleeing from battle gone wrong, hence his alliance with her husband would put them all at risk. Sheltering him would risk the Hebrews treating them as enemies too, with the consequences that Sisera's mother imagines for captured women at the end of chapter 5. Jael's motives are not made explicit; leaving them to the imagination invites readers into the story, to wonder and explore possible dynamics.

Initially the scene plays on motherly imagery, as Jael reassures Sisera, soothing him like a child, 'have no fear!', taking him to bed and tucking him in with a blanket, then giving him milk and watching over his sleep. Even though it is her tent, Sisera gives orders. He commands her, a woman (a liminal other), a Kenite (a liminal ethnic other) to guard the entrance of the tent (a liminal space). He has put someone whose identity is by definition beyond his grasp in charge of the boundary between himself and safety. He never sees her as a true 'other'. She is simply a product of his prejudices and expectations, someone he cannot imagine behaving as she is about to. And, of course, he assumes that his status is such that others will work to save him, even putting themselves at risk for him, with no understanding of the choices facing those without his privileged status. Ironically, he tells her to answer any pursuers who ask, 'Is there a man here?', with 'no'. No, there is no man – because he is like a child; and no, because he will be dead by then. The scene then turns dark. Just like Eglon, Sisera is penetrated by a weapon and feminized; just as with Eglon, the violence is graphic and possibly excessive. The sword went so far in Eglon's belly that it was completely swallowed; here, the tent peg is driven with so much force that it nails him to the ground. Unlike with Ehud however, the murder of Sisera is a murder of opportunity, using whatever weapon was at hand. Women may not have been skilled in war, but it was their job to put up the tent (Mandolfo, 2019, p. 349) and therefore Jael would have had skill and strength invisible to Sisera. As with Sisera, Jael now goes out to meet Barak. This time, she displays her handiwork to the victorious general. Within the logic of patriarchy, Jael has deprived both men of honour, as she killed a warrior and overcame the most prized enemy. Yet nowhere is this then commented on, or problematized, either here or in Deborah and Barak's song. Commentators rush to conclude that the events show Israel in weak and negative terms, with no real men left (Bal, 1988a, p. 93; Butler, 2009, p. 85; Conway, 2019, p. 123). Commentators also disagree on assessing the nature and impact of Jael's action. Is she an example of treachery and betrayal? Does she violate sacred rules of hospitality (Block, 1999, p. 209)? Or is it Sisera who does so, by imposing himself on a woman in her own space and ordering her about (Smit, 2018, p. 83)? The tension between hospitality and survival is key and reappears in Judges 19. Sisera is in survival mode, Jael may be too. The nature of war and situations of extreme danger is to blur boundaries and undermine normal rules of social interaction, leading to unpredictable actions and individuals violating their normal social codes. We cannot simply assess Jael and Sisera's actions via peacetime standards.

The importance of Sisera's death is unclear. Symbolically, it mattered, but strategically it was unnecessary, perhaps as Eglon's had been. What it does is reinforce the new identity of Israel by shaming the Canaanite general and, by extension, his entire people. Victory is complete and attributed to divine action in 4.23, though using God (*Elohim*) rather than Yahweh. The attribution of victory to God reinforces that asking who, out of human protagonists, was going to get glory was the wrong question. Victory is brought to 'the sons of Israel', the pan-Israelite formula, even though only two tribes were summoned in 4.6. A victory statement is part of the framework, but an additional element appears – 'the hand of the Israelites bore harder and harder on King Jabin', a statement that appears to reverse the poles of oppression, with Israel doing to Canaan as Canaan had done to Israel. The question for Israel is whether they will have learnt anything from the episode, and whether they will be a different type of nation to the one they have vanquished or adopt their political practices. The renewed mention of King Jabin highlights his absence from the war but heightens the parallel between Sisera and Barak as the military chiefs who receive orders from others. It would be natural to assume that the corresponding parallel would be between Jabin and Deborah – however, Deborah is Yahweh's representative, so that Jabin is fighting directly against Yahweh as the real king of Israel.

5: Victory song

5.1–11: Call to worship

Deborah and Barak now sing together, as happens elsewhere post battle. Deborah's name comes first, unusually for a woman, but they are still presented as working together. In battle, Deborah followed Barak, the military man, and now Barak follows Deborah, the prophet, in memorializing the event in ways that give glory to Yahweh and shape the identity of Israel. The song combines several different genres, as Butler points out: 'epic narrative, battle calls, cultic blessings and curses, tribal evaluations, and poetic satire' (2009, p. 123). Martial imagery dominates, and Yahweh's actions take centre stage. Yahweh plays the role that Canaanites would usually attribute to their own gods, giving the song a cosmic feel. It opens and closes with blessing, and blessings and curses are woven through the text, in 5.9, 24, 23, 31. Israel features strongly, with an emphasis on tribal participation and unity as a wider group, accountable to Yahweh for participation or non-participation. The poem interprets the story theologically, but also seeks to shape the national identity of Israel by reinforcing the importance of cohesion and shaming those who did not participate. The song is old, with many archaic words, and therefore difficult to interpret.

The first verse extols willingness to follow Yahweh's lead in two different ways. The reference to long hair may be a reference to Nazirite vows, a willing, usually time-limited, vow for a specific purpose; the second part 'when the people offer themselves willingly' repeats the sentiment of the first line, in typical Hebrew poetry parallelism. It could refer to offering for military service, but the first line, together with the expression 'the people', rather than the men/sons of Israel, suggests wider openness to serving Yahweh. The singers then call kings and rulers to worship, an ironic statement since they have just brought down an oppressive ruler and his chief commander; the defeated enemies are enjoined to bless Yahweh for their own defeat. Yahweh now enters the scene, depicted as a cosmic warrior with the natural world at his command. The storm imagery is often associated with Baal, the Canaanite deity, but here is repurposed for Yahweh, whose distinctive identity is stressed repeatedly in 5.5 with the parallelism, 'before the face of Yahweh, the one of Sinai, before the face of Yahweh, the God of Israel'. The formula is redolent with covenant terms, pointing to the self-revelation of Yahweh at Sinai, and his close relationship with Israel. Hence the underlying message is a religious polemic that claims that it is Yahweh who is the cosmic king, and none of the local deities control natural phenomena. 5.6–8 then recounts the gradual worsening of conditions in Israel. The two people used as chronological markers – 'the days of ...' – are Shamgar and Jael, two liminal figures whose ethnic status is unclear and loyalty to Yahweh never mentioned. Their inclusion into the victory songs reprises the motif of the inclusion of foreigners and blessing of the nations. The parallel also puts Jael, a foreign woman, on a par with a deliverer of Israel, suggesting approval for her actions. The rest of the pericope is slightly unclear, but most commentators see it as a depiction of oppression, with travelling becoming dangerous, thereby hampering trade, in 5.6, farmers possibly afraid to go into the fields in 5.7 (Block, 1999, p. 225), or entire villages simply disappearing. Overall, normal life ceases until Deborah rises. Deborah's role is recounted in the first person (contra the NRSV translation which bizarrely uses 'you' in this verse, then 'my' in 5.9) and described as 'a mother in Israel'. Beldman (2020, p. 92) criticizes her for it, arguing she is exalting herself; however, Deborah had been self-effacing in 5.6, as in the narrative, and her words could just as easily reflect her surprise that someone like her was chosen, or a simple acknowledgement of the way in which Yahweh worked to bring in deliverance. The word 'mother' may evoke mothers as fierce protectors and guardians (cf. the frequent image of the she-bear and her cubs, 1 Sam. 8; Prov. 17.12; Hos. 13.8), or evoke affectionate feelings and safety (Ps. 131.2). It could also simply be used as an honorific for her role as prophet, though there are no obvious biblical parallels for such a practice.[1] Here, the close link between 'mother' and change for the better suggests it is the fierceness of mothers in providing for their children that is in sight, a fierceness that often challenges patriarchy from the inside (Fewell and Gunn, 1990, p. 402). Whether the term is used both literally and metaphorically is unclear. Deborah may well be a mother, literally, but this is not central to the meaning. 5.8 is a notoriously difficult verse, with an equally obtuse translation in the two LXX versions. The phrase 'he chose new gods' does not have any clear referents in the rest of the poem; it could point to Israel's apostasy, but that is not obvious, unless we make a causal link between 'new gods' and 'war at the gate'. 5.9–11 forms an inclusio with 5.2–3. 5.9 echoes 5.2 and willing service, while 5.10–11

1 Cities are occasionally called 'mother', and the term 'mother in Israel' is applied once to the city Abel, in recognition of its wisdom in 2 Samuel 20.18–19.

echoes 5.3 and the appeal to the rich and privileged to bless the Lord – i.e. ironically inviting the enemy to rejoice in their own defeat. 5.10–11 also graphically contrasts two sets of people: the rich, well-dressed privileged, probably city-dwellers, who 'walk by' and possibly ignore the other group, the farmers at the watering holes. The mention of gates then reinforces the contrast because the city gates mark the separation between town and country, and symbolically exclude the people of Israel from the prosperity of Canaanite city-states. Israel is portrayed as the underdog against cruel, privileged opponents (with no acknowledgement that city states would have had to rely on a vast agrarian economy). The characterization will carry through to the contrast between Jael the tent-dweller and Sisera's mother the palace-dweller.

5.12–18: Roll call

The next section of the song recounts the involvement of various parts of Israel. First, Deborah sings as prophet, while Barak as military leader deals with captives. Given the later musings of the mother of Sisera on the treatment of captive women, together with the fact that all fighting men were said to have been killed in 4.16, one may wonder who Barak and his men have taken captive and whether they will be treated in the same way as Canaanites would treat their prisoners of war. The Torah is specific in Deuteronomy 21.10–14 on how female captives that men find sexually attractive should be treated. The passage is distasteful to modern eyes but stands in contrast to 5.30 and the violence towards women captives there by ensuring some protection, a period of mourning and a place within the kinship system. 5.13 shows the preparations for war, with Israel again characterized as weak and oppressed. Deborah's call, better translated as 'rouse yourself for action!' than 'awake!', reinforces that the impetus for war comes directly from Yahweh, through the prophet. The ensuing list of participants does not name all 12 traditional tribes but misses some and uses some clans or subgroups: tribal identity fluctuates over the biblical corpus and the vocabulary for tribal and kinship groups is fluid, with subgroups or clans occasionally referring to the whole tribe, and tribes not strictly defined by the territory they occupy but often overlapping (Butler 2009, p. 144). Many respond, but not all, which prompts the question, what does it mean to call Israel, Israel? What is it that keeps this group of tribes together, beyond need and self-interest? The lack of interest from some of the tribes shows deterioration since the Shechem covenant, though the number of tribes shows that a sense of unity and interdependence still exists. There is a reasonably solid coalition of northern tribes: Ephraim, Benjamin, Issachar, Zebulun and Manasseh (Machir represents the eastern portion of Manasseh). Unity starts to break down with Reuben, who searched their hearts and tarried. It is unclear whether they joined or not, but if they did, solidarity is not an obvious or immediate choice. The image of their listening to piping suggests that they could not be bothered joining in. Dan, Asher and Gilead (poetic name for Gad) completely failed to help and are named and shamed. Judah and Simeon, the leading tribes of chapter 1, are conspicuous by their absence, in an incipient north/south division. The inclusion of the tribes' responses implies that the song also functions as a mechanism of social control, shaping corporate identity and memory. Those that respond and fight enthusiastically are depicted as closer to Yahweh and to an ideal (imagined) Israel.

5.19–22: Battle report

The poem expands on the shorter battle account of 4.15, but equally stresses the defining role of Yahweh, here emphasizing the simultaneous marshalling of human and heavenly resources. 5.19 taunts the defeated people, who had seen themselves as great and strong, with an exaggeration of their status for effect, 'the kings of Canaan', when we know Jabin did not make it to the battlefield. Their status is then dwarfed by Yahweh's marshalling of the hosts of heaven, with the dual assault of sky and waters. The song employs poetic licence to convey the magnitude of victory and awe at Yahweh's intervention. The use of the Wadi Kishon to sweep away horses and chariots echoes

Israel's history in Exodus, thereby hinting at the reliability of Yahweh, whose mighty acts of deliverance are consistent. Yet Gideon, the next judge, will question what Yahweh has done since the Exodus and apparently does not know this story. Yahweh's control over nature is a recurrent feature of divine power and action in the OT (see Job and Psalms, in particular), and extends into the NT as nature miracles are a particular locus of revelation, for instance with Jesus calming the storm (Matt. 8.23–27) or walking on water (Matt. 14.22–33).

5.23–24: Curses and blessings

The next two verses form a bridge between the main battle and the killing of Sisera. First comes the cursing of Meroz for not going into battle. This is consistent with shaming non-fighting tribes. As such, it functions as social control and identity delineation. Meroz does not appear anywhere else in Scripture; we do not know where it was, who the inhabitants were, or why the messenger/angel of Yahweh appeared, though his appearance reinforces the sense of a battle at two levels, earthly and heavenly. The curse makes sense in its placement in an antithetic parallelism with the blessing of Jael. Meroz represents Israelites (or friends of Israelites) who have not taken a stand against Canaan, while Jael is a non-Israelite who did take a stand with Israel. This in turn forms an inclusio with the final verse of the poem, which calls for enemies to perish and friends of Yahweh to prosper; taken together, these two verses problematize the identification of friend and foe, away from simple ethnic boundaries and into the realm of ethics and wider loyalties. Jael is singled out for the highest praise as 'most blessed', first among women as a whole, then, with an intensifying parallel, among 'women who live in tents' (since the word 'tent' is also used for houses, it is likely to be primarily a poetic device rather than a restriction of her blessedness). The use of 'most blessed' is unusual, as it is usually applied to male warriors, or to women in connection with motherhood.

5.25–31: The death of Sisera

The next part of the story, the killing of Sisera, is explored through two women connected to him, Jael who killed him, and his mother who gave him life, both located in private, domestic spaces. First, Sisera's death is retold in dramatic ways that enhance Jael's courage and Sisera's shame. The language and imagery are more brutal than in the prose, with multiple verbs emphasizing violent action in 5.26: strike, crush, shatter, pierce. The song omits the depiction of a drowsy Sisera falling asleep, which masculinizes Jael's attack by removing the emphasis on deceit (Fewell and Gunn 1990, p. 405). In the prose, Sisera gives orders, a constant acting subject. Here, he appears unnamed in 5.25, after which all the verbs have Jael as subject, until Sisera falls dead to the ground. His name is only used as an object of Jael's actions, 'she struck Sisera a blow'. Sisera, the passive actor here, is feminized within a patriarchal framework where, symbolically, men are 'active' and women 'passive'. Feminization is enhanced by the sexual overtones of the encounter in 5.27. The word for 'he lay', *šākab*, is often used to denote sexual intercourse; he then lies 'between her feet'. Given that feet, in Hebrew, are a frequent metaphor for genitalia, we could translate the expression as 'he lay between her thighs'. Sisera, the aggressor, the man whose mother will, in the next pericope, picture as taking 'wombs' captive, is himself attacked, penetrated and killed without fighting back. His humiliation and shame are complete. Such depictions of a 'feminized' enemy death are frequent in ancient literature (and in Judges itself see Abimelech's death) and reinforce concepts of hegemonic masculinity in war, while delineating identity by valorizing the self and demeaning the other. Whether such identity constructs are helpful is questionable. The discrepancy between prose and verse accounts prompts questions about the way characters conceptualize their actions over and against the narrator's depiction.

The narrative then shifts to a different domestic space and a different woman, in a palace rather than a tent. The cameo is a surprising acknowledgement of the shared humanity and suffering of the 'other side', though no doubt intended to comment ironically on enemy expectations. The mother of Sisera, surrounded by other women, is anxiously waiting to see her son, expecting to celebrate his victory. Unlike Deborah and Jael, she has stayed where women were seen to 'belong', though that does not stop her from indulging in violent war fantasies. Her traditional portrayal has her at a window, gazing out onto the public world of men and war, passively waiting for Sisera's return. She is hidden from the male gaze, behind a lattice or curtain. But she herself gazes onto the world of men, both imagining and condoning its violence. It is worth wondering here whether an actual woman would fantasize in the way she does here, or whether she is presented as the 'perfect' woman in the construction of masculine identity: reflecting to a man the qualities he wants to see in himself, approving his actions, rather than with her own subjectivity. Equally, the picture is one familiar to women throughout history, waiting anxiously and mourning the loss of loved ones in wars they themselves had no say in. The simple picture of a woman waiting for her son draws out sympathy, heightening shock at the next verse. The contrast between her palatial surroundings, with her own attendants, and Jael suggests a subtle comment on justice and echoes the biblical theme of bringing down the proud and rich and lifting up the lowly, found most powerfully in two other women's songs, one by Hannah (1 Sam. 2.1–11), the other by Mary, the Magnificat (Luke 1.46–55). Deborah's song is more complex in that she and Barak are now the victors who will go on to oppress Jabin in chapter 4. Can they still conceptualize themselves as lowly and weak?

5.30 then shatters the image of a mother's worry over Sisera's delay. The verse is somewhat difficult but boils down to a crude imagining of men taking the spoils of war, particularly focused on women: war rape and taking away their clothes. The word for women or girl is not even used, but replaced by *raḥam*, from the word for 'womb', thereby reducing women to their forcible sexual use by soldiers, 'a womb or two'. The coarseness of the language, together with the complete disregard for the women's fate, undermines reader sympathy and highlights the toll of war on women. Irony abounds as readers know that Sisera was vanquished, and it is Canaanite women that are potentially at risk of the fate she imagines. Her disregard may be born of callousness, or an effect of privilege and entitlement that suggests she is not at risk. Once again, power and privilege are shown as fragile and transient. Sisera's mother is complicit in a war that would bring her spoils too, in rich cloth or jewellery. Ethnicity trumps gender in her reveries. At this point in the book, it is a picture of the Canaanites. By chapter 21, it will be a feature of Israelite internecine war.

The song finally concludes with an imprecation on Yahweh's enemies and a call for blessing on Yahweh's friends. The line may function as a final liturgical response. Theologically, it presents as a typical for/against statement: either for Yahweh or against him. The story, of course, has already problematized the concept of easily dividing people into 'camps', with the cursing of Meroz the friend and Jael the supposed ally of Jabin. The rest of Judges, and the wider sweep of Scripture, problematize the statement further, with countless stories showing that those who love Yahweh may be unexpected and those who think they are friends of Yahweh may become complacent and forget what 'love of Yahweh' truly means. It is ironic that the verse starts with a curse on Yahweh's enemies, given that this is the position Israel occupied at the very beginning of the story, doing what was evil in the eyes of Yahweh. The song, focalized through its human characters, shows that they are unaware of the source of their earlier misfortune. There is also irony in that, as Judges progresses, Israel will increasingly find itself on the wrong side of Yahweh, showing they do not 'love Yahweh', hence Deborah and Barak's song may unwittingly bring a curse upon Israel itself. The word translated as 'friends' in the NRSV is, literally, 'those who love him'. The use of 'love' is reminiscent of Deuteronomy, where the word is used frequently, overwhelmingly about the Yahweh–human relationship (in both directions, from Yahweh to Israel in Deut. 4.37; 5.10; 7.13; 10.15; 10.18; 23.6 and Israel to Yahweh in Deut. 6.5; 7.9; 10.12; 11.1, 13, 22; 13.4; 19.9; 30.6; 30.16). There, love involves the entire person (Deut. 6.5; 10.12;

11.13) and closely links to walking with Yahweh in obedience to covenant living, often associated with keeping commandments (Deut. 7.9; 10.12; 11.1, 13, 22; 19.9; 30.16; 30.20) and extending care to other humans who may be less fortunate (Deut. 10.19; 15.6; 21.15–16). While Deuteronomy is largely addressed to Israel, Yahweh's love is not contained by Israel alone and extends to those who keep his commandments more widely (Deut. 5.10; 7.9) as well as those in need (Deut. 10.18), hence holding together justice and mercy. To 'love Yahweh' is therefore a deeply covenantal concept with salient ethical ramifications, undergirded by faithfulness to Yahweh alone (Deut.6.4–5; 11.22; 13.4). The earnest singing of the final verse therefore strikes a discordant note within the wider sweep of the book. It contributes to the problematization of Israelite identity, caught between the ethnic and the covenantal, and that of fluid enemies who can turn into friends of Yahweh. The singer(s) seem to relish violence and the downfall of the oppressor, and the level of violence may have a cathartic element for a people who saw themselves as smallerand less sophisticated than the city dwellers who oppressed them. But just as with Ehud, the fragility of power and privilege means that the risk of simply reversing the poles of oppression lies just below the surface. The figure of Jael focalizes the ambiguities of ethnicity and creed: is she Canaanite, like her husband? Does she want to be a friend of Yahweh, or the Israelites? Is she merely working for self-preservation? What is the root of her murderous rage? She is caught between conflicting oppressive forces, with possibilities for violence on every side, yet equally, possibilities for alliance on both sides. She is called 'most blessed', suggesting that even though her status may not be resolved from the point of view of socio-economics, she may be shown mercy by Yahweh regardless of her motives.

The song as a whole has made explicit Deborah's prophetic understanding of the events that occurred under her watch; it is first and foremost a hymn of praise to Yahweh. Some have argued that Yahweh's place in the song is underdeveloped compared to other victory songs and human actors are given too much prominence (Beldman, 2020, p. 100; Fewell and

Gunn, 1990, p. 401); human beings are not depicted as heroes, however, and there is very little of the epic poem recounting great human deeds. Instead, the song opens and closes with direct addresses to Yahweh and unambiguously attributes victory to his saving action on the battlefield. At this point in Judges Yahweh is still mentioned frequently, given complete recognition for his leadership in battle, and covenantal language is prominent. The framework formula, 'the land had rest' closes the entire account, outside of the poem. Neither Deborah nor Barak's deaths are recorded.

Reflections

The richness of a dual perspective

Read together, the dual prose and song accounts offer different foci and function as prompts to question our grasp of the narrative. Intriguingly, having both accounts means that a later editor gives us a glimpse on how early Hebrews theologized their experiences. The different emphases open up a gap between the narrator's perspective and that of the composer(s) of the song, a gap which raises theological questions. Jael's actions are recounted neutrally in the prose; in the song, they are much more violent, as well as extolled as positive. Was Jael right or justified? Should her actions be praised? Is the graphic violence of the song necessary? In chapter 4, the violence is more muted and part of the logic of war; chapter 5 delights in the violence. Is either approach justifiable? And does chapter 4 justify chapter 5? In addition, the double account offers a glimpse of the process of identity-forming through remembrance and the creation of a public narrative. Why is the song so much more violent? Does this mean that violence is a key part of identity-forming for Israel? How much do facts matter, given the differences between the two Jael accounts? Are those differences discrepancies, or simply drawing on different information? The inclusion of the roll call is a crucial detail for the identity-forming aspect of the song and its importance in social control. Conversely, common emphases highlight key questions for Israel, presumably at different times in its history: the role of women is prominent and unusual in both; both texts draw the readers into feeling a degree of sympathy for the 'enemy'; neither text elucidates Jael's motivations; both show a high degree of cooperation between different leaders, without assigning a pre-eminent role to any (Jael is neither judge nor prophet, but participates in deliverance; Barak is military leader/deliverer, though not said to judge, and does not deliver alone; Deborah is prophet and judge, but not military deliverer). Reading the two accounts together therefore gives them more depth, creates more ambiguity and draws the reader into doing more work than one or the other account would do on its own.

Gender and violence

Judges 4—5 is often highlighted for its unusual depiction of women, particularly in connection with war and violence. Traditional fears of men and women are both explored here: male fears of female sexuality, particularly used against them; fear of lack of loyalty and betrayal; fears about the performance of masculinity, particularly in battle. And on the other hand, women's fear of losing loved ones while they are silently waiting, powerless, and the fear of becoming enemy prey. Men and women are both heavily affected by the culture of warfare, and no alternative is offered to violence. The passage engages with the question of female violence, and does not depict it altogether negatively, which is unusual (since women in patriarchal cultures are more likely to be depicted positively as the feminine ideal, either mothers or virgins). Rather, it shows women as capable of violence, with a proactive stake in war and survival. Scholars have clearly felt uncomfortable with a text that praises Jael and allows Deborah to lead in war (Schneider, 1999, p. 76), and even feminist scholars often dismiss them as 'patriarchal patsies', preventing an acknowledgement of violence as empowering women – however distasteful the thought (Mandolfo, 2019, p. 342). Many commentators condemn Jael as violent, inhospitable and a traitor, yet fail to consider her place within the wider culture. Women were often used to seal alliances they had no say in; they were expected to follow their husbands' loyalties regardless of what it meant practically and ethically for them. It is possible to read Jael as a traitor to her husband and to Sisera, but equally possible to suppose she has great moral integrity and favoured loyalty to Yahweh or at least to Israel as other Kenites had. The ambiguity underlines the fact that women are not consulted or seen as subjects when it comes to political dealings. What Jael does do is act politically for herself. Commentators, in addition, have consistently highlighted that women occupy men's roles in the narrative (e.g. Butler, 2009, p. 100), yet the text itself exhibits considerably less tension about women's performance than interpreters do (Mandolfo, 2019, p. 342). To interpret women's violence as simply either acting like men, or being forced to act violently because they are potential victims, removes women's ability to be moral and political agents within this violence. They may be *seen* as taking on a male role, but, as Deborah's song shows, women's own interpretation of their actions shows considerable divergence from typical patriarchal expectations, which challenges patriarchal structure by transforming women from object into subject. Both Jael and Deborah, each in her own way, willed violence. Deborah, by relaying instructions for war, going to war and celebrating it in song; Jael, for her own unknown reasons. As such, they are complicit in the violence described, as the final stanza of the song explicitly shows. The biblical text overall treats women and men equally as to morality, ethics and spiritual responsibility. If we question the violence of women then we need to question the violence of men also. If we condone the violence of men as politically necessary, or adjunct to survival, then we must do so with women's violence too. The text, in addition, begs us to consider the complicity of women in the violence inflicted upon other women, as Sisera's mother fantasizes about her son, and Deborah about Sisera's mother. Neither shows mercy, and both are set to profit from the demise of the other. This portrait of moral ambiguity is consistent with that of women more generally in the OT. There is no theologized moral difference between men and women.

Women are described as 'intelligent, strong-willed, capable and endowed with the gift of persuasion' (Bird, 1997, p. 38); in many places they have judgement, wisdom, practical skill and religious discernment, and at times have particular skills that enable specialization and recognition (García Bachmann, 2013). In narrative terms, women often play an important and at times equal role, have the same moral and religious obligations as men and are therefore fully responsible for their actions, which makes them, by default, civic and legal persons (Hamley, 2019, p. 117). The theological view of men and women here is therefore one where they stand equal before Yahweh; Yahweh works with both, despite the ambiguity and brokenness of human persons and cultures.

Patriarchy not only affects the portrayal and interpretation of women: it affects men and understandings of masculinity. Many commentators highlight the success of women and the related humiliation of men, with different weightings to both elements (Hanselman, 1989, p. 104; Rasmussen, 1989, p. 79). Some also argue, contra chapter 5, that Deborah never even went into battle (Soggin, 1981). It has been the tradition to highlight Barak's perceived failure and to see Israel being saved by a woman as a failure of leadership. While this may be true at the level of the ancient culture, should we necessarily assume that cultural phenomenon equals theological meaning? Could the text – and therefore Yahweh – work in the margins and seams of the culture to challenge its assumptions, and actually value courageous women? Critics like Butler continuously emphasize the weakness of Barak for not going out to battle on his own and see him as a failure or at least less of a man and hero. But the main drive of Judges is to show that the confident male warrior type is not necessarily the best and that it is Yahweh who delivers and should be king. The narrative therefore may be unexpected within a patriarchal culture, but it does not mean that its main thrust would be the inadequacy of Barak. The tendency to berate Barak shows the ongoing dependence of ancient culture and interpreters on ideas of human force, power and violence as ways towards liberation. The poem does not stress the loss of glory motif in any way, though it foregrounds Deborah over Barak. In the same way, commentators often argue that glory goes to Jael and not to Deborah (Butler, 2009, p. 107; Frolov, 2012, p. 146). Again, the poem's balanced retelling of different elements of the story does not bear this out; the narrative leads directly into the hymn of praise, where elements of shame and failure are not present and glory is shared between human protagonists, but mostly – and properly – directed to Yahweh. Within the canon, it is Barak who will be consistently mentioned as leading at the time, which could be a reflection of patriarchal rewriting of history, or an acknowledgement that Deborah called, Barak led, and Jael helped. The tendency of interpreters to use patriarchy as a lens to interpret the story, rather than look for the wider biblical picture, is encapsulated in Frolov's comment that 'men are supposed to protect women and come to their rescue, not the other way round' (2012, p. 143). This view, however, draws more on Western notions of chivalry than the biblical corpus, where men almost never kill to protect women but to protect themselves and their honour, the state, other men and their honour, or even Yahweh and his honour (Mandolfo, 2019, p. 351). There are many stories of men *failing* to protect women in the OT: David refusing to act following the rape of Tamar (2 Sam. 13), the old man and the Levite using women as human shields (Judges 19), Judah refusing to provide for Tamar as a widow (Gen. 38), to name a few. Indeed, men occasionally kill women to protect all these interests, as we will increasingly see in the rest of Judges, with the sacrifice of Jephthah's daughter (protecting his honour), the burning of Samson's wife (because of his rash actions), the rape and murder of the concubine (human shield), the murder of the majority of the girls and women of Jabesh-Gilead in Judges 21 (to ensure the ongoing integrity of the twelve-tribe structure).

The story of Barak instead undermines notions of hegemonic masculinity – the cultural and psychological construct that is dominant in cultural and political power structures (Haddox, 2016, p. 179). Hegemonic masculinity is oppressive because it relies on agreement and enforcement of its own standards;

a story like that of Barak and Deborah, collaborating and choosing not to endorse hegemonic masculinity's idea of the lone warrior, strong leader, who gets glory by killing the enemy, is deeply subversive and unsettling, a fact that Deborah points to in 4.9. Images of hegemonic masculinity are obvious in comments that anything that falls short of masculine control (such as a woman killing the enemy leader) or a man being killed by a woman (Sisera) is in effect feminizing. The prevalent culture therefore is, indeed, patriarchal, but the story and the song deconstruct this normative ideology by giving a woman in her tent the final blow (Thelle, 2019, p. 446). In the end, this is yet another embodiment of the freedom of Yahweh in effecting deliverance, and of Yahweh's deconstruction of human ideas of power and who should and does wield it. As such, commentators' frequent deliberations on who the main character is may be missing the point; rather, as the song points to, it is Yahweh who is the main character, working in partnership with human actors, none of whom is perfect, but whose faith is good enough. The importance of Yahweh is shown with the foregrounding of Deborah, with her lengthy introduction and prominence in the song ('I, Deborah'): she initiates and participates in deliverance, not through violent military action but through prophecy; it is the word of Yahweh, ultimately, that saves, a word transmitted by a willing listener.

3

Gideon (6–8)

The peace following Deborah and Barak's leadership is short-lived: by the opening of chapter 6, Israel's situation is worse than it has ever been. The next deliverer, Gideon, marks a new stage in Israel's decline, from an unexpected deliverer to a more obviously flawed one, whose son, Abimelech, will embody 'doing evil in the eyes of Yahweh' right at the centre of the book. The stories of Gideon and Abimelech belong closely together as the first overall story of (failed) dynastic leadership. They focus more on cultus, idolatry and an exploration of faith, fear and doubt. Issues of justice, violence and proportionality become more pressing, as do questions around appropriate leadership, all of which will bloom in the Abimelech narrative.

Chapter 6: Call and response

6.1–6: Israel at breaking point

Judges 6.1 opens with the formulaic, 'Israel did what was evil in the eyes of the Lord'. The wording of 'continuing to do evil', together with the much shorter length of oppression, implies a possible positive reset following Deborah and Barak (Smit, 2018, p. 89), though the nature of the oppression has hardened considerably. The Midianites are now the oppressors, an interesting development given that the Kenites, who have just participated in deliverance for Israel through Jael, are connected to Midian, as descendants of Moses' father-in-law, the priest in Midian. Once again, boundaries between friends and foes are fluid and unsettled. Other oppressors, the Amelekites and the Easterners, nomadic groups from the Arabian desert (Butler, 2009, p. 197), are people who should have been 'driven out' of the land as Israel settled in. Israel's choice to make treaties, intermarry or dwell with the Canaanites directly results in their present situation.

The picture is desperate, worse than before Deborah. Then, roads were empty and farmers scared to go into the fields. Now Israelite crops are destroyed and the people forced to take refuge in hills and caves; Israel appears on the brink of extinction. The narrator focalizes the story through the eyes of Israel, describing the Midianites in hyperbolic terms, a plague of Midianites to match the mosaic plague of locusts. The enemies are described as thieves and raiders in opposition to the peaceful Israelites simply planting crops. The picture underscores the nature of war as linked to land and survival, and the interwoven nature of the theological, social and economic aspects of human life: the land, God and the people are intimately linked in every aspect of the story. The oppression goes beyond trying to gain labour or goods in 6.4, to wanton destruction of crops and livestock. The complete destruction of Israel's agrarian economy undermines their survival, suggesting that what the Midianites and Amalekites are after is the extermination of Israel. 6.5 stresses the intentionality of the oppressors, coming into the land 'to destroy it'. The hyperbolic 'too many to count' and the comparison with locusts echoes the story of Exodus, now reversed. It is the enemies that are too numerous, and the locusts are attacking Israel rather than Egypt. The description also echoes the covenant curse of Deuteronomy 28.38, 'You shall carry much seed into the field, but shall gather little in, for the locust shall consume it.' The curse is attached to warnings around breaking the covenant – a covenant Israel had now breached by doing evil in the eyes of Yahweh. The end of 6.5 emphasizes that it is not just Israel that suffers, but the land too. Ironically, part of Israel's sin is the worship of local gods, usually gods of the land associated with agrarian rituals and fertility to ensure better crops. Now they turn to Yahweh and ask for help, though no repentance is mentioned. The situation is desperate, and if Yahweh does not help then Israel is doomed. Questions abound: what will Israel be prepared to do? Spiritually and practically? What kind of action is justifiable in response to the threat of extermination of an entire people? (of course, the answer to the question can be flipped to argue that the Canaanites are justified in their response to Israel's invasion). The terms of the story are set up for another account of justifiable violence in response to unreasonable gratuitous violence.

6.7–10: Along came a prophet

Israel's lack of repentance is emphasized by the break in the framework sequence. They cry out to Yahweh, but their cry is utilitarian and fails to acknowledge the cause of their distress. Unlike earlier, Yahweh does not immediately raise a deliverer or lead the people into a war of liberation. Instead, he sends a prophet to tackle the root problem rather than its recurring symptoms. In the first pericope, with respect to the Midianites, Israel was simply 'Israel'. Now in 6.7, in relation to Yahweh, they are 'the sons of Israel', a frequent idiom that locates Israel back into history and relationship – a human history as descendants of Jacob, and a history with Yahweh who elected to work with Jacob and renamed him Israel. 'Sons' suggests a father, continuity and relationship, as well as common values and shaping of behaviour. To call on Yahweh presumes a relationship, and Yahweh reminds Israel of what that relationship was supposed to look like. An unnamed prophet appears, at the same point as Deborah had appeared in the previous narrative. The use of the unusual "*'îš nābî*", man prophet, strengthens the echo of Deborah, the woman prophet (*'iššâ nĕbî'â*). The parallel highlights the differences: the prophet here is unnamed, is not known or respected, the Israelites do not go to him for judgements and he is not a judge of any kind, which shows the dramatic deterioration in Israel's cultic and social life between the two episodes. Israel starts from a lower point here than it had in chapter 4. There is no sense that anyone is actually listening to this prophet, or that there is any social cohesion around seeking Yahweh. Where Deborah immediately transmitted Yahweh's call to a deliverer, here the prophet calls Israel as a whole to repentance and is ignored. His message is introduced as a typical oracle, with 'thus says the Lord', and follows the lines of a paradigmatic retelling of Israel's story, with an indictment of their failure to heed the covenantal relationship. The speech echoes the angel's intervention in chapter 2. The paradigmatic story is one of justice and mercy, as Yahweh graciously answered Israel's cry for help in Egypt, confronted the oppressor and delivered the people, in response to which they were invited into a covenantal relationship of exclusive love for Yahweh. The speech is cast in the second masculine plural: the people are addressed as 'you', thereby collapsing time. The acts of yesterday are the story of the people of today.

This captures Israel's dilemma: how does a new generation come to 'Know Yahweh' for itself? How can stories be more than 'history', and shape Israel's history in the present? Can faith be successfully handed down? This collapse of time will be relevant to Gideon's question in 6.13: he will, in effect, say that these stories may well be true about the past, but what about the present? The lack of experience of Yahweh's acts in the present is problematic, as is the underlying perception of who Yahweh is. Yahweh is consistently described as the 'God of Abraham, Isaac and Jacob', that is, a God whose profound nature and commitment do not change. Hence his commitment to justice, mercy and deliverance will be the same today as in the past. Yet Gideon's perception is that it is God who has changed, rather than Israel who has walked away. The final sentence, 'you have not listened to my voice', is heavy with irony. Yahweh's voice is one of justice and freedom for the oppressed. The people have been following other gods, gods of tribe and empire who have led them into oppression and not delivered them. Why are the people crying out to Yahweh now, rather than these other gods? Are they crying out to any god who may listen? Or does the memory of the Exodus still lurk within the nation? The parallel with chapter 2 creates an expectation that the people will respond in similar ways – by repenting. However, things have changed, and they do not.

This section therefore sets the scene for the call narrative of Gideon, showing that raising a deliverer is undeserved, an act of gracious liberation from Yahweh, and setting up a picture of Israel that will show Gideon not as a man set apart for his holiness or faith, but as a man of the people who comes to meet Yahweh for the first time.

6.11–18: The call

Prophecy is followed by a call narrative, though unlike with Deborah it is not the prophet who transmits the call. The messenger, who in chapter 2 had delivered a similar message to that of the prophet, now plays the role that Deborah the prophet played with Barak. The transition from prophetic speech to call narrative is abrupt, without any response from Israel. Early in Judges, Israel actively sought Yahweh's mind. Now, Yahweh must send not just one but two messengers, a prophet followed by an angel, for the people to begin to listen. The narrative is much longer than Deborah's, with Gideon's doubts and fear taking centre stage: fear of the Midianites, of not being up to the task, of Yahweh not fulfilling his promise, of other Israelites. The pericope contains the usual structural elements of a call narrative: confrontation with God/messenger, introductory address by the person called, divine commission, raising objections, divine reassurance, sign to authenticate experience (Block 1999, p. 257).

The messenger/angel waits under a tree, as Deborah had. Yet no one is expecting Yahweh to appear or send anyone, despite crying out to him. The tree is an inverse link to Deborah's story, linked to a pagan altar rather than to Yahweh's judgements. Enter Gideon, the 'hacker' whose name prefigures his role later in the story, and Joash, his father, who sponsors Baal worship despite his Yahwistic name. They are Abiezrites, a clan whose name means 'my father is help', which could either refer to Yahweh or prefigure Joash's role in saving his son from the villagers. Gideon is threshing in the wine press – a symbol of the fear that shapes his entire life. Because of Midianite oppression, key agricultural tasks had to be carried out in secret. The opening pericope had stated that Israel was hiding in caves, their entire crops destroyed. The story here suggests the situation may not have been quite this dire, since Joash has land and buildings and there are crops to process. Since no one notices the angel under the tree (unlike in the story of Abraham in Genesis 18), the angel appears to Gideon where he is in the wine press, an intimate, domestic environment, so that the coming of Yahweh to help Israel is as hidden as agricultural tasks. The angel's greeting, 'The Lord is with you', is unusual as a greeting, occurring only here in the singular, in Ruth 2.4 in the plural, and in the angel's address to Mary in the New Testament (Luke 1.28). It is more commonly used as a parting blessing. The designation 'mighty warrior' is ambiguous: is it honorific? A clue about Gideon's abilities? Does it foreshadow what is to come? Or is it ironic, given Gideon's later protestations and paralysing fear?

Gideon's answer is combative, and unexpectedly theological. He immediately picks up on whether Yahweh really is with him, or with his people. The messenger had not said, 'the Lord is with you [plural]', but 'the Lord is with you [singular]'. Gideon immediately goes from the personal to the national and questions Yahweh's presence with Israel, without considering the implications of Yahweh being with him as a person. On the surface, Gideon's question is a classic theodicic question (why do bad things happen to the people of God?), or the kind of question that may be found in psalms of lament (why have you forgotten us?). However, lament is usually undergirded by covenant language. Here there is a sense of entitlement to Yahweh's help, without any sense of an underlying relationship of reciprocity and mutual obligations. It is ironic that Gideon accuses Yahweh of abandoning Israel, when it is Israel who chose to walk away from Yahweh. Gideon refers to the Exodus as the paradigmatic event of Yahwistic faith, but casts it as a distant memory and does not refer to any of Yahweh's 'wonderful deeds' since, such as Joshua's conquest, or Othniel, Ehud, Deborah and Barak. Yahweh's actions are reduced to one single long-ago liberative event. On the positive side, it shows an awareness of Israel's history still being passed down the generations and an understanding of Yahweh as saviour/liberator. On the other hand, Gideon assesses Yahweh like a tribal god, who should be with his tribe regardless of their actions and can be discarded for another god if it seems good in Israel's eyes. Clearly, Gideon does not see the worship of other gods (in his own backyard!) as an issue, nor does he have any inkling that Israel may have been the architect of its fate – his words echo the words of the prophet but miss out the command of 6.10. There is an air of doubt about the faith that was handed down: did God really do this?, which harks back to Genesis and the serpent sowing seeds of doubts, 'did God really say …'. Each generation struggles to trust the word of Yahweh and the testimony of others. Yahweh's actions are reduced to 'wonderful deeds' because Gideon does not consider that the presence of Yahweh may have wider implications than military victory and prosperity. The interaction is robust, in line with much Old Testament prayer, from Abraham to the Psalms to the prophets. Yet it also reveals the need for the very possibility of faith to be re-established, broadened and deepened. A mechanistic understanding of faith does not sustain the people at a time when their practical experience suggests the absence of God, regardless of the reasons for this apparent absence. Gideon makes the common mistake of thinking that the presence of God can only be found in prosperity and blessing, linking material circumstances to the presence and approval of God. The Hebrew Scriptures as a whole repeatedly explore this question, most powerfully in the book of Job. Job is articulated around the prose narrative's ambiguity about the word for 'blessing', which is used both to speak about blessing and, euphemistically, for curse. Hence there is a core ambiguity in Job: are riches a blessing or a curse? Is Job's traditional piety, with his pre-emptive sacrifices, a way of blessing God, or is it in fact a curse that restricts God to a mechanistic relationship? Can a relationship between Job and God thrive outside of the realm of actions–consequences? Gideon is an opposite type to Job, as he is completely unaware of the demands of covenant living and the depth of Israel's sin; yet he is very similar to Job in having a straightforward expectation from God that links prosperity with God's presence and approval. Because he cannot protest Israel's innocence, he instead protests God's absence and charges him with abandoning his people.

Yahweh is not fazed by Gideon's reproaches. Yahweh now speaks directly, in a complete identification of Yahweh and the messenger, a common feature of OT texts featuring angels (e.g. Genesis 18). Yahweh's answer is unexpected. There is no reassurance but a commission. Gideon is told that he is part of the answer to his own question. He is invited to trust Yahweh and partner with him on bringing about change, rather than expecting an independent 'marvellous deed'. 'Have I not sent you?' is a typical commissioning formula (Butler, 2009, p. 203), which gives Gideon authority for the task and assures him that Yahweh has heard Israel's cry. However, the formulation of the command is odd, 'go in this strength of yours'. Is this an affirmation of Gideon's skills and resources because he doubts himself, or is it a challenge to recognize that he needs Yahweh's strength? The ambiguity creates space for a question that will thread itself throughout the rest of the narrative: will Gideon go in Yahweh's strength, or his own? Will he give glory to Yahweh, or to himself?

6.15 has more protestations from Gideon. On the one hand, they are the right answer – Gideon recognizes that he cannot deliver Israel, though he locates his inability not in his lack of strength, skill or worth but in lack of social status ('least in my family') and political power ('weakest in Manasseh'). He does not understand that it is Yahweh's power that will deliver, by going with him: 'how can *I* deliver ...'. His claims regarding lack of social status and strength are questionable. His father owns property and supports a place of worship, which suggests he is the head of a clan and hence wields both economic and political power (Butler, 2009, p. 203), and the family have enough resources that Gideon can easily sacrifice animals (a kid in 6.19 and a bull in 6.26). Gideon calls ten of his servants to help him in 6.27 and his father clearly has sway over the townspeople (6.28–32). Gideon therefore seems to be trying to avoid responsibility, while also failing to acknowledge his own privileged position at a time when Israel is struggling. Gideon has also failed to recognize the motif of Yahweh choosing the weaker members of families and tribes as leaders in the history of Israel so far – his objections, if they have any truth, would make him more likely to be chosen, rather than less. Yahweh's response is in line with traditional call narratives, assuring Gideon of his presence with him, as in the stories of Moses (Ex. 3.12) or Joshua (Josh. 1.5). Yahweh will not endow Gideon with additional strength or skills, but go with him in a restoration of Yahweh's presence alongside Israel, reversing the dynamics of withdrawal that follow Israel's evil. Yahweh's response is emphatic – Gideon will strike 'every one of the Midianites'. Given the description of the enemy as a great multitude, Yahweh here is stressing the magnitude and completeness of the victory to come, surely a 'marvellous deed'. The Midianites were too numerous to count, but they will not be too numerous for Yahweh, working with Gideon, to strike down one by one. Gideon now has a choice; divine presence does not guarantee success but simply makes it possible. Gideon must take a step of faith, but he doubts. Just as the stories of past generations were just stories to him, now Yahweh's words are just words and he wants more, so asks for proof. Gideon's doubts are different from those of Moses in Exodus 3. Moses doubted himself and his own ability – his speech, whether others would listen to him, and whether he really was up to the job. Gideon, in contrast, doubts Yahweh – is Yahweh really who he says he is? Is he really with Israel? Will he deliver? Does he really have power? The revelation of who Yahweh is comes early in the Exodus account. Here, Gideon has clearly recognized his interlocutor, as we see in 6.15 with the use of my Lord (*'adōnāy*) for Yahweh, rather than my lord (*'adōnî*), a simple honorific address, yet this recognition of Yahweh does not yield faith in what Yahweh may do. While the sign Yahweh spontaneously gives to Moses is there to prove to the rest of Israel that Yahweh has truly sent him (Ex. 4.1–5), here it is Gideon who asks for a sign of his own choosing to test whether Yahweh has true power and he, Gideon, has his favour. Gideon wants proof to assuage his doubt, because he struggles with faith; yet many successive tests simply give way to a need for more proof. The nature of faith is explored here as something that cannot be simply tested and proved beyond all doubt. At some point Gideon will have to stop asking for signs and take a step of faith. His recurring demand for signs, testing Yahweh, shows his poor knowledge of the Torah and the problems of Israel wandering in the desert, or the clear prohibition of Deuteronomy 6.16, 'do not put the Lord your God to the test' – a prohibition that will be repeated many centuries later by Jesus, also tempted in the desert, in Matthew 4.7. The temptation is to reduce faith to reason and, together with it, to reduce Yahweh's presence and covenantal partnership to the performance of marvellous deeds. Gideon asks for a sign, though he does not specify a sign of what; he says he will prepare a gift (*minḥâ*, the word used for tribute in Ehud's story), a word usually used in the context of worship. The size of what he prepares is much more than what is needed for a meal prepared in hospitality, which suggests that Gideon intends it as a sacred offering.

The echoes of the call of Moses highlight the differences between Moses and Gideon. Gideon's attempts to refuse his commission are about doubts and fear, not humility. Moses had recognized the God calling, whereas Gideon asks for a sign to prove that Yahweh is truly God; Moses led the people to Sinai and covenant, Gideon will lead them into apostasy; Moses remained a nomadic leader who died in the desert whereas Gideon will accumulate riches, a harem, and die in wealth and plenty, attempting to create a dynasty. Gideon, unlike Moses, seeks the credit and glory that belong to God, whereas Moses asked to see more of God's glory and veiled his face before the Israelites. Overall, Gideon seems to echo more of Pharaoh's characteristics than those of Moses.

6.19–24: Theophany

Gideon's words in 6.17, 'if I have found favour with you', are reminiscent of Abraham's words to the messengers/Yahweh in Genesis 18, asking them to rest under the tree for a little time while he prepares to tend to their needs (somewhat more comprehensively than Gideon does, but with unleavened cakes and fresh meat in common). The scene, however, takes a different direction. The messenger gives specific ritual instructions to Gideon; the giving of ritual instructions is reminiscent of the times of the patriarchs, before the giving of the law. Gideon must be taught again what to do, and a rock is turned into a makeshift altar, underlining the fact that even though there was an altar to Baal and an Asherah pole, there was no altar to Yahweh in the house of Joash. The angel sends fire to consume the offering and goes 'from before his eyes'. Here is a link between seeing and faith, repeated in 6.22, 'Gideon *saw* that it was the angel of the Lord'. Gideon keeps needing to see, touch or experience with his senses. This reliance on the senses is linked to the mechanistic faith explored earlier and its link between actions and material consequences. Gideon struggles with faith as a concept that he cannot entirely rationalize or control through reason. The discrepancy between faith as believed and life as experienced is a continual one in Scripture, and not necessarily negative. The psalms of lament are based on the tension between faith in the God of the Covenant and an experience of reality that denies or masks the presence or activity of God and his love for his people. Israel's struggles to embody the covenant in the Promised Land are also seen through their struggle between their faith identity, an identity they imagine and strive towards, and the reality of their situation and the pull towards a different embodied identity. The tension is never solved in the biblical corpus but reflects a key aspect of humanity – a normal component of faith. The early disciples in the NT struggle to believe even though they have seen the risen Christ (John 20.29), and the writer of the letter to the Hebrews expands on the nature of faith in chapter 11 as 'the conviction of things unseen'. They will even refer to Gideon as an example of faith (11.32), suggesting that Gideon's struggles with doubt were part of his faith journey with Yahweh, rather than an insuperable obstacle or character flaw. 6.22 ushers in a deeper level of seeing, of recognition, in the mode of a theophany. Gideon still refers to the messenger as 'the angel of the Lord' – a fearful figure if one thinks back to the Exodus and the angel of the Lord spreading the final plague on the firstborn. Gideon's reaction is very similar to those who see Yahweh directly and fear they may die, in line with Torah (Gen. 32.30; Ex. 33.20; Num. 17.12–13; Deut. 5.24–27) and multiple other scriptural examples (Judg. 13.31–33; Isa. 6.5; Luke 5.8; 1 Tim. 6.16; Rev. 1.17). In the OT imagination, divine holiness is incompatible with human uncleanness or impurity, and this incompatibility puts the human person at risk, hence the need for elaborate purification rituals for priests in the sanctuary or prophets meeting God (Isa. 6.5). Sin rather than uncleanness is emphasized in the NT, for instance with Peter's exclamation 'Go away from me, Lord, for I am a sinful man!' (Luke 5.8). Accounts earlier in the canon do not stress sin as clearly, but stress the otherness and glory of Yahweh as the source of the danger. Yet interwoven with fear of death are consistent stories of those who see Yahweh, and live – such as Jacob, Moses, Gideon, Samson's parents, Isaiah. The human–divine distance is breached by Yahweh's grace in forming covenantal relationships. The source of Gideon's fear seems located simply in the awesomeness or transcendence of Yahweh; there is no acknowledgement of sin on Gideon's part. Neither does Gideon ask for divine help or mercy, as suggested by the NRSV's 'help me' in 6.22. Rather, he exclaims, 'alas!' (*'ahāh*), an expression of self-pity or despair. Yahweh himself answers, presumably now in a disembodied voice since the messenger has disappeared. Yahweh's response comes in answer to Gideon's cry of fear, hence Yahweh's words, 'peace to you, do not fear'. As with Moses or Joshua, the command not to fear is not based on the fact that there is nothing to fear, but rather on the presence of Yahweh. It is this presence that reassures and enables human action in the face of impossible adversity. Peace, of course, is the opposite of fear. Gideon again responds in typical patriarchal fashion, building an altar whose name reflects the experience. The town now has two rival altars, one to Baal and one to Yahweh, a fact that sets up the next segment of the story, though this altar is the one that is said to endure. This is Gideon's first positive response to Yahweh, with the apparently unbidden construction of an altar in an act of practical worship. An altar is then an invitation to continue worship, or in this case to redirect worship away from pagan gods to Yahweh. The altar also shows that Gideon's meeting with God is not simply about Gideon, but will have significance for others who will be invited to worship differently, though Gideon may not quite see this yet. Gideon's theophany has changed him, and with this change comes the possibility of a new start for Israel.

6.25–32: Bringing down the altar of Baal

At this point in a call narrative one would expect a confirmatory sign from Yahweh and for Gideon to take up his calling. However, the narrative takes a double turn: first, with Yahweh's testing of Gideon's loyalty, and then with Gideon's testing of Yahweh's power. Many key elements in Gideon's story happen under cover of darkness: Yahweh speaking to him, the tearing down of the Baal altar, testing Yahweh on two successive nights, reassurance before battle, and the attack on the Midianites. Night comes to symbolize Gideon's state of mind – he is afraid, seeking to hide or avoid his calling. Fear dominates the narrative, just as fear of the Midianites dominates Israel's life. It is not fear of the Lord, the beginning of wisdom, that motivates Gideon. He was afraid momentarily after realizing the messenger's identity, but now his deeper fears reassert themselves: fear of the task at hand and fear not just of Israel's enemies but of Israel itself. The two town altars symbolize the depth of syncretism in Israel; Gideon is asked to choose and declare loyalty to Yahweh by destroying the pagan altar. In doing so, he would address the final part of the message of the prophet in 6.10, by calling Israel to stop worshipping foreign deities and leading the way in showing Israel that it is Yahweh, not Baal, who answers their cry. Yahweh's instructions are an act of war on foreign deities. Gideon is asked to destroy the religious paraphernalia at the heart of the community, and not just destroy them but replace them with an altar to Yahweh, using the wood of the Asherah as kindling for a sacrifice. The symbolism is clear: Yahweh is more powerful than Baal and

Asherah, who are no more than firewood, and has reasserted his place at the heart of Israel. Gideon is asked, specifically, to deal with the source of Israel's problems (idolatry) rather than just its symptoms (oppression by other nations). For Gideon, this is not just about his personal religious loyalties, but a command that risks alienating him deeply from his entire kinship group, family and tribe. What Yahweh asks of Gideon, in a household-based system, is to potentially tear his own world apart and put his own life on the line. What faces Gideon is a test of faith: he must trust that Yahweh will act on his promise, even though the very thing he is asked to do seems to negate the possibility of the promise being fulfilled. Gideon's obedience may be reluctant, but it is a remarkable statement of faith. It is quite understandable that he acts at night, as he probably would have been stopped during the day. At this point, it looks like Gideon may turn out to be the right kind of deliverer at last.

Focalization shifts in 6.28–29, and the scene is conveyed through the eyes of the astonished townspeople, who react as Gideon had feared. They not only do not understand what Gideon has done, but do not even try to elucidate what may be going on. They do not mention the new altar but are only concerned with the deities that have been removed. The men approach Joash, as head of the household and therefore responsible for his son. The demand for Gideon's life ironically mirrors the command to put to death those who lead Israel into idolatry. Here, Israel wants to put to death the one who is trying to lead them away from idols. Despite the depth of Israel's unfaithfulness, Yahweh still cares and seeks to deliver. The level of love for Baal and Asherah, however, problematizes the people's earlier cry to Yahweh, and suggests that it was very unlikely to have been directed to Yahweh only, and/or accompanied by any kind of repentance or renewal of covenantal life (or even the intention of it).

Joash's response forms the theological climax of this part of the narrative. Joash defends his son, in a rare positive picture of intergenerational relationships and support. Just as Gideon had to make a choice between Yahweh and his Baal-worshipping clan, the clan must make a choice between Baal and their Yahwist kin. It is unclear where Joash himself stands religiously. His speech is heavy with irony, questioning whether a god really needs people to defend and 'deliver' (*yāšaʿ* in the *Hifil*) him. It is unclear whether Joash is showing allegiance to Yahweh, protecting his son, or simply hedging his bets, by encouraging the people to let the gods work it out between them. His speech is not a covenantal speech, but it does undermine the ascendance of pagan deities in Israel, questioning their divine status. The representation of foreign gods as non-gods, who cannot see or hear, is frequent in the OT, and is a Deuteronomic motif, appearing in Deuteronomy 4.28 as part of the warning against forgetting Yahweh and becoming complacent in the land: 'There you will serve gods, the work of man's hands, wood and stone, which neither see nor hear nor eat nor smell.' Similar statements appear in the Psalms (115.4–7; 135.15–16), Isaiah (44.9; 45.20; 46.7), Jeremiah (10.2–5) and Daniel (5.23). The battle therefore is not a battle of the gods, but a battle between Yahweh as subject, and the pagan deities as projections of the people's wishes and desires, with no reality of their own. Yet in Joash's speech we see a similar impulse to Gideon's earlier: allegiance to a god, any god, needs to be won by this god proving himself. Gideon had asked Yahweh to prove himself, Joash asks Baal to do the same. It is therefore ironic that it is Gideon whose name is changed to reflect the struggle with Baal, given that it is his father who stood up against Baal before the villagers. Characters often undergo a name change following a theophany and promise (Abram becomes Abraham in Gen. 17.5, Jacob becomes Israel in Gen. 32.27, Saul will become Paul in Acts 13.9), yet here Gideon's name is not changed following a theophany, but in response to his actions towards Baal. His new name does not include a Yahwistic element but the name of the pagan god. Jacob had been renamed Israel as a reflection of his struggling with God and with humans. Gideon struggles with Baal. The name change does not necessarily augur well. The exact meaning of the name Jerubaal is contested; often translated 'let Baal contend against him', it could equally be 'let Baal contend for himself'. The ambiguity of the name remains an open question for the rest of the narrative: it may appear to have one meaning at this point, but will it shift as the narrative goes on? Which name will Gideon really live up to? Which heritage will ultimately define him, Gideon, the 'hacker' who brought down the altar of Baal? Or the one who keeps being drawn to Baal and shows that Baal does indeed contend for himself – and maybe wins?

6.33–35: Drawing up the battle lines

Now the narrative resumes its usual course: the Midianites, Amalekites and Easterners gather their military forces, though we are not told why (or whether) they intended to attack Israel. The narrator emphasizes that it is *all* the Midianites, Amalekites and Easterners, repeating the earlier picture of the multitude rising against a handful of Israelites. Once again, the narrative strategy to gain reader approval of Israel's war violence is to paint a David and Goliath picture, with the 'foreigners' as aggressors. The impression created is that of an overwhelming force, until 6.34 breaks the picture with a *waw* disjunctive, 'but'. This 'but' is the turning point of the narrative; the call narrative was important, and so was Gideon's response, but this is the crucial moment when Israel's fortunes turn. The reality of Yahweh's presence with Gideon and, by extension, with Israel is now confirmed with Yahweh's sending of the Spirit. Gideon is now a charismatic leader – yet seemingly unaware of it. The gift of the Spirit seems strangely disconnected from the faith community, and there are no obvious markers of how it may be recognized or known. While in the NT gifts and fruit of the Spirit are explicitly highlighted and nurtured, in the OT the work of the Spirit is woven through more discreetly, empowering Israel for action, service and prophecy. Here, the coming of the Spirit seems to lead directly to the gathering of Israel. If Gideon had been as insignificant as he had claimed in 6.15, why would so many respond to his call? Had he actually already proved himself as a 'mighty warrior'? And how come his clan so quickly turn from wanting to kill him to following him? Is this a direct result of the coming of the Spirit? Yahweh's direct action? Both Yahweh and Gideon are at work, without a clear definition of how divine and human elements interweave. A different configuration of tribes comes together, Manasseh, Asher, Zebulon and Naphtali, giving a localized feel to the story and highlighting the fact that Israel does not work as an overall entity at this point.

6.36–40: Testing Yahweh

But ... Gideon has second thoughts. Just as the narrative flow had stopped for Yahweh to test Gideon, now it stops for Gideon to test Yahweh. It may be reluctance to obey, but it also illustrates the divine–human partnership as a true partnership: Yahweh does not overpower Gideon in order to use him, but works with him and makes space for Gideon's own agency. The sending of the Spirit had empowered him, but it had not taken him over or changed his deeper nature. He stills struggles to believe and wants more proof, either because earlier proofs do not seem strong enough before 'all' the enemies, or because the effect of 'seeing' proof does not last. Sensory experience is pitted against what Yahweh has said (6.37), so that the word of Yahweh needs to be backed up by signs that human beings can touch, see or feel. 6.37 seems to suggest that what Gideon doubts is Yahweh's word itself, or Yahweh's power to match his word with actions. It is not a test to find out God's will, because this will is clear enough already. Gideon's view of Yahweh seems closer to the depiction of the capricious gods of the Canaanite pantheon than to the God of the covenant, a perspective enhanced by Gideon's choice of test: Baal was a weather-god, who claimed lordship over dew and even had a daughter called Dew (Smit 2018, p. 98). Gideon is testing out whether Yahweh is stronger than Baal. A distance has opened between Yahweh and Gideon because there is no dialogue; Gideon addresses Yahweh simply as 'God' (*Elohim*). Gideon is doubting the words of Yahweh, so Yahweh does not speak but acts instead, communication that Gideon needs and understands. Gideon's choice of words is interesting: he wants to 'know that you will deliver Israel by my hand'. The focus is on himself and his role within deliverance, rather than on Israel; unlike Moses, he does not express doubt about himself as a leader or share his vulnerability. He simply wants certainty. Yahweh obliges, without blaming Gideon for his lack of faith. His words come true, in an echo of the story of creation, 'and it was so'. Genesis 1 uses the phrase repeatedly to highlight God's creative power: God says what he will do, 'and it was so' (Gen. 1.7, 9, 11, 15, 24, 30). The trustworthiness of Yahweh's word and promises had also been a strong feature of the end of the book of Joshua (12.43–45), and Gideon's distrust is another sign of Judges reversing all that had been achieved in Joshua. Gideon must relearn about the trustworthiness of Yahweh. Yahweh does not simply answer, but answers with generosity and abundance: an entire bowl of dew is obtained from the fleece, a sign of his complete commitment to blessing Israel. Yet reason again hampers Gideon, as he realizes that the test he had set was somewhat dimwitted: a fleece would naturally have retained the damp long after the ground had dried out!

Gideon's request is phrased in a way that shows he knows exactly what he is doing – testing God. It is quite appropriate for him to ask Yahweh not to be angry, given the reaction to testing that is recounted in Exodus, in particular at Rephidim, using the same word for testing, *nāssāh* in the *Piel* (Ex. 17.1–7), and Yahweh's impatience with Israel's chronic disbelief. Yahweh is patiently reshaping Gideon's view of God and imagination for what God can do, by showing patience and grace for Gideon's foibles and responding to Gideon's doubts in a way that Gideon can understand. Gideon's spirituality is shaped, not by the Yahwistic covenant and its profoundly 'other' God, but by the Baal stories of anthropomorphic gods who can be treated, tested and evaluated just like human beings (Smit, 2018, p. 94).

7: The main battle

7.1–9: Whittling down the troops

7.1 mirror images 6.33: the Israelite troops had set up camp just as the enemy armies had. Gideon is still consistently called Gideon, not Jerubaal, suggesting that hacking down Baal's altar should shape his identity, rather than struggle with Baal. The two armies are now described in similar terms rather than the asymmetric awe of the enemy multitude of earlier verses. This may be a focalization through Gideon's eyes, now feeling more confident thanks to the troops that rallied and the sign Yahweh gave. Yet newfound confidence is exactly what provokes the need for what comes next. Yahweh proceeds to whittle down the troops so that the armies are no longer symmetrical, and it becomes clear that an Israelite victory can only be ascribed to Yahweh's miraculous intervention. Yahweh is challenging the myth of independence and self-sufficiency among his people and those who watch them, challenging them to take their proper place in the world and assign Yahweh his proper place in relation to them. Yahweh's point is not about infantilizing Israel or diminishing them, but rather enabling them to flourish within a healthy covenantal framework that leads to peace and rest on all sides, as in the vision of Joshua 21. A corollary of Yahweh's teaching is to challenge the nation's confidence in what violence and war can achieve and curb independent desire for war, which is likely to enable more peaceful living in the long term. Yahweh's statement is highly ironic and paradoxical – one would expect that the Midianites are too numerous for Israel, but instead it is the opposite, it is Israel who are 'too numerous'. Yahweh may have yielded to Gideon's demands for proof, but he is now developing a strategy that will rely on faith and fly in the face of the reason that Gideon so prizes. Gideon wanted proof that Yahweh would deliver by his hand; Yahweh is clear that it will be the divine hand that will deliver. Irony deepens with Yahweh's command to Gideon, based on the very thing that plagues Gideon himself: fear. Those who will be able to opt out of battle are those who own their own vulnerability, something Gideon is obviously unable to do.

Modern translations often add 'thus Gideon sifted them out', but this is not present in either MT or LXX; both MT and LXX are clear that it is Yahweh who initiates the sifting, and men self-identify as afraid and turn back.

Yahweh is acting as commander-in-chief, deciding on the organization of troops, and now argues that the troops are still too numerous so that another sifting exercise ensues. Gideon does not get a say. This time, the sifting is completely arbitrary – drinking posture. It will be impossible for those who do go to battle to say that they were kept for their better skills, courage or strength, which also means that those rejected won't suffer a slur on their masculinity or willingness to fight. 7.5–6 are unclear in Hebrew; translations normally include facilitations to clarify meaning. The men are picked according to how they drink, but the text seems to contradict itself as to how they do so, who laps, who uses hands etc. Various explanations have been proposed and the text amended accordingly, often to argue that certain ways of drinking show men that are more alert – therefore more ready to fight. This surely misses the point. It is not human skills that will deliver victory but Yahweh's presence. Hence the choosing is not conducted along the lines of military readiness, but to teach the people about war with Yahweh (Judg. 3.2), one in which they are dependent on Yahweh's help and grace. This help is evident with Yahweh's dramatic announcement in 7.7, that 'with the three hundred that lapped, I will deliver you'. Here is the theological high point of the story. Yahweh is about to initiate one of the 'marvellous deeds' that Gideon thought were something for the past and only stories. In the previous story, the enemy had been militarily and technologically superior and Yahweh had shown that this superiority meant little. Here the people are having to learn again that greater strength or skill is not a determinative factor. In the previous story, Deborah and Barak willingly gave praise to Yahweh; here, Yahweh must engineer the situation to leave no doubt that it is Yahweh who brings about deliverance.

7.9–14: Reassuring Gideon

Once again, Yahweh takes the initiative as commander-in-chief, giving the order to attack, with the usual divine commitment formula, because 'I have given them into your hand'. Victory is a *fait accompli*, because Yahweh has already decided the outcome. Yet Yahweh makes provision for Gideon's humanity, as Gideon once again struggles to trust Yahweh's word. Yahweh had anticipated Gideon's fear following the downsizing of the army and now acts as a patient teacher to him. Ironically, what Yahweh specifically makes provision for is Gideon's fear. Gideon had not acknowledged his own fear earlier, when men who were afraid got leave to go home. But now, under cover of night, when he can hide once again, he takes up Yahweh's offer. Yahweh's gentle care and guidance come through with the provision of a companion to go with Gideon (the companion may be a servant, though the word used, *na'ar*, simply means young man, and therefore could be a military attendant or a younger friend). A companion would help him feel safer and provides someone else as witness to Yahweh's sign, but also acknowledges the loneliness of leadership and the burden that Gideon is being asked to carry. Gideon himself hadn't reached out to anyone, resuming the lone, independent leader motif of the earlier judges. 7.12 resumes focalization through Gideon's eyes, looking at the enemy and feeling overwhelmed by the multitude, with an echo of 6.5. The men eavesdrop on conversations in the camp and overhear a dream and its interpretation. Dreams are a frequent way for Yahweh to communicate and there is a pattern of Yahweh communicating with foreign rulers through dreams (Gen. 20.37; 41.1–36; Dan. 4); in the latter two cases, however, an interpretation for the dream is provided through a Hebrew. Here, it is a foreign soldier who has a dream and another who gives its interpretation, and it is Gideon, a Hebrew, who is the recipient of the divine message. The dream is interpreted through word association, a traditional Ancient Near Eastern divinatory technique (Niditch, 2008, p. 98), holding together the word for bread, *leḥem*, with that for making war, based on the same tripartite root, *lḥm*. The bread therefore has dual symbolism: on the one hand, it is a symbol of plenty, the life that the Midianites are taking away from Israel; on the other, through its shared root, it represents Israel as an army coming up against its oppressors. The interpretation is intriguing at two levels. First, how have the Midianites heard of Gideon? Once again, we wonder whether he already had a reputation as a 'mighty warrior', justifying the angel's greeting and further problematizing his claims of weakness. Second, which 'god' is the Midianite referring to? It could be a tribal god whom he thinks will defend Israel against invasion, in a system where different ethnic groups claimed protection from local territorial deities. Yet this Midianite seems to recognize the sovereignty of Yahweh, however skewed his understanding, at a time when Israel itself doubts it. It is curious that Gideon should be convinced by this overheard conversation – why would the words of the Midianites carry more weight than the words of Yahweh himself? Gideon, who had been all about logic until now, is convinced by a completely illogical dream. It may be that the affirmation of his own fear-inspiring presence to the enemy has boosted his confidence. Nevertheless, Gideon recognizes Yahweh's hand and 'worships' (7.15). At this point Gideon comes across positively as a man who has engaged with Yahweh and is gradually learning to listen, trust and worship in response to his expanding experience.

7.15–25: The battle

Gideon wastes no more time; he is finally convinced and shares his new-found certainty with the troops, in much the same way that Ehud had. He places the battle to come under the sign of Yahweh's favour, affirming that Yahweh had given Midian into their hands. Gideon's plan and instructions are sketchy, with a simple instruction to do as he does. There is no indication of where his ideas came from, but it is noticeable, in comparison with the battles of Joshua, that he has not asked for or received specific divine instructions on either the conduct of the battle or how to deal with its aftermath (such as instructions on booty). The plan seems to be to create fear in the middle of the night, leading the Midianites to think that Yahweh is coming with thunder and lightning (Baal imagery again). The dynamic of fear is now reversed: instead of Gideon being afraid of Baal's supporters, the foreign oppressors are afraid of Yahweh. It is psychological, rather than physical, warfare, appropriate for a small band of fighters against a much larger enemy. Gideon's battle cry, 'for Yahweh and for Gideon' (7.18) reflects his understanding of the dream he overheard, that he leads and Yahweh will deliver the enemy into his hand. He puts himself on a par with Yahweh; in one way, this reflects the covenantal partnership and double causality in the way in which Yahweh works. Yet in another, this is a warning signal about Gideon's growing confidence – his eagerness to take glory for himself, the act that Yahweh had warned against in 7.2. In the previous story, Barak had forfeited his glory; here, Gideon threatens to take for himself the glory belonging to Yahweh. The three companies execute the plan, enabling Gideon's own words to come to pass. They attack in deepest night, cloaked in darkness; the noise and light give the impression they are far more numerous than they truly are. An enemy just waking from sleep is much easier to trick. The Israelites repeat and embellish their war cry, 'A sword for Yahweh and for Gideon!' The mention of the sword echoes the interpretation of the soldier's dream in 7.14, that the bread symbolized 'Gideon's sword'. Yet it is also ironic, because the tactics just described mean that the men are holding jars and lights but no swords! Verses 21 and 22 then paint a strange contrast: each man stands in his place, while Yahweh is the agent that sets swords going, internally, in the enemy camp. The narration emphasizes that it is not Israel's swords that gain victory, but Yahweh's actions. Swords and violence don't solve conflict, trusting Yahweh does. Without instructions to do so from Yahweh, the army pursues the fleeing enemy, calling for reinforcements. It is unclear whether the pursuit was either necessary or desirable. The call for reinforcements suggests that Naphtali, Asher and Manasseh had not gone home as instructed by Yahweh but stayed for backup, thereby undermining Yahweh's cull of the army. Like Gideon, the rest of the army seeks their share of glory. Zebulon is not mentioned again – they may have gone home while the others had stayed. It may have been considered cowardly by other tribes but was the only example of full obedience to Yahweh's instructions.

Gideon then compounds the men's actions by actively sending out messengers to Ephraim (geographically near), asking them to join in the fight. Gideon had quickly forgotten the point of reducing the size of the army, his own confidence replacing dependence on Yahweh, and his own plans, divine directions. Ephraim responds enthusiastically. Gideon is clearly trusted and his leadership not questioned here. Every detail of the narrative reinforces the picture that Gideon may have already been a recognized local warlord, so that his initial protestations were not about humility or doubts about his abilities, but a lack of trust in or willingness to follow Yahweh's command. The narrative technique of Judges consistently employs this ambush style, leading the reader to see a character or story in a certain light, then gradually revealing information that forces a re-reading and re-evaluation. As a narrative technique, it is highly effective in drawing readers into meaning-making and asking deeper questions of ethics and theology. '*All* the men of Ephraim' respond (a counterpart to '*all* the Midianites, Amalekites and Easterners' of 6.33), and they pursue the enemy leaders, a pattern becoming established in the major judges cycles, as Barak had done with Sisera. Both men, Oreb and Zeeb, are killed in symbolic places, and their heads are brought back, which marks a ritual killing together with the type of corpse mutilation that prevents the proper burial of the dead and therefore enhances shame, inspires terror in enemies, affects the afterlife of victims and proclaims complete victory. Mutilation of the living and desecration of the dead emerge as a consistent theme in Judges, and reflects the practices of surrounding nations rather than obedience to the laws of *ḥerēm*.

8: Things fall apart

8.1–3: Dispute with Ephraim

The taking of army leaders at the end of the chapter 7 should have signalled the end of the Gideon cycle, yet new action is initiated, this time by Gideon rather than Yahweh. A short cameo relates the first complication, a dispute with Ephraim. Ephraim was called after the initial attack, to help prevent the Midianites from fleeing to safety, but 'the *men* of Ephraim' now complain that they should have been called in time for the offensive. The dispute is typical of tension around the distribution of spoils and attribution of glory. It relies on a war culture that prizes aggression and competition between men, where honour is won or lost on the battlefield. Fragmentation is starting to show in Israel; as in chapter 5, participation in warfare is an important component of tribal identity, and how tribes conceptualize the belonging of others within the wider group. Tensions around participation and non-participation will continue to mount throughout Judges until chapter 21, when non-participation eventually leads to the massacre of Jabesh-Gilead. Israel's sense of kinship and shared identity has little to do with Yahweh or the covenant here, and Ephraim is more concerned with its own status and glory than the liberation of Israel from oppressors.

The argument is heated, they 'upbraided him violently', and Gideon shows himself a skilled negotiator, diminishing his own achievements to enable others to affirm their own sense of personhood and honour. His calm response, appeasing anger, bodes well for his ability as a statesman. His response, however, jars with the theological drive of the narrative. He gives some credit to God (*Elohim* rather than Yahweh), but does not share anything of Yahweh's leading or Yahweh's instructions on paring down the army. Nor does he acknowledge that his calling for reinforcements fell outside of Yahweh's instructions. Instead, he diminishes his own accomplishments but still casts them as accomplishments, and praises the Ephraimites. It seems that Gideon still thinks that military prowess is more impressive than Yahweh's victory. Yahweh as agent has disappeared from the narrative; this is Gideon's campaign now, on Gideon's terms, for Gideon's purposes. The earlier doubting, fearful Gideon was closer to Yahweh; as his confidence grows, he will depend increasingly on himself.

8.4–21: Friends and enemies alike

The next turn of the narrative is articulated around the pursuit of the Midianite kings and the remnants of their army, interwoven with another story, that of Israelite towns Succoth and Penuel. The juxtaposition of the stories highlights Gideon's treatment of friend and foe, blurring the boundaries between them. The narrator paints a picture of the exhausted Israelite army pursuing the enemy, working hard to free Israel, begging kin in Succoth for some sustenance on the way. Gideon could have confiscated provisions (Block, 1999, p. 289) instead of relying on hospitality and solidarity, yet the people of Succoth refuse. At this point, reader sympathies lie with Gideon and his men. The people of Succoth are belligerent, possibly sneering. They may be afraid of helping Gideon before victory is clear, risking reprisals from the Midianites and Amelekites. While the request to feed an army is not unusual, it is a big ask for a people who had been described at the beginning of the story as desperately struggling to eke out a living under Midianite raids. Poverty and oppression here do not lead to solidarity but to everyone trying to survive for themselves. The men of Succoth demand proof of victory before they part with scant resources; they clearly do not see Gideon as a liberator or have faith in his actions; nor do they see themselves as part of a bigger Israelite whole being helped by Gideon, as the designation 'your army' shows. For them, this is about Gideon, not about Israel. They react very differently from the men who enthusiastically followed Gideon after the coming of the Spirit; one wonders whether Yahweh's presence has receded, hence Gideon no longer has the charismatic authority needed for his role, replacing it with threats and brute force. Gideon, who himself had doubted Yahweh, now sets out to punish the people who doubt him, calling it justice or a lesson. Gideon has learnt little from Yahweh's patience and kindness in helping him build up his trust. There is no grace in Gideon's response. A personal experience of grace does not necessarily shape the recipient into being gracious themselves, a theme that will appear more prominently in the NT, from the Lord's Prayer's 'Forgive us our offences as we forgive those who offend against us' to the parable of the unjust steward (Luke 16.1–13). While the imitation of God is a strong NT theme (Matt. 16.24; Mark 8.34; Luke 9.23; John 13.15, 34; Eph. 5.1; 1 Thess. 1.6; 1 Peter 1.16; 2.21; 3 John 1.11), it is far from absent in the OT, as the characteristics of Yahweh's relationship with Israel come to be the characteristics that should shape Israel's life too – see, for instance, Leviticus' insistence, 'be holy, for I am holy' (Lev. 19.2; 20.7), an injunction always embedded in wider ethical commands for good living. But Gideon does not learn from Yahweh's grace towards him or Israel. Instead, he threatens to 'trample [their] flesh on the thorns of the wilderness and on briers'. Death in the wilderness symbolizes a return to pre-conquest reality, a roll back of life in the Promised Land and, implicitly, an othering of Succoth as cast out of covenant and promise. Gideon is effectively policing the boundaries of Israel according to political allegiance to his leadership. His actions become erratic and self-interested: in making an example of Succoth, he consolidates his own power through fear. His words 'the Lord has given Zebah and Zalmunna into *my* hand' also reveal a lot. The narrator never reported such a promise from Yahweh. Gideon extends the promise to justify his later actions, claiming divine authority to assert his own, a clear abuse of the position he holds. Power and status corrupt his sense of self and his ability to listen to Yahweh. 8.8 rehearses a parallel story in Penuel. At the root of both is an evaluation of Gideon's leadership. The image of the thorns and briers foreshadows the parable of Jotham in chapter 9, and its evaluation of the bramble king; his threat to tear down the tower of Penuel also links him to the Abimelech story and Abimelech's abuse of his own people. His threat to Penuel is ironic, 'when I come back in peace …'. He promises to bring destruction as he comes back in peace; there may be external peace, but Gideon will cause internal strife rather than peace for Israel, strife that endures beyond his lifetime and continues with his son Abimelech. Gideon's first days as ruler do not bode well and tarnish the optimism of chapter 7.

Gideon leads the army onwards in relentless pursuit of the Midianites. The narration hyperbolically depicts the magnitude of Israel's victory over the enemy that had seemed so overwhelming. Now the David and Goliath dynamic has been reversed, and the people of the east cower before Gideon. Gideon leads another surprise attack, which enhances fear and gives the advantage to what should still be a smaller force. There is no obvious need or imperative to pursue the fleeing army, other than logic, war and politics. Killing all the enemies may make Israel feel safer, but it risks worse reprisals from their allies. To pursue the kings, rather than just the generals, is to attack the real seat of power in an attempt to undermine the enemy's ability to regroup and rebuild. Peace may last longer, yet so will enmity. There is no mention of Yahweh here, and no hint that he has given this victory.

Having captured the enemy kings, Gideon now returns to Succoth and captures (*lākad* in both 8.12 and 8.14) a boy/young lad and makes him give them a hit list. It's unclear whether the young lad gives out the names of the elders willingly, though the use of 'capture' together with the differential of power between seasoned military leaders and a boy suggest coercion rather than willing betrayal. Gideon's words in 8.15 show that this is not justice but revenge for a personal slight, 'you taunted me'. He does not stress the impact of their refusal on his troops, nor his commission to deliver Israel, which would have deserved support; and he does highlight kinship. But instead, he objects to how they have treated him, angry for wounded pride. He then does as he said he would. The phrasing of 8.16 is interesting in Hebrew; LXX^{A} has the word for threshing to describe what Gideon did. LXX^{B} is unclear. In MT, the word is *yāda'*, to know, in the *hiphil* meaning 'declare/teach/make known'. The emphasis in Hebrew is on teaching them a lesson or making an example. What is it he is saying, and to whom? Gideon seems focused on those who refuse him what he needs, who do not take him seriously. Not siding with him is the equivalent – or worse – of siding with the enemy. The audience is the wider people of Israel: Gideon is starting to rule by fear by making known how he treats those who resist him. The man once dominated by his own fears now rules through fear. The account of Penuel ('the face of God') is terse and factual, but no less brutal or disproportionate. Penuel was named by Jacob in Genesis 32 following his struggle with God. Here, Gideon struggles with other Israelites and never seeks the face or approval of God. He breaks down the tower of Penuel, the same verb used for his breaking the altar of Baal: symbolically, Israelites who do not obey him are treated in the same way as foreigners. Succoth and Penuel mark the first time in Judges that Israelites kill other Israelites, a trend that grows exponentially in the rest of the book. Israel apart from covenant living seems bound for self-destruction. Gideon's actions foreshadow the failure of leadership, first in Judges, then with the monarchy, initiating a pattern of leaders who abuse their position and use it for their personal ends. Gideon used Israel's army for personal revenge. His language increasingly features the first person singular, as his self-importance grows and his focus shifts away from the common good and into tyrannical rule. A striking feature of chapter 8 is Gideon's differential attitude towards the weak and the strong. Towards the strong – whether Ephraimites or Midianite kings – he is deferential and respectful, even if he intends to kill; with the weak, he turns into a bully (Klein 1989, p. 61), failing to distinguish between justice and revenge.

The final pericope in this section returns to the kings of Midian. More is revealed of Gideon's background. He had brothers who were killed at Tabor. Why they were killed is unclear, or whether their death happened in war or peace (in a raid on Israel). Either way, this is the first record of the violent death of an Israelite in Judges, and the only record of Israelites being killed by foreigners. From then on, all Israelite violent deaths will be at the hands of other Israelites. The information about his brothers illuminates some of Gideon's motivations and the depth of his anger, letting no one, not even other Israelites, stand in the way of revenge. Some have argued that Gideon may be acting as *go'ēl*, avenger of blood, along the lines of the provision for justice after the murder of kin in Numbers 35.24 and Deuteronomy 19.4–13 (Webb, 2012, p. 260). Yet in the legal material the emphasis is on justice and due process, including safeguards about places, witnesses and intent. It is unlikely that the provision was intended to be applied in war settings, and the wider thread of the Judges narrative, interwoven with Succoth and Penuel, strongly suggests that this is not about justice but about revenge. Until Gideon, judges were motivated by the plight of Israel. From now on, their motives will be increasingly mixed, with a high proportion of them seeking personal gain. Parallel to this change, the first hint of dynastic monarchy occurs in the book here in 8.18. The kings' comment on Gideon's brothers, 'they resembled the sons of a king' may be a simple statement of fact, a taunt, or a shrewd observation on Gideon's bearing and behaviour. The narrator introduces additional doubt about Gideon's description of himself as of no status, and gives more credibility to the messenger's salutation of 'mighty warrior', while foreshadowing what comes next in Gideon's and Abimelech's stories. The Midianite kings talk of Gideon's brothers as a prize kill, with no regret. The dialogue follows the course of a ritual exchange of insults between warriors (Webb, 2012, p. 258). Gideon taunts the kings back with a lost possibility for mercy, had they themselves shown mercy to his brothers. Yet everything in this chapter shows that Gideon does not deal in mercy. Gideon orders his son to kill the kings. The boy is described as *na'ar*, a lad or youth, the same word used for the boy in Succoth. Young people are used by older men in war. One was intimidated in Succoth, and here the young boy is a pawn in the trading of insults, since being killed by a boy rather than a seasoned warrior would have been an insult to the kings, adding humiliation to their coming death. Gideon may have also meant it as a rite of initiation, inviting his son into leadership after him through the symbol of killing the most important enemies. But the boy comes across much as

Gideon himself had in the first part of his story, hesitant and afraid. Gideon tries to teach war to his son, but his teaching does not follow the way of Yahweh. Rather, his way of waging war is that of the surrounding nations. Reader sympathies ebb further away from Gideon as he abuses his authority both as leader and as father, a theme developed further in the Jephthah narrative. The kings taunt Gideon again, with a slur on his masculinity should he not kill them himself and shame his son for his failure. Gideon kills them coolly, taking away their jewellery as booty. He appropriates the symbols of kingship for himself and takes booty after the manner of the Canaanites, rather than dedicating a share of it to Yahweh. What had started as a holy war of liberation has quickly degenerated into a bloodbath and the pursuit of a personal feud, together with the accruing of personal power and riches. The picture of Gideon's quick journey to abusing power problematizes war and leadership by showing the inability of human beings to keep to the boundaries set by Yahweh, and their propensity to confuse their own wishes with those of God. These interwoven narratives chronicle Gideon's propensity for anger and revenge and his increasingly self-interested actions. The parallel shows him treating foreigners and Israelites with profound brutality, based on his own judgement of what they deserve. As is often the case in war, the military value of the enemy is acknowledged (as this will enhance the value of those who defeated them), but the harshest treatment and disputes occur within the in-group (Niditch 2008, p. 103) as the war effort needs total cooperation and the ability to delineate clearly between self and other. Dehumanizing the other enables the rationalizations needed to justify killing; yet by default, it means that a strong in-group identity is needed, over and against which the identity of the 'other' is constructed. Liminal figures with divided loyalties, and those who do not exhibit loyalty to the in-group and its values, threaten this construction of identity and are therefore treated with the greatest brutality. The tensions of constructing the identity of Israel, particularly in war, will increase and bloom to their full catastrophic consequences in Judges 21.

8.22–35: Gideon the ruler

The necessary aftermath of war is the building of peace; previous deliverers were simply said to have judged Israel and the land had rest, but against expectations, Gideon's story does not conclude after the capture of the kings, but introduces Gideon's peace-time leadership, setting the scene for Abimelech. As Israel comes to Gideon to ask him to rule (*māšal*) over them, they make no reference to Yahweh. They offer dynastic rule in the style of local kings, though the word for reigning as a king (*mālak*) is not used. Their choice of Gideon seems based on his military leadership, rather than on being Yahweh's chosen deliverer. They fail to understand the real source of deliverance (and Gideon does not correct them), assuming that military strength is what a ruler needs, rather than knowing Yahweh through close study of the law and following the covenant, and being chosen by Yahweh, as prescribed for a king in Deuteronomy 17.18–20. They offer Gideon rule, not straight after battle, but after he has turned against fellow Israelites and killed and taken booty from the Midianite kings. How have those stories shaped the Israelites' actions? It is unclear why the people want to move to a dynastic model. They may have reflected on the leadership vacuum that followed previous judges; they might find the theocratic, more dispersed model too difficult; they may envy the Canaanites' apparent success in the land without connecting their political model to the oppression they visited on Israel, or inequality within the city-states. Gideon appears to have united a significant portion of Israelites, but are they united around the right thing? Around Gideon, or Yahweh? There is no indication of how big the delegation is, or who they may represent. It may simply be those who were in battle with Gideon, wanting to secure their own status and power by gathering around him as a private militia. While they do not use the word for king, *māšal* is nevertheless often used of kings and linked to hereditary rule. Gideon's refusal implies that it is kingship that is offered. Deuteronomy 17.14–20 makes grudging provision for kingship – grudging because it is linked to wanting to be like the people of the land, and clear restrictions are placed to limit imitation of local kings. Firstly, Yahweh should choose the king, a principle the people have ignored. Gideon's response has the appearance of piety, acknowledging that Yahweh should have pre-eminence. The refrain in the epilogue, 'in these days there was no king', picks up on this motif, suggesting that by the end of Judges there was neither human nor divine king, in contrast to earlier aspirations. Gideon's words are tinted with dark irony when read in the light of chapter 9. His eldest son won't reign but be killed by a younger son who will claim kingship in accordance with his name, Abimelech, 'my father is king'. Gideon gives a superficially right answer but does not enquire of Yahweh as to what kind of leadership he should be offering Israel, if any. His actions then immediately contradict his words, as he claims booty along the lines of a Canaanite king establishing his royal treasury. Gideon had been acting increasingly like a king, with summary punishment on those who defy him, taking glory for himself, addressing other kings as equals and taking their royal symbols. The Midianite kings had already referred to him and his brothers as having the likeness of a king (in Canaanite eyes, rather than Yahweh's), and Gideon strengthens the picture. Asking for his share of gold amounts to asking for symbolic submission from other Israelites (Beldman, 2020, p. 124), as a king is given tributes by vassals. Gideon mirrors the behaviour of Canaanite kings. Until Gideon, delivering Israel had been its own reward. Now Gideon gains status, power and wealth.

Let's compare this passage to the battle with and defeat of the Midianites at the time of Moses in Numbers 31: in Numbers, Moses follows the principles for holy war set out in Deuteronomy 20 (Klein, 1989, p. 64). All the men are killed, and Moses determines the fate of human captives. Spoils of war are purified and brought before Yahweh for atonement, before being distributed with a portion for Yahweh, a portion for warriors, and a portion for the congregation. Moses does not take spoils for himself. In contrast, Gideon gives Yahweh neither share nor glory, and only warriors profit, rather than the entire people. Gideon is not just building his own power, he is establishing that of his warriors too, and disregards the welfare of the wider people. There is no attempt here to shape the community according to the covenantal principles, and the people adopt Canaanite practices without understanding how socio-political arrangements shape patterns of oppression and abuse.

Gideon's failure to lead Israel into covenant faithfulness is enhanced by the cameo in 8.27, as he leads the people into idolatry. The exact nature of what he makes is unclear. In OT terms, an ephod was an elaborate high priestly garment that the high priest put on to seek God's will (Ex. 28, 35, 39; Lev. 8; 1 Sam. 23.9–12; 30.7–8). Yet here no priest is mentioned, and neither is Yahweh. An ephod is mentioned again in association with idolatry in the story of Micah in Judges 17—18. The Akkadian cognate term, *epattu*, may help illuminate the use of the term. An *epattu* was a cloth spread over idols, sometimes used as a shorthand for both cloth and idols (Block, 1999, p. 300). It may be that the ephod was initially dedicated to Yahweh or meant to symbolize that the victory and booty belonged to Yahweh, though this is not explicit, and if so, the meaning of the ephod changed over time. In a story redolent with contrastive parallels to Moses, this echoes those of the bronze serpent (Num. 21.6–9) and the golden calf (Ex. 32.2–4). In Numbers 21, Moses is ordered to make an image of a serpent as a reminder of the people's sin and of Yahweh's healing. The serpent is used appropriately under Moses, but later becomes a snare to Israel (2 Kings 18.4). Unlike Moses, Gideon was not instructed to make the ephod, nor did he invest it with specific meaning pointing to Yahweh. His actions are therefore closer to Aaron's in making the golden calf. The ephod and its worship are condemned in paradigmatic covenantal terms: Israel 'prostituted itself' before it, an image of illicit activity and covenant breach. The narrator underlines the breadth of the problem with 'all' Israel. Joash's local pagan shrine has become a centre for national idolatry sponsored by Gideon. Once again the picture is of a Canaanite king, with sponsored sanctuary and priestly duties. Gideon the iconoclast now promotes idolatry, in a complete ironic reversal, and the place in which he had seen Yahweh and set up his altar returns to its original use, as if neither revelation nor deliverance had occurred. Gideon's readiness to forget Yahweh's marvellous deeds epitomizes the state of Israel as a whole. Yahweh has not abandoned Israel, however, as 8.28 reminds the readers with a return to framework formulas. First, 'Midian was subdued before the Israelites'. The narrator uses the passive, reminding readers that it is not Israel or Gideon who subdued the enemy, but Yahweh. Gideon is not said to have judged (*šāpaṭ*) Israel – the implication is that he reigned instead. Yet despite Gideon's flaws, the land has as much rest as with Deborah, another sign of Yahweh's mercy. This is the last time in Judges that the land will have rest.

Gideon's legacy is explored further, with details of his descendants. He had a perfect number of sons, 70, and clearly aimed to establish his family for the long term through his many wives. It is unclear why he had a concubine (*pilegeš*) as well; she is singled out, of a different status and from a different location, which signals trouble. Gideon's overall life-style contradicts every prescription in the code for kings in Deuteronomy 17.14–20: kings were forbidden to amass large fortunes, have multiple wives, or contravene covenantal principles and worship. Gideon's large family (and the likelihood of sibling rivalry), together with the account of his death and burial, echo patriarchal times, preceding the giving of the law. Gideon's legacy is ambiguous. 8.33 suggests that after his death the people returned to the Baals. Gideon may not have led them into covenantal faithfulness, but it appears that worship under his rule was syncretistic, with Yahwistic traits, whereas after his death, the people turned entirely to Baal and Gideon suffers the same fate as Yahweh, forgotten, his work towards deliverance disregarded. Idolatry takes a new turn in 8.33 as Israel ironically starts worshipping 'Baal-berith' (the Lord of the covenant); it is unclear who this god exactly was: either a deeply syncretistic conflation of Yahweh and Baal, or a complete turning away from Yahweh and his covenant towards a rival lord of the covenant. Gideon's work is still praised in 8.35. Just because Gideon was not perfect does not mean he was discarded completely, or vilified. Instead, his story is told candidly and honestly, and recognition of his achievements is encouraged, which places this story under the sign of grace, promoting a healthy culture of how to talk of leaders with both honesty and loyalty. Gideon focuses all the ambiguities of Israel, pulled in several directions, towards Yahweh and away from him, at times understanding and at times oblivious, ambiguities made obvious in the frequent switches of names between Gideon and Jerubaal. Gideon symbolizes the state of Israel towards Yahweh in his ambivalence, and in the way he and his descendants are rejected by Israel. 8.35 condemns Israel for failing to show loving-kindness (*hesed*), a deeply covenantal term, to the house of Jerubaal. Israel has broken an implicit covenant with Gideon as well as Yahweh. This final pericope, oscillating between Jerubaal and Gideon, points to underlying questions: Did Baal contend with Gideon? Did Gideon contend with Baal? Did Baal contend for himself? Who won?

Concluding reflections

Judges 6—8 paints a careful, detailed and nuanced pen picture of a leader, in his strengths and weaknesses, as he seeks to step into the role Yahweh has called him to. New questions on leadership crystallize around choosing leaders, reasons for fighting, the appropriateness of rewards, and legacy and succession. The character of leaders is examined more closely than in previous accounts, with character flaws threatening to derail their leadership yet not necessarily a barrier to Yahweh's gracious action. Gideon struggles with the balance between faith and reason, he has deeply mixed motives, abuses his position to pursue personal vendettas, acts as a bully with no mercy, and uses his position to establish himself and his household rather than benefit Israel as a whole. A recurrent theme of Gideon's story is the correspondence between words and actions. Gideon constantly struggles to believe that Yahweh will make good on his word. Yet in Gideon's life a gap opens between word and deeds. He seems to take on board Yahweh's instruction to reduce the army, but then seeks to share in

Yahweh's glory, disregarding divine command as he mounts a campaign to pursue Midian; he claims not to want kingship, but in every way acts as a king; appearing to fight for Yahweh, but leading the people into idolatry. The intertext with Deuteronomy 17.14–20 suggests that the root problem with Gideon is his lack of schooling in the ways of the Lord:

> When he has taken the throne of his kingdom, he shall have a copy of this law written for him in the presence of the Levitical priests. It shall remain with him and he shall read in it all the days of his life, so that he may learn to fear the Lord his God, diligently observing all the words of this law and these statutes, neither exalting himself above other members of the community nor turning aside from the commandment, either to the right or to the left, so that he and his descendants may reign long over his kingdom in Israel. (Deut. 17.18–20)

Gideon has experienced the presence of Yahweh but does not deepen his experience through study of Scripture and habits of life. His experience was emotional and significant, but ultimately shallow. Gideon failed to guard his heart against the temptations of power; his reliance on Yahweh is inversely proportional to his self-confidence: instead of Yahweh's marvellous deeds inspiring his faith and leading him deeper into the covenant, they become accessories in his quest for power, and he quickly fails to distinguish what is his and what is Yahweh's. Hence, he claims victory for himself, takes the strategic lead and fails to acknowledge his vulnerability and dependence. The more confident he becomes, the more he disregards others around him, with untold brutality at first, and later as a privileged leader amassing treasures for himself at the expense of the common good. Yet Yahweh's faithfulness nevertheless shines through: Yahweh sends a prophet and a messenger despite Israel's lack of interest; patiently answers Gideon's questions and requests for proof, working with Gideon to give him the best possible chance of leading faithfully and not claiming glory that is not his; even as Gideon moves away from working in partnership with Yahweh, Yahweh is still faithful to Israel and grants 40 years of peace. And ultimately, Gideon is remembered as a deliverer and a man of faith, despite his shortcomings, a memory that shapes the community in grace and hope because human frailty is never the last word.

The story of Gideon stands at the heart of Judges: Gideon is the first judge to confront idolatry, first to lead in idolatry, first to deal with internal tensions violently, first Israelite to kill other Israelites, first king. And last to bring the land rest. At the heart of the book is the question of kingship and rule, and what it means for Yahweh to be the true king of Israel, as Gideon promotes in words but denies in actions. This story is the most explicitly theological story in the book, with its focus on cultus and a high proportion of dialogue with Yahweh. Israel's religious life is explicitly pictured as the root of the problem, and deliverers as part of the problem as well as the solution. Gideon works with Yahweh on deliverance, but then takes on the role of saviour single-handedly, begging the question, will Israel be saved by Yahweh or try to save itself? (Gillmayr-Bucher, 2009, p. 696).

4

Abimelech (9)

Chapter 9 stands at the centre of Judges, after the Deborah/Barak and Gideon sequences and before Jephthah and Samson. It works as a sequel to Gideon's judgeship, yet is separated from it by the rest formula in 8.28. Many of the themes of 6—8 are extended and magnified here: the growing absence of Yahweh; questions of character and leadership; self-interest and self-centredness; abuses of power; the consequences of ruling through brute force; jostling for power; brutality towards non-combatants; disregard for the people; justice and revenge. And threaded all the way through, the question of kingship.

9.1–6: Seizing power

Not unusually for a biblical narrative, a younger son, rather than the obvious heir, moves into the limelight. It is the first time in Judges that power moves along bloodlines. Abimelech was introduced at the end of chapter 8. His name, meaning 'my father is king', is ominous. While it could be a pious reference to Yahweh as king, the discrepancy between Gideon's words and actions when refusing kingship suggests that the name probably reflects Gideon's real-life status. Abimelech is a rare name in the MT; its only other uncontested uses are for the Canaanite kings of Gerar (Gen. 20, 21, 26), and one reference in Psalm 34.1 to the king of Gath, elsewhere called Achish (1 Sam. 21.3–15).[1] Both have 'Abimelech' as a Canaanite name or title,

1 1 Chronicles 18.16 has an Abimelech as son of Abiathar, but the parallel passage in 2 Samuel 8.17 names him as Ahimelech.

which compounds questions about Abimelech's mother. She was a *pilegeš*, a term often translated as 'concubine' but more akin to a secondary wife, whose status is formal but lower (for the status of *pilegeš*, see Hamley, 2017). Children of *pilegeš* are sometimes included in genealogies and share in inheritance, but this is not consistent. Abimelech is differentiated from his siblings from the start. In 8.31 his mother is said to be 'in Shechem'. Given that Israelite families were normally both patrilineal (genealogy and inheritance going through the paternal side) and patrilocal (women live with their husbands and their families), the location of Abimelech's mother suggests a different social status, possibly a different ethnicity with different marriage customs (matrilineal), and a sharp differentiation of siblings along maternal lines. The positioning of Abimelech's mother, together with the surfeit of family-related terms in 9.1 (son, mother, kinsfolk, clan, family) suggests an uneasy relationship at best between the one isolated boy and the large clan of 70 brothers. In addition, 9.2. implies that those 70 brothers ruled over the region, whereas Abimelech had not been granted shared power. The brothers are not said to rule over Israel as a whole, yet their sphere of influence extends beyond their own tribe (Ophrah is in Manasseh but Shechem is in Ephraim). Gideon might have married a Shechemite as an attempt to unify the tribes, or to extend his power base. Abimelech comes across as unwanted and possibly dispossessed, which shapes his disposition and actions. At this point, reader sympathy lies with Abimelech, whose important name clashes with the reality of his social position. Depending on what comes next, he could fit the pattern of unexpected leaders through being a younger, more liminal heir.

The status of Shechem is unclear. The later description of the lords of the city, their religious practices and their characterization as descending from Hamor suggest that they may be Canaanites, or Israelites who have gone completely native (Chisholm, 2013, p. 314; Fokkelman, 1992, p. 34; Webb, 2012, p. 270). If they were Canaanites, or a mix of locals and Israelites, then Abimelech's ethnicity may be mixed, so that his status in Israel is lower and liminal. Shechem has high symbolic significance due to its place in Old Testament history. Abraham and Jacob both worshipped there (Gen. 12.6; 33.18); clearly a Canaanite place in Genesis 34, it is the locus of the rape of Dinah and her brothers' bloody revenge, though it remained a sacred place for Jacob (35.4; 37.12); Moses continued this tradition and planned to worship there (Deut. 11.29; 27.4); it is a sacred place in Joshua, made a Levitical city (21.7) and a city of refuge (21.21) and twice the place of a major renewal of the covenant (8.30–34; 24); Joseph's bones are buried there (24.32). Later, in 1 Kings 12.1–14, Rehoboam goes to Shechem for Israel to declare him king, a chain of events that will lead to the division of the kingdom. Shechem holds within itself the best and worst of humanity, and its place in the story of Israel is highly ambiguous, as a sacred place and a place of wickedness, a place of hope and despair, a place of great beginnings and tragic endings. Its place within this story belongs to the negative strand of Shechem stories, with pagan worship and distortion of the covenant, where families are broken apart and loyalties severed. Just as in Genesis 34, it will prompt the massacre of many brothers.

9.2 expounds Abimelech's arguments for rule. He wants it to be heard by 'all the lords (*baal*) of Shechem'. He is addressing the important, wealthy and powerful, rather than the assembly of all the people. Power is becoming concentrated in the hands of the few, with an underlying assumption that it should pass down the generations. Abimelech's argument is solely based on family and kinship, rather than character, fitness to rule, or Yahweh's choice. The power of the covenant as the uniting and shaping force at the centre of Israel is waning, gradually replaced by tribalism and blood ties. Furthermore, Abimelech presents having one ruler, rather than a collaborative team, as self-evidently better. He is self-interested, but also embraces and plays on cultural acceptance of a hierarchical model of social organization that will, over time, create vast inherited privilege. This kind of system stands in direct contrast to the picture of the covenantal community drawn through the laws of the Torah, 'the whole congregation' regularly addressed and tasked with shaping their covenantal life (Ex. 35.1, 4; Lev.

4.13; 19.2; Num. 8.9; 13.26; 14.7; 15.25; Josh. 18.1; 22.12) in ways that were profoundly subversive of hierarchical and inherited privilege, despite their setting within a patriarchal system. Leviticus offers a powerful case study in looking at the imagined, idealized community of what Israel could aspire to be: despite a strong patriarchal culture where the head of the household rules, the laws of Leviticus limit the authority and reach of family heads; more widely, the Jubilee laws (Lev. 25) set out a proposal for a society not allowing inherited wealth to be accrued and passed down the generations, but enforcing a reset of the distribution of wealth at regular intervals, preventing advantage being taken of those who struggle because of life circumstances and encouraging proactive care for them (in particular the 'orphan, widow and stranger'). While there is no evidence that these laws were ever implemented, they are held as ideals that should shape the socio-political and theological consciousness of the nation. Abimelech's socio-political imagination is clearly not shaped by the Torah and its close link to the character of Yahweh as seen through his liberating action, but rather through the norms of surrounding cultures. Abimelech uses 'Jerubaal' to speak about his father, and the name is used throughout the narrative, enhancing the Canaanite feel of the story. Loyalty to lineage, family and clan take prominence in forming alliances and the ascendance of leaders. Gideon himself set the scene for such a shift through his kingly lifestyle, and his children work out his legacy. 9.4 takes the story even further out of covenantal Israel as Abimelech's rise to kingship is funded by the proceeds of the pagan temple of Baal-Berith, though support of Abimelech will ironically lead to its destruction. He is given 70 pieces of silver, a currency frequently associated with betrayal and wrongdoing (see Delilah in 16.5 and Micah in 17.2). The money equals one piece of silver per brother – a much lower price for their lives than Delilah will be paid for Samson's. Abimelech uses the money to hire mercenaries, 'worthless fellows' (*'anāšîm rêqîm ûpōtăzîm*), literally 'empty and arrogant men' (Butler, 2009, p. 237). Abimelech surrounds himself with people who have no interest in contributing to society, do not care about others, and have nothing better to do. They 'follow him': Abimelech's leadership is characterized by the type of people ready to follow. It is unclear whether the rulers of Shechem are aware of his specific plans at this point.

In the idolatrous worship centre sponsored by his father, Abimelech kills all his brothers 'on one stone', a parody of ritual sacrifice enabled by Baal money. His father is consistently called Jerubaal from now on, and implicitly the message is that Baal contended and won. Abimelech's appeal to the importance of blood and kin clearly does not extend beyond what is useful to him. Turning against his brothers suggests that he does not want to rule Shechem only, but the entire tribe and, possibly, all Israel. Abimelech's actions are not fully explained; readers can only conjecture that his motives involve an unhealthy mix of thirst for power and anger and resentment. He appears as an extreme caricature of his father's worst traits and an illustration of the underlying theme of the impact of one generation upon the next. Themes of sibling rivalry and violence run through much of the OT, particularly through the patriarchal narratives (Cain and Abel, Ishmael and Isaac, Jacob and Esau, Joseph and his brothers) and will feature powerfully in the succession narratives of King David. Preferential treatment of mothers and siblings consistently leads to disaster and exposes the flaws of a patriarchal system centred around a strong head of household whose power is only passed to one other; and where multiple mothers are used to separate and rank the children of one father (García Bachmann, 2018, p. l). The narratives themselves question and undermine the culture that they portray. Abimelech's actions stand together with another similar event in the canon, the slaughter of Ahab's 70 sons in 2 Kings 10. The fathers of the sons killed both ruled oppressively, murdered fellow-Israelites and sponsored pagan worship; both had 70 sons; in both cases a conspiracy is led by one individual, who secures the support of local leaders; and the leader of the conspiracy is proclaimed king (Block, 1999, p. 312). However, differences sharpen the meaning of both events. Jehu is portrayed as an agent of justice against a king and his family who had sponsored idolatry and worked to destroy the social fabric of Israel through injustice and oppression, whereas Abimelech acts out of selfishness, greed and resentment. Gideon had not been perfect, but he had delivered Israel and led it into peace in ways Ahab never did. Family and descendants were a much greater threat within an established hereditary monarchy than in the wake of Gideon. Placing the two stories together highlights a recurring feature in Judges: the people act in ways that mimic justice, sacrifice, or just war, yet are not sanctioned, let alone commissioned, by Yahweh. Abimelech kills only his brothers, leaving widows and orphans vulnerable and without protection. His brothers are all described as 'men', implying maturity and settled life, in contrast perhaps to Jotham, the only brother to escape the massacre and, fittingly within biblical logic, the youngest one. Readers may hope that this brother will come back and avenge both father and brothers, taking up the mantle of leadership as many younger brothers do.

The rulers of Shechem, now Abimelech's brothers are dead, proclaim Abimelech king, suggesting a transfer of power from the brothers onto Abimelech. Abimelech is the first person to be named king in Israel, though it is only a partial kingship whose sphere of influence seems restricted to Shechem and Beth-Milo, in the style of Canaanite city-states. The significance of kingship is shown through the root word for king, *mlk*, being used three times – they 'kinged' him king, My-father-is-king. It is also the first time in Judges that leadership is determined entirely by human action, rather than through divine intervention. The ceremony is conducted by an oak tree; trees that once were markers of divine encounter and the administration of justice (Abraham, Gideon, Deborah) are now associated with the making of an illegitimate, murderous king. Israel has forgotten its past, and is now jeopardizing its future.

9.7–21: The intervention of Jotham

News of the coronation reaches Jotham, the surviving younger son, and he intervenes. Rather than resorting to military challenge, Jotham engages in prophetic action, appealing to God

(Elohim) for justice. The two brothers contrast sharply; Abimelech's (possibly Canaanite) name embodies his ambitions, whereas Jotham's Yahwistic name means 'the Lord is perfect/true'; Abimelech uses brute force and surrounds himself with worthless men, Jotham stands alone and uses words. Neither uses Yahweh's covenant name and both define themselves in relation to their father, one in opposition, the other claiming continuity and loving loyalty (*ḥesed*). Jotham's choice of Mount Gerizim to deliver his speech is loaded. In Deuteronomy 27, Mount Gerizim and Mount Ebal were used to seal the covenant through ritual blessings and curses, which makes them highly symbolic for important speech and social critique (Niditch 2008, p. 116). Gerizim was the mount of blessing, where blessings for obedience were proclaimed in Joshua 8.30–35. As Judges reverses the achievements of Joshua, Mount Gerizim becomes the mount of curse for Israel's unfaithfulness to covenant principles, and to the house of Gideon (Jotham, like his father in his war cry, links Gideon/Jerubaal and God). Jotham uses a parable or fable as a commentary on kingship, the importance of character, and the responsibility of the people in choosing their leaders.

The genre of the speech is generally classed as fable: it uses inanimate objects speaking and behaving as human beings (Block, 1999, p. 316). Trees from the Middle East, central to Israel agrarian economy, are used here. 8.8 has them simply deciding to have a king; it is unclear why, and the move seems random and possibly unnecessary, echoing the purely human choice of Abimelech as king. Several trees are asked to reign in turn, each highly symbolic of the sources of Israel's wealth and well-being and often used in paradigmatic pictures of blessing and as symbols of what cruel kings take from common people (Deut. 6.11; 8.8; Josh. 24.13; 1 Sam. 8.14; 2 Kings 18.32). First, the olive tree. Olives were central to the economy as a staple food that also produced oil for cooking and lights and was used in medicine and for anointing kings. Olives therefore brought strength, health and honour to others. Figs symbolized peace, safety and prosperity (Butler, 2009, p. 240). In a land without sugar, figs were used as sweeteners for food, to make containers with the leaves and poultices in medicine. Finally, the grape vine, consumed fresh or dried and turned into juice or wine, symbolizes life, fertility and joy. All three are symbols of covenant blessing, and their absence of covenant curse (Deut. 28.39). Symbolically, the labour of farmers is the source of Israel's wealth and well-being. All three trees consider their agrarian contribution of greater worth to the common good than kingship. Kingship is portrayed pejoratively as 'swaying over' the other trees, in an echo of the Deuteronomic prohibition of kings from 'exalting themselves above other members of the community' (Deut. 17.20). Now 'all the trees' join together – the trees as a whole are responsible both for the decision to have a king to start with and for the king they end up choosing. They ask the bramble to reign. Brambles grow where nothing else does, symbolizing the wilderness. They have little use apart from firewood – they are wild, not cultivated. The bramble's answer is arrogant and misleading. First, it demands 'lasting faithfulness', in a perverted echo of covenant language, a reminder that this is exactly what Israel failed to give Gideon, their deliverer, who had been offered kingship first. Second, it offers protection in its shade, a frequent image for the protection of the king in the Ancient Near East (Butler, 2009, p. 241). Yet brambles are not trees; they stifle trees, and their shape and thorns mean that they cannot offer shade or protection. The bramble does not speak of the common good, but focuses on its own longevity in power, with a demand for faithfulness and a threat to those who default. The threat itself is arrogant, setting the bramble over the most majestic trees of the region, the cedars of Lebanon, and it foreshadows Abimelech's use of fire in battle later in the chapter. The parable seems to equate Abimelech with the bramble king, comments on his supporters' lack of wisdom and highlights the risk of natural justice coming back to hold them accountable for their choices. It is unclear whether the parable is a generic critique of monarchy as a system, or a critique of a particular brand of self-seeking kings. What is missing, however, is any sense that only Yahweh rules and should designate leaders. Unlike Gideon, Jotham does not even try to acknowledge Yahweh's kingship.

Jotham then explains his own parable. His speech is clearly addressed, not to Abimelech, but to the people of Shechem, who have betrayed the house of the man who liberated Israel, and he calls for their actions to be rewarded with just deserts, in a classic action–consequence framework. Jotham conflates lack of faithfulness to Jerubaal's house and the choosing of Abimelech as king. Yet the two things are not co-terminous; Jotham seems to equate faithfulness to Gideon with continued rule for his descendants, a Canaanite rather than Yahwist concept at this point in Israel's history. It is the killing of the brothers, and the conspiracy, that evidences the lack of integrity and faithfulness. Jotham repeats Gideon's mistake in 9.17, in claiming that it is his father who delivered Israel, erasing Yahweh out of the story. Jotham uses his father's military credentials to underlie a claim to inherited privilege, contra Yahweh's specific instructions that the people should not take credit for a victory that belonged to Yahweh. This once again problematizes Gideon's inheritance: he has taught his sons principles that lead them to compete for inherited power, which might bring victory. Gideon's disproportionate use of force in response to disloyalty is also reflected here, as Jotham invokes a curse on all who support Abimelech. 'Justice' is therefore problematized. Gideon was not perfect, but does this justify Abimelech's actions? If Abimelech is also a son of Gideon, why was he not treated in the same way as his brothers? Abimelech's actions are evil, but does this justify the widespread death of his supporters? If everyone gets their just deserts, who will be left? Who decides who deserves what, and how does one distinguish between just deserts and revenge? The rest of the narrative will explore the logic of violence and death, suggesting that the cycle of deserts and revenge is ultimately self-annihilating.

Jotham is perceptive and clever with words. He downgrades Abimelech to 'the son of a slave' (9.18) rather than a concubine, a calculated insult that highlights Abimelech's otherness, and downgrades the status of the men of the city who call him 'brother'. By the same token, he distances himself from Abimelech, asking for faithfulness towards himself as true son and dismissing Abimelech's sonship. As far as Jotham is concerned, Abimelech and the rulers of Shechem are equally guilty, and his curse calls for them to destroy each other. The curse involves a form of natural justice where violence meets violence and bargains between parties with no integrity are doomed from the start. Jotham delivers his sacred curse in defence of his father, not in the name of Yahweh. The status of his speech is ambiguous. On the one hand, it draws on the prophetic tradition of social critique, and the punishment he calls for will come true, suggesting divine approval, though he never claims to speak on behalf of Yahweh. Yet on the other hand, there are deeply problematic elements to his speech, and Jotham himself will not reappear at any point and, most significantly, never be king or ruler, so that the chain of inherited rule and privilege is broken. He simply escapes without changing the situation and goes to live in the wilderness, never to be heard of again. In many ways he delivered his rebuke to Israel much as the prophet did prior to the call of Gideon, and the response is identical – there is none.

9.22–25: God intervenes

A framework element appears unexpectedly in 9.22 with the length of Abimelech's leadership; however, he does not judge Israel but rules (*śārar*), a verb not used yet for leadership, though the noun has described military leaders, usually second-in-command such as Sisera. In Judges the word usually occurs in contexts of violence and war, suggesting a possible translation as warlord (Webb, 2012, p. 280). The narrator does not acknowledge Abimelech as king. It is unclear whether 'Israel' means all Israel or, more likely, uses the local area as symbolic of the entire nation. Abimelech reigns for only three years, the shortest leadership in the book, and the mention of his rule comes not at the end of the story but at the point where oppression of Israel is usually mentioned: Abimelech functions as an oppressor of Israel, and Yahweh himself delivers. Abimelech is not validated as ruler by Yahweh, and the sending of the Spirit on the deliverer is replaced by an 'evil spirit' sent by

God (not called Yahweh, in a reminder that the nation has all but abandoned the covenant). The 'evil spirit' is not defined; its appearance simply reinforces the men's existing disposition, leading them to act as Jotham had predicted, faithlessly and without integrity. It is the character of leaders that produces strife, and God uses this character to bring about judgement. 9.24 underscores the link to justice. God himself brings justice, specifically for the killing of Gideon's sons, not the taking away of inherited rule. The theme of God as avenger of innocent blood emerges early in the canon with Cain and Abel (Gen. 4), is reinforced in the law (Deut. 32.35, 41), stressed by the prophets (Isa. 34.8; 35.4; 61.2; 63.4; Jer. 50.28; 51.56; Nah. 1.2) and picked up in the NT (Rom. 12.19; Heb. 10.30). The use of the Hebrew *ḥămas* for violence in 9.24 implies strong condemnation of Abimelech and the lords of Shechem. The verse also underlines corporate responsibility. Abimelech is not treated as a scapegoat, or representative, and those who have supported and enabled his rule are held jointly responsible. The lords of Shechem now initiate guerrilla warfare to undermine Abimelech's rule, with complete disregard for the welfare of those who are neither lords nor rulers. As in the time of Deborah, the highways are now unsafe: Abimelech's rule leads to oppression, not liberation. The shortness of Abimelech's rule therefore points to Yahweh's mercy in intervening and preventing Israel from self-destructing and widespread harm on ordinary people.

9.26–41: Gaal, son of Ebed

Focus moves away from Abimelech and onto the lords of Shechem, and their repetition of the Abimelech pattern with a new possible ruler. Like the trees of the parable, they go from potential leader to potential leader with no real rationale for their choice. The shift is so quick from one favourite to the next that one wonders whether another will come and Shechem will be trapped in a perpetual cycle of political strife and violence. The new friend in whom the lords of Shechem place their confidence is Gaal, son of Ebed. The meaning of the name is contested; on the one hand, 'Gaal' is linked to the word for loathing (*gāʿal*), and the patronymic to 'slave' (*ʿebed*), which may set up a negative expectation of this 'loathsome son of a slave' (Schneider, 1999, p. 143). Conversely, Block (1999, p. 325) argues that while the first name is linked to that for loathing, it also bears a resemblance to that for redeemer (*gōʾēl*), while the patronymic is more likely to imply 'servant of a certain god'. Gaal uses similar arguments to Abimelech's: clever persuasion, an appeal to self-interest, playing on kinship and genealogy as an overriding criterion, but he argues that his credentials are stronger. Unlike Abimelech, who reigned 'over Israel', Gaal stresses the Canaanite identity of Shechem and its founder Hamor, over and against the outsider from Israel. Unlike Abimelech, who sends relatives to speak on his behalf, Gaal is present in person, surrounded by his kinsfolk, belonging. The men celebrate before anything has been done or achieved. Their celebration is marked by excessive drinking and loose talk, a warning sign in the world of the OT. The narrator's disapproval is strengthened by the place of their celebration – 'the temple of their god'. This is no Yahwist celebration, and the men are cast as Canaanites, or renegade Israelites. Gaal boasts of what he would do if given leadership, and his drunken talk is taken at face value. His final words, 'increase your army', is a call to war, without good reason or consideration of the cost to the wider nation.

The next pericope, 9.30–33, shifts the focus back to Abimelech. He does not reside in the city that has made him king; a deputy, Zebul, rules the city for him, which would have made it easier for Gaal to exploit the social gap between the rulers of Shechem and Abimelech. 9.31 is unclear: Zebul sends messengers '*bətārmâ*', sometimes translated 'in Tormah',[2] but could equally be 'treacherously'. By inciting war, Zebul is acting treacherously towards the lords of the city whose interest he is supposed to look after; equally, his message to Abimelech could be less than honest. So far, there has been nothing but

2 Some translations have 'Arumah' here, but this is a facilitation obtained by harmonizing Abimelech's residence with the place he goes back to in 9.41.

drunken talk, yet his message makes it sound as if the entire city (rather than its drunken leaders) is on the verge of rising up. Is Zebul trying to set Abimelech on the offensive? He counsels an ambush against the city. The strategy is simple and relies on the element of surprise, though assuming that troops will be ready to fight. The attack seems disproportionate, and there is no attempt at fact-finding or reasonable judgement from either Zebul or Abimelech. Once again, it is not justice but revenge and self-interest that motivates the characters. The end of Zebul's instructions, 'do to him as your hand finds' feeds into Judges' increasing focus on characters making decisions, particularly moral decisions, based on their own evaluation and desires rather than by reference to the covenant or the God of the covenant.

Zebul and Abimelech put their plan into motion. Through carefully crafted taunts, Zebul incites Gaal, together with his supporters, to go out and fight Abimelech. The fighters on both sides are called 'the people' (*ʿām*), with no distinction between opposing forces. They are all equally Israelite, equally Canaanite, and equally misused by their leaders. Zebul throws Gaal's boasts back in his face, in an illusion of poetic justice, but the two men are equally corrupt and self-interested. For all we know, Gaal had never intended to fight and did not seem to expect an attack, yet he does go out leading his supporters and fights Abimelech. Israelites kill many Israelites again, and with each story in Judges the death toll on Israel increases. The narrator amplifies pathos with the image of wounded soldiers forming a path all the way to the entrance of the city, the threshold of safety. Victory is attributed to Zebul, and Abimelech once again leaves the city, having apparently achieved what he had set out to do, though Gaal has finally escaped him. The episode has achieved little, other than inflame the anger and bloodlust of the bramble king.

9.42–49: *Massacre in Shechem*

No explanation is given for Abimelech's actions from then on; he appears animated by a killing frenzy that makes no attempt to justify its actions. He repeats the tactics of the day before with an ambush outside the city. This time, no enemy comes out to fight. Instead, ordinary people go to work in the fields. They, again, are simply 'the people' but a different group from either Abimelech's troops or Gaal's supporters. These are not the 'lords of the city', Abimelech's adversaries, but simpler, less wealthy or powerful folk working the land. The narrator amplifies the dissonance of the scene through the juxtaposition of military vocabulary ('three companies', 'lying in wait') and a thoroughly domestic, pastoral scene. The attack seems incongruous and unjustified. The people are slaughtered and the way to safety blocked, before the city itself is taken and everyone killed – presumably, men, women and children. Furthermore, Abimelech makes the place uninhabitable by sowing it with salt so nothing can grow there again. Sowing with salt was a common feature in Assyrian war annals (Wright, 2015, p. 153), a ritual act signifying curse and permanent desolation (Webb, 2012, p. 90). The nihilism of Abimelech's actions is striking. The city he had fought to gain for himself as king he now lays waste and ravages. He has no emotional connection with its inhabitants, no care for their welfare. Having destroyed the line of his father, he destroys the line of his mother in the people of Shechem, making the centre of his kingdom a wilderness. The bramble king has lived up to his name; brambles stifle good crops and devastate the land if unchecked. Meanwhile, the lords of Shechem do not come out to defend ordinary people as they had for Gaal. Instead, they go to safety. Like Abimelech, they show no solidarity or proactive care for the people they rule. Shechem exemplifies the worst of leadership and unequal social structures. It is the lords of Shechem whose choice brought Abimelech to the city, yet they fail to take responsibility and protect the city from the consequences of their own choices. They flee to the temple of El-Berith, whose treasury had funded Abimelech's initial campaign and whose god does not have the power to save. True to Jotham's curse, fire comes out of the bramble king and consumes them. There is a certain poetic justice to their finding death where it all started. And yet, unease remains with the tally of total deaths – presumably for all who died in Shechem, men, women and children, rather than just in the temple.

9.50–57: Thebez

Abimelech's frenzied rampage continues and he attacks another city, not mentioned so far, with no apparent motive. He is out of control, perhaps not entirely sane, but nobody tries to stop him and his troops follow. What level of responsibility should they bear for the leader they still choose to follow? Abimelech and his men are swept into a spiral of violence and power, as victory spurs them to attack others. Abimelech's confidence grows from his initial victories, and he reckons without the intervention of Yahweh in human history. His godlessness comes back to haunt him as, ultimately, God shows that only he grants or withholds victory. Thebez stands in sharp contrast to Shechem. It does not have a temple, but a tower. Its leaders do not desert ordinary people; they seek safety together, a fact emphasized by the narrator: 'all the men and women and all the lords of the city' (9.50). Abimelech is blind to the difference, assuming that what worked in Shechem will work here. The bramble king is ready to unleash fire again, but he is stopped. Not by the lords of Shechem who stood against him, but by 'one woman'. The man who had killed his 70 brothers on 'one' stone is killed by 'one' woman; the man who had argued it was better for 'one' to reign, rather than 70, shows the fragility of his argument, as 'one' woman, without a force of worthless men, kills him. The man who killed his brothers on a stone is killed by a stone dropped on his head. The narration is beautifully ironic as Abimelech's sins turn against him. It is somewhat fitting, too, that it is a woman, a non-combatant, with a domestic object (likely a hand-held millstone), who kills a man with so little regard for ordinary people. The woman is unnamed, unlike Jael, possibly indicating a drop in the position of women in Israel, though she may also stand as a symbol of 'the people', nameless and invisible to Abimelech, who nevertheless mattered. Being killed by a woman, whom he would have considered inferior in every way, is something Abimelech, a hypermasculine warrior in a patriarchal culture, fears beyond anything. Hence he commands his armour bearer, a young man, another *na'ar*, to kill him, the king, just as Gideon's son was told to kill the Midianite kings. Whereas Jether had refused to kill an enemy king, this young man does not hesitate to kill his own. Despite Abimelech's last wish, his death will be remembered exactly as he wanted to avoid; the story illustrates the inability of men who think themselves powerful and invincible to control either their death or the memory they leave behind. Abimelech did not foster the kind of loyalty and goodwill that would have been remembered positively, neither did he help Israel enough that he could at least be remembered as a mixed blessing, as his father was. His legacy lies in the ruins of Shechem. Even the loyalty of his troops evaporates: as soon as he dies, they give up. Their desertion shows they had no loyalty to a cause, but only followed a man. 9.56–57 forms a theological conclusion to the episode, setting God firmly in control over human history. Abimelech's schemes were thwarted by the real king of Israel, whose name still is not used. The dominant principle here is a sense of natural justice, people reaping what they have sown. Justice is rendered via double causality: God uses Abimelech and Shechem's own faults to bring about their downfall. There is a sense of common responsibility still running through these verses. The people had got the king they deserved, and the king had got the people he deserved. The final sentence enhances the fact that God works for victims, and his justice fulfilled the curse of Jotham. God has mercifully cut short the destructive reign of Abimelech, but the land does not, and will not again, have rest, as danger comes as much from within as without.

Reflections

Abimelech's tale weaves together numerous theological themes that have occupied Judges so far. The line between Israelites and Canaanites is so blurred that it collapses altogether into an amorphous 'people'. The construction of gender identity is raised again, as it was in the story of Barak, Deborah and Jael. Questions about justice, revenge and proportionality abound, as do questions about leadership and character.

It would be easy to leave notions of gender and masculinity out of theology, to treat them merely as anthropological or sociological. Yet if the Bible is a sacred text and gender is configured in specific ways, then, whether implicitly or explicitly, gender is theologized and this theologizing needs to be reflected upon. The story of Abimelech is a story of hypermasculinity, or hegemonic masculinity, and Abimelech's struggle to assert a legitimate identity (in his eyes). Hegemonic masculinity creates a template for what it means to be a man and denigrates or delegitimizes any alternatives (Carman, 2019, p. 305). Abimelech's understanding of masculinity is in sharp focus in the death scene (9.54), where he is more concerned with preserving his image as a 'real man' than about preserving his life. Abimelech oscillates between performing well against his own criteria, and failing. Battle, war and the ability to beat down opponents all feed into hypermasculine ideals in the Hebrew Bible (Carman, 2019, p. 306); Abimelech wages war and often wins; he kills most of his rivals (his brothers), yet one escapes; again in Shechem, Gaal escapes, possibly explaining Abimelech's fury then misdirected at all the people of Shechem. Abimelech is successful on the battlefield, yet, theologically, military prowess is not the ultimate measure of a man, as Gideon's story showed. Self-control and restraint are marks of successful men, rather than unbridled violence on the battlefield. The second half of the chapter chronicles Abimelech's complete loss of self-control, so that he moves from battle to massacre. He is no longer a warrior but a killer, and the stories do not enhance his masculinity but rather undermine his value as leader. Abimelech fails to have children, another mark of the 'ideal man', and cuts off the possibility of kinship through both paternal and maternal lines. He has nothing to hand on to another generation and no one to keep his memory alive in the way Jotham keeps his father's. Abimelech may be powerful and express this through both words and actions, but his words in the narrative all lead to deeply violent acts, unlike Gideon, whose legacy was mixed in this regard, having used speech wisely to appease the Ephraimites yet turned to violence against Succoth and Penuel. Abimelech consistently misdirects his power, showing his complete lack of discernment and wisdom. Abimelech's instantiation of masculinity is destructive at every point, failing to give him what he is seeking throughout, the honour that belonged to his father. As a younger son from a secondary wife, he could not start life in the best possible place to embody hegemonic masculinity; he could have sought to build his status through developing skills, wisdom and a household of his own, but instead seized on the one aspect of masculinity most embodied by his father, valour in battle, and hyperextended it into a caricature of hegemonic masculinity.

Abimelech struggles to find his place within the kinship system, distorting it in trying to rectify the wrong the system inflicted upon him. Abimelech's ambivalent relationship to family is seen through his desperate desire to inherit his father's status and live up to his name, and his turning away to his mother's kin and attempting to erase his father's line through killing his brothers. Ultimately, Abimelech's appeal to kin is shallow and he annihilates most of his kinship group. He symbolizes the fragility of a political system that rests on kinship and tribal alliances rather than a shared vision for life together. The kinship system was a bedrock of stability and survival in ancient agrarian societies; the move from a household-based system to one that favours wider leadership and association is here shown as complex and full of pitfalls. At its best, Israel is an interconnected system of tribes and households, whose cohesion is strengthened by the kinship system yet does not rely solely upon it. Cohesion is meant to rest on a common covenantal vision, to which kinship is tributary. As covenantal participation wanes, kin and tribe grow in importance and local rifts and competition become increasingly deadly, culminating in civil war in Judges 21.

The wider political system is under scrutiny in the Abimelech narrative. The parable questions kingship. It is not implied that it was wrong for the trees to want a king, yet their desire seems pointless and possibly misdirected. The parable issues strong cautions about kingship, in line with the concerns about Canaanite-style kingship developing at the end of the Gideon narrative. The fable shows the best people as already busy involved in service and refusing to step into leadership roles; the story overall suggests that leaders often aspire to power for the wrong reasons and end up seizing it through the wrong means; both fable and story place heavy responsibility on the people who choose leaders unwisely, without consultation with God. Most of these cautions could be levelled against any kind of leadership, rather than being specific to kingship. Placing the actions of Gideon against the prescriptions of Deuteronomy was a much clearer critique of kingship itself, though restricted to certain ways of inhabiting the role. It was these abuses, characterized as Canaanite, that were the focus of critique. Chapter 9 is more interested in wider questions of leadership: who chooses leaders, according to what criteria? Neither blood nor might are depicted as legitimate ways towards leadership; the only legitimate way is the one that is consistently ignored: divine selection. Jotham and Abimelech are equally wrong in seeing their father's military record as legitimizing leadership, and their father's blood as legitimizing inherited leadership. On a wider level, the people of Israel are responsible for choosing the wrong leader. The notion of corporate responsibility stands out as significantly different from Ancient Near Eastern traditions surrounding kingship; within the covenant, all Israel is responsible directly under Yahweh as king, and responsible for upholding the law (Lynch, 2020, p. 175). The entire people are covenant partners, so that there is no hiding behind a leader and their actions. The text works with great nuance in its depiction of 'the people' and how those who choose leaders are the privileged few, guided mostly by self-interest that will lead them to disregard most of the people their new king is supposed to reign over. Where self-interest is the primary motivation of both king and supporters, loyalties have no solidity as they shift according to the parties' perception of what will advance their own interests (Assis, 2005, p. 173). Rulers are shown as self-interested and ruthless, and it is ordinary people who suffer the most under their rule. As Judges progresses, every Israelite will become implicated in the dynamic of self-interest, with 'every man doing what's right in his own eyes', with anarchy and systematic victimization of the most vulnerable. In a context where leaders have forgotten their responsibilities, care for the nation is left only to Yahweh's mercy.

As a sequel to the Gideon material, the story of Abimelech proclaims that, in the end, Baal contended – and lost. His people, the baals of Shechem, and their temple are destroyed, and Abimelech, who acted on their side, disappears. Gideon, who had sponsored pagan worship, loses his inheritance via his sons and their conflict. Loyalty to Baal and acceptance of Canaanite norms of social organization has cost Israel dearly; from here on, the nation will descend into deeper internecine troubles, as loyalty to the covenant, once renewed in Shechem, recedes even further.

5

Jephthah and the Minor Judges (10–12)

10: Call to repentance

After Abimelech's story at the centre of the book, the narrative returns to framework elements that set the scene for the second half of Judges. Chapter 10 enables the transition away from the defunct line of Gideon to a succession of minor judges, before introducing the third divine message in the book inviting Israel to repentance.

10.1–5: Tola and Jair

Bracketing the Jephthah episode in 10—12 come a series of short accounts of different Judges: Tola and Jair in 10.1–5, Ibzan, Elon and Abdon in 12.8–15. They are often called minor judges due to the brevity of the accounts, which mention their judging but no delivering. Noth claimed that the minor judges had a different role, administrative or judicial rather than military deliverance, but there is little narrative evidence for the claim, which relies on source criticism (Mullen, 1993, p. 187). Judges 3 had a very short account of another judge, Shamgar, who delivered but did not 'judge'. In contrast, many of the longer accounts still share the phraseology 'X judged Israel' (Othniel, 3.10; Jephthah, 10.7; Samson, 15.20 and 16.31), while Deborah and Barak split judging and delivering. Finally, Tola, the first of the minor judges, is said to have risen 'to deliver Israel'. The only consistent distinctions between major and minor judges are length and literary style. They are not characterized as fully and no exploits are recounted. It is the overall structure of the book that places each individual leader in the category of 'judge', though role and relevance differ according to context. Leadership is the question that runs through all the different accounts, including those of the minor judges. In a book chronicling the life of a nation, it is unremarkable for narrative time to slow when recounting major events and speed up in periods of relative calm.

Tola is the only judge from Issachar and lived in 'the hill country of Ephraim', providing a geographical link back to Gideon's story. There are no details of what or who Israel needed delivering from, of whether deliverance was achieved through armed conflict or negotiation, or of Israel's religious and ethical state. He 'rose to deliver', an active verb of which he is the subject, rather than Yahweh raising him up. It may be a simple stylistic variant, but may also point back to Abimelech's rise to power and the parable of the trees: people choosing leaders without consulting Yahweh. The framework elements (he rose, he judged, he died, he was buried), here and in other minor judges, link these narratives stylistically and thematically to the rest of Judges. Next, Jair, a Gileadite, provides a geographical link back to Gideon and Manasseh and forward to Jephthah. Tola and Jair break the dynastic chain, in line with the negative evaluation of hereditary leadership in 8—9. Jair followed in Gideon's footsteps, however, in building up a harem, amassing wealth (Deut. 17.16 specifically forbids kings to accrue many horses; here there are donkeys, somewhat less grand but in the same category) and seemingly extending kin-based leadership and capital via his 30 sons and their 30 towns. There is no mention of Yahweh here either and no comment on their religious allegiance. The land is not said to have rest – while there is no mention of strife, there is also no sense of political stability as the death of Jair ushers in a vacuum of power, with no leader and no apparent system for identifying one.

10.6–9: A reprise of the cycle

10.6 returns to the language of the framework, as Israel continued 'doing evil in the eyes of Yahweh'. Evil is clearly defined as worshipping other gods, now listed. Yahweh is not even one among the gods, but left aside and abandoned, specifically not worshipped. The gods mentioned are all linked to nations that have oppressed Israel in the past (Aram and Moab) and will do so in the future (Philistines and Amorites), which enhances the treachery of turning to them as opposed to Yahweh who had delivered them. Symbolically, Israel is choosing death over life, and gods associated with deeply oppressive social practices and configurations of power. Israel has entered a religious marketplace, where religion is a consumer choice in a rather modern way, according to what is right in their own eyes, without deferring to what is right in the eyes of Yahweh as true judge. Perversely, complete abandonment of Yahweh may suggest that Israel has finally understood something of Yahweh's utter otherness and demand for complete loyalty. Ironically, the Israelites are 'sold into the hand of the Philistines and the Ammonites', whose gods they had worshipped. The connection between the people and Yahweh is broken, so he lets them go to another – instead of belonging to Yahweh they are sold to other nations and their gods. The link between gods and oppressors underscores that it is not possible to separate worship of a god and the cultural and social systems that are associated with them. Religion is not privatized, but deeply shapes the communal lives and values of nations. The introduction of Ammonites and Philistines paves the way for the two stories to come, first Jephthah, then Samson. Details of tribes most affected see Judah and Benjamin mentioned for the first time since Othniel, though it is 'all Israel' that is 'greatly distressed' at the level of oppression they once again endure.

10.10–16: Israel and Yahweh

Yahweh, called by his covenant name, now re-enters the narrative as agent. In 2.1–5 he had sent an angel/messenger, in 6.7–10 a prophet, and now he comes in person to call his people back to him. As before, the Israelites cry out because of the pain of oppression and Yahweh answers first by inviting them to deal with the root cause of their distress. Given that the people had been said not to worship Yahweh, why do they cry out to him? Is Yahweh a last resort? Do they remember the past, or are they trying every option available? Their cry to Yahweh is, for the first time, accompanied by an acknowledgement of sin. It is unclear why, and whether their confession is heartfelt or what they know they 'should' say. 10.11–13 is terse and clipped, reminding the people of Yahweh's faithfulness in history and noting the ironic link between their specific oppressors and the list of gods in 10.6 – seven oppressors for seven deities. Yahweh repeats the narrator's statement that the Israelites have abandoned him. The language is emotional and feeds into the picture of divine pathos in the covenantal relationship. Yahweh concurs with the facts of Israel's confession, but his response is unexpected. He will not deliver again. Israel broke the covenant, despite Yahweh's repeated attempts to draw them back. Yahweh had already acted on their behalf, again and again, to deliver them from the very same oppressors that they have now joined in worship. Yahweh's answer now is to let them experience the consequence of their breaking of the covenant. The refusal takes readers by surprise; a confession was what they were waiting for. Yahweh's response prompts them to question whether the confession was genuine or just utilitarian, another attempt to manipulate Yahweh to be on their side in the manner of a tribal god. The manipulation of God will loom large in the narrative of Jephthah. The divine response betrays both impatience and anger, as well as inviting the Israelites to see the lack of logic in their position: if other gods are better, why not cry to them?

Israel's response is both resigned and deeply covenantal: it recognizes that Yahweh can do as he wishes, but that the covenantal relationship provides the context for their asking for help. They offer nothing in return, seeming to have realized that they are coming empty-handed and only grace can bring deliverance. Their words are, 'do to us what is good in your eyes', a clear contrast to their earlier 'doing evil in the eyes of Yahweh'. Now they submit themselves to what is good in Yahweh's eyes, though they seem to have no idea of what this may look like. The expression draws us into the deep faultline of the framework. What is 'good' at this point, what would be just or fair, would be for Israel to bear the consequences of their actions; but what has been shown as good in the eyes of Yahweh, time and again, is a move away from the action-consequence framework, and towards an economy of grace and mercy. Israel then changes its way, without an assurance of divine deliverance to come. The second part of 10.16 is contested. The verse is usually translated as, 'he could no longer bear to see Israel suffer', or, literally, 'his soul was shortened by Israel's troubles', in line with divine pathos in response to suffering enabling the transition from justice into grace. The verb (*qṣr*) indicates extreme impatience – Yahweh could no longer tolerate. Yet the word used elsewhere, distress (*ṣārâ*), is replaced by *'āmāl*, which could mean either pain/trouble or hard work/efforts. Hence some commentators (Beldman, 2020, p. 140; Block, 1999, p. 349; Polzin, 1980, p. 177) argue that the translation should convey Yahweh's impatience with Israel's feeble or misguided efforts. Whether Yahweh is tired of their attempts at manipulation and half-hearted repentance, or of the pain that their waywardness is causing, or both, it is divine pathos that enables the passage into an economy of grace, though the raising of a deliverer is delayed.

10.17–18: Looking for a leader

The culmination of chapter 10 sets the scene for the arrival of Jephthah. Ammonite and Israelite forces face each other, though the Israelite army seems to have no overall leader, despite having 'commanders' (*śar*, the term used for Sisera, Midianites Oreb and Zeeb, and Zebul). The passage echoes

Judges 1.1, when the people ask Yahweh who should go first, but here the commanders (rather than the Israelites as a whole) are asking one another, rather than Yahweh, and offer a reward to whoever is brave enough to lead. Despite their confession, Israel has not gone back to full covenantal living and are keeping up the way of selecting leaders that had given them Abimelech. The people are preparing for battle with neither human nor divine leader.

11.1–12.7: The rise and fall of Jephthah

11.1–3: Meeting Jephthah

11.1 opens with a contradiction. It introduces Jephthah as 'a mighty warrior and the son of a loose woman'. Jephthah's name simply means 'he opened', which could reflect gratitude towards a god who, in biblical imagery, opened the womb of his mother, though we do not know which god. However, as the story progresses, Jephthah keeps opening his mouth with increasingly catastrophic results. Beyond his name, the first qualifier, 'mighty warrior', seems a potential answer to the commanders' question and echoes the angel's address to Gideon. Jephthah's military credentials, however, do not stand alone but are placed in parallel with his questionable parentage. Where a father's name would normally be we find a statement of illegitimacy. The description of his mother, *'iššāh zōnah*, is often taken to refer to a professional prostitute. The root *znh* could refer to a range of inappropriate sexual behaviours, usually by women (Hamley, 2015, p. 41–43). *zōnah* on its own usually refers to sex workers, though its meaning is sometimes extended (as in the English 'whore') to speak pejoratively of women who do not fulfil traditional expectations of female behaviour. The composite noun form *'iššāh zōnah* includes a wider semantic range that includes women living outside the patriarchal household (García Bachmann, 2013, p. 26). Jephthah's two main characteristics, military man and illegitimate child, create dissonance from the start and sets the scene for a leader constantly caught between his skills and confidence as a military man and the deep lack of confidence and desperate need to belong of a rejected child. The next part of the verse further problematizes Jephthah's descent. Is Gilead, his father, an actual individual, or does it represent the city as a whole (Fewell and Gunn, 1993, p. 126)? 11.2 makes it more likely that Gilead is a man who had extra-marital relations, though his name being Gilead symbolizes the self-righteous attitude of an entire town, who accommodate the life of a prostitute/loose woman but will not care for her child. Jephthah's father is absent in all but name and leaves his child rejected and ostracized. Gideon's father, despite his syncretism, had defended his child; Gideon himself was closer to Gilead, with multiple partners and one child considered of lower status. Fathers consistently have a profound impact on the next generation. Jephthah himself will kill his own daughter, and in the final episodes of Judges Micah's father is completely absent, while the young woman's father in chapter 19 indirectly contributes to the events that lead to her gruesome death. Judges' downward trajectory increasingly affects all aspects of social and individual life. Jephthah's status is even lower than Abimelech's, and his brothers are openly hostile rather than distant. Once again, the choice of a head of household to have multiple sexual partners leads to strife between brothers and a brother being driven away (see Ishmael, son of Hagar, Gen. 21.14–21; Joseph, son of Jacob, Gen. 37). Unlike Gideon's *pîlegeš* in Shechem, Jephthah's mother has no legitimate status with regard to Gilead. Yet the brothers drive him away so that he does not inherit, which suggests that Gilead must have recognized paternity. They do not say that his mother is a prostitute but that she is 'another woman', implying she may be Canaanite, of non-Israelite ethnicity (Kamrada, 2010, p. 19). The dispute is violent enough that Jephthah runs away. Readers are invited to hold two different pictures of Jephthah in their mind: the outlaw and man of war, leading worthless men, and a bullied child driven away from home. The mighty warrior does not fight but flees and leads a questionable life. He surrounds himself with 'worthless/empty men', the same word as for Abimelech's men. The parallel suggests that the stories may run the same course. Yet Abimelech had chosen such men, whereas here they simply gather around Jephthah. The description of their activities is rather vague in Hebrew: 'they went out with him'. Translations often render the phrase as 'they went raiding', but this is not clear. The verb is often used for an army going out to war, but as the object of their warrior skills is not mentioned it can only be inferred. They may have raided or have hired themselves out as mercenaries. In any case, they are men on the margins, worthless men ironically gathered in the land of Tov, meaning, 'good'.

11.4–11: Choosing a leader

Meanwhile, the people don't have a leader, partly because they themselves drove away the one person who could help. The insertion of Jephthah's back story shows that life story and character form a crucial part of leadership, and again emphasizes collective responsibility. Here the community will not just be responsible for choosing Jephthah, they are also directly responsible for the kind of man he has been shaped into. It was Jephthah's brothers who ran him out over inheritance rights, yet the community stood by doing nothing, though they are aware of his current whereabouts. He is a 'mighty warrior', and the elders now go to find him. They go in person rather than send messengers. Jephthah, being illegitimate and rejected, had low status and low honour. By going themselves, the elders signal willingness to ascribe honour back to him, that he could be reintegrated into the community. Honour and belonging are key to successful bargaining here. However, asking Jephthah suggests that no one had volunteered and they are scraping the bottom of the barrel. Jephthah clearly knows this. The elders do not pray or consult with Yahweh before asking Jephthah. They make their request with no preamble or apology, maybe thinking Jephthah is bound to accept because he will be desperate to be welcomed back. They show themselves as mercilessly exploiting a man whom their community has abused. They do not offer him what they had offered one another. In 10.18, they had said that whoever led in battle would become head (*rōʾš*) over them, i.e. leader of the city in peace as well as war. Yet here they offer Jephthah commander status (*qāṣîn*), that is, to lead the troops in war but with no long-term benefit. They clearly think he is desperate, and possibly expendable. Considering Jotham's parable, the offer raises fears of another bramble king. No one else wanted to lead, and the people turn to someone who leads worthless men. Jephthah responds combatively (11.7); his reply is as terse and cutting as the elders' offer. Even though his brothers rejected him, he widens responsibility to the elders, who had the power to intervene yet chose to stand by: you 'rejected me'. The verb translated as 'reject' in the NRSV is actually 'hate' in Hebrew (*śānēʾ*), a more forceful expression of feelings. Jephthah brings out the contradiction in their offer: either they were wrong then, or they are wrong now. The prospect of liberating Israel does not figure in the exchange. It is Jephthah's personal needs that shape his decisions. His pointed reference to 'my father's house' reminds them of his birthright, implying that he is looking for his due, not a favour. The elders are the ones who are desperate, so they increase their offer and hold out the same proposal as they had to their own people. Symbolically, the proposal restores Jephthah as full citizen. Nevertheless, the elders never apologize or admit wrongdoing and simply increase the incentive for Jephthah to agree. The bargaining is not about doing what is right, on either side; it is a political and personal power struggle. Leadership had previously been used to achieve deliverance, but now deliverance becomes a way to assert leadership (Beldman, 2020, p. 145). DeMaris and Leeb (2005, p. 183) argue that honour comes in two varieties, ascribed (through birth and place within the kinship system) and acquired (through deeds). Jephthah had little ascribed honour, and what he had, through his father, has been taken away from him. His dispute with the elders is about regaining some of his ascribed honour. At the same time, Jephthah ties their offer to victory in 11.9. He will accept the offer, conditional on his success on the battlefield, which now binds together ascribed and acquired honour. He repeats the terms of the bargain, making it his own, and brings in Yahweh. The mention of Yahweh as one who gives victory further strengthens his position: if he is victorious, it is not simply because of his skill but because his leadership is endorsed by Yahweh. It is unclear whether mention of Yahweh displays Jephthah's piety and understanding of war in the Promised Land, or whether it is an additional bargaining tool. Not to be outdone, the elders now invoke Yahweh as guarantor of the deal they have struck. Again, it is unclear whether this a convention to seal a formal agreement, or a genuine – though belated – appeal for Yahweh's participation. Either way, both sides expect Yahweh to bless their existing choices rather than consult, listen or work in partnership. 11.11 moves to a public ceremony to establish Jephthah's leadership – before any battle has taken place. The timing of his being made head over Gilead matters little: as leader of the army, defeat in battle would most likely lead to his death. The people had gathered at Mizpah, which is not said to be a worship centre. It may be where the troops have assembled and the ceremony aims to ensure loyalty to their new commander. Jephthah 'spoke all his words before Yahweh', but we do not know what his words were, or what they meant. Once again, Yahweh is used as guarantor of human plans rather than active partner. Parallels between chapters 10 and the beginning of 11 are as significant (Beldman, 2020, p. 143; Block, 1999, p. 354; Webb, 2012, pp. 313–14): where Israel rejects Yahweh, the Gileadites reject Jephthah; where Israel is oppressed by the Ammonites, Gilead is oppressed by the Ammonites; the Israelites appeal to Yahweh whom they had rejected, the Gileadites appeal to Jephthah whom they had rejected; the Israelites turn away from other gods and repeat their appeal, the Gileadites turn to Jephthah and appeal to him; Yahweh refuses to help, Jephthah refuses to help; Yahweh stays silent, Jephthah agrees to help. The parallel suggests that Jephthah now occupies the place that properly belongs to Yahweh and that the people are putting their faith in him rather than Yahweh, in a repeat of the values of the Gideon story.

11.12–28: Negotiating with the Ammonites

This next section chronicles Jephthah's negotiations with the Ammonite king. For the first time, a leader seeks to negotiate rather than go straight into war. Jephthah's negotiating technique mirrors his bargaining with the elders: he uses questions to draw his opponents into his own perspective, challenges opponents on truth and principle, highlights instances of rejection (11.20) and differential treatment, making it personal (11.27). Jephthah the outsider knows the history of Israel far better than anyone so far in Judges and shows himself a skilled speaker and negotiator. He starts by sending out messengers, following standard diplomatic procedures, approaching the king as an equal and speaking as if the land belonged to him. His speech follows the Ancient Near Eastern lawsuit tradition (Butler, 2009, p. 284), looking at facts and history to establish that the Ammonites are the aggressors, hence in the wrong (11.12). Jephthah initially shies away from framing his argument in covenantal terms. The king is skilled in negotiation too and responds in kind, asserting his own right to the land. Both leaders behave as often seen in war, each asserting that their war is just and trying to cow the enemy into backing down. Ethnic groupings are not entirely clear throughout the exchange and confuse or conflate Ammonites, Amorites and Moabites. In 11.13, the *Ammonite* king claims that Israel took away his land, when the biblical tradition says that this land was taken following the defeat of the *Amorite* king Sihon (Block, 1999, p. 359). A battle of public narratives ensues, as each nation defends its own construction of history and derived geographical integrity. Jephthah goes back into Israel's history, yet he eschews the traditional formula 'when the Lord brought us out of Egypt' in favour of 'when they [Israel] came up from Egypt' (11.16). Yahweh's actions on behalf of Israel are erased while the people take credit. Jephthah has effectively dissociated the political and spiritual history of Israel, against the grain of covenantal faith. Jephthah draws on the stories behind Numbers 20—21 and Deuteronomy 2; in his survey of the state of the land when Israel first arrived, he does not even mention Ammon, invalidating their claim to historical ownership. His retelling of the story of Israel in 11.19–21 reminds listeners of the configuration of power when Israel supposedly entered the land: they tried to respect surrounding nations but were rebuffed; other nations are depicted as callous towards a desperate group of refugees, not only failing to grant them safe passage but attacking them. Finally, in 11.21, there is an acknowledgement of Yahweh: the small people in their battle against a much stronger enemy could only win thanks to supernatural help.

Having made a historical argument, Jephthah now makes a theological argument in 11.23–24. Victory in battle was generally attributed to the favour of tribal gods in the Ancient Near East, hence Jephthah rests on a culture understood and shared with his interlocutors, rather than covenantal concepts specific to Israel. Jephthah's logic is clear: the land never belonged to the Ammonites but to other tribes; these, through their own actions, lost the land in a battle they had initiated; since victory is granted by divine fiat, the land belongs to Israel at a cosmic level. The land does not belong to the king by right of historical possession, nor by battle, nor by the favour of the gods. Jephthah sets up an opposition between the nation's two gods as equal tribal gods favouring the interests of specific peoples and locations, rather than taking the covenantal approach of arguing that Yahweh gave all nations their territories. Some critics see the argument as polytheistic (e.g. Webb, 2012, p. 322); however, Jephthah may simply be using concepts familiar to his opponent in order to make a good argument, and echoing Yahweh's sarcastic comment in 10.14 – 'Go cry to the gods you have chosen!' Jephthah's mention of Chemosh is odd, since Chemosh is the god of Moab not Ammon (that would be Molech). If other texts such as 2 Kings 3.27 are right in their assertion that Chemosh (and the Ammonite god Molech) demanded human sacrifice, then the mention of this god is a dark allusion to what is to come. Jephthah's apparent mistake could be a simple one; it could also be part of his argument that the land never belonged to Ammon or their god, and that even if the land had belonged to Moab, their god Chemosh relinquished it long ago (Chisholm, 2013, p. 350); Chemosh would be the correct territorial god (Webb, 2012, p. 322).

Jephthah now moves to a personal attack on the king, comparing him negatively to a Moabite king and questioning his reasoning: why not invade earlier, if the land is yours? Jephthah concludes his argument in highly personal language in 11.27, asserting the justice of his position against a king who has 'done evil' to him. The underlying values of the exchange illuminate cultural understandings of war: Jephthah is keen to assert that his cause is just; matters of aggression are central to questions of justice; history shapes the present and is fundamental in deciding disputes; victory in war is a theological matter and entitles the victors to land (Niditch, 2008, p. 132). Jephthah shows his own vulnerability in the emotional language of 11.27, of sinning against and being wronged, as if everything revolved around him – a tendency that will reappear in his exchange with his daughter. He then invokes Yahweh as judge. Just as with Gideon, who recognized (if he did not practise) that it was Yahweh who was the true king, here Jephthah nods to the understanding that it is Yahweh who is the true judge. Yahweh, however, is not consulted but merely used as arbiter of a human dispute. One wonders whether Yahweh was indirectly the real audience of Jephthah's speech. The king, however, disregards the message, either because he has no good answer or because negotiation was never his aim. The exchange may have simply been two opponents sizing each other up and testing the other's resolve to go to war. Jephthah has demonstrated that he is more than a military leader and has the stature of a statesman, worthy to be 'head' of Gilead. Whether his actions were right, however, is unclear. What would have happened if negotiations had led to an agreement for peace? Would he have made a covenant with the Ammonites, in contradiction to Yahweh's orders (Ex. 23.32; 34.15)? Would he still have won the leadership of Gilead, without battle?

11.29–33: Internal and external battles

Jephthah's finals words to the king invoked Yahweh as judge of their dispute. In 11.29, Yahweh renders judgement by sending his Spirit on Jephthah. It is the first time in the narrative that Yahweh is active in Jephthah's life and in the Gileadite search for leadership. Yahweh has not chosen the leader of Israel, but he blesses their choice, however poor, and empowers Jephthah with his Spirit, which will give him the resources to lead the army. It is unclear whether Jephthah is aware of the coming of the Spirit; he does not consult with Yahweh, and Yahweh does not act as commander-in-chief. Jephthah receives no verbal divine message or commission. Discerning the presence of Yahweh does not necessarily come instinctively in the world of faith. There is no indication that Jephthah has been formed in the type of practices that would enable him to recognize the work of Yahweh; the beginning of the book of Samuel will later reflect that 'the word of the Lord was rare in those days; visions were not widespread' (1 Sam. 3.1). The setting is in continuity with that of Judges; the story of the call of Samuel suggests that neither Eli nor Samuel were well prepared to hear, listen and recognize the voice of Yahweh, even though they were dedicated to his service. Positive faith formation goes back to the Deuteronomic vision of raising children in the ways of the Lord (Deut. 4.5–9; 6.1–24), steeped in stories of the covenant, diligent in engaging with the Torah and, above all, loving the Lord. Jephthah knows the history, but there is little evidence that he understands its theological significance, has knowledge of the Torah, or sees Yahweh as covenant partner. Whether Jephthah knows of the Spirit's empowerment or not, the event is presented as directly prompting the move towards battle.

A battle account would normally ensue, but the narrative flow is broken as Jephthah interrupts the leading of the Spirit to make an unsolicited vow. No reason is offered for it. Yahweh has already sent his Spirit, hence given approval, yet Jephthah is uncertain and bargains for more security. If Jephthah was not aware of the Spirit, he may be seeking to manipulate Yahweh and control the outcome of the battle; if aware of the

Spirit, he may be trying to gain a dominant position within the relationship, or ask for additional assurances, as Gideon had. Jephthah's view of Yahweh seems based on a mechanical relationship that can be sealed through bargaining and gifts; his picture of God is closer to that of Canaanite gods and, in the nature of what he offers, closer to Chemosh (god of Moab), said to demand human sacrifice.[1] Jephthah's doubts about Yahweh's approval are clear in his use of the conditional, 'if you will give the Ammonites into my hand ...' He then promises that 'whoever comes out of the doors of my house to meet me, when I return victorious from the Ammonites, shall be the Lord's, to be offered up by me as a burnt offering' (11.31). Some have argued that Jephthah had an animal, rather than a person, in mind. This is grammatically possible, given that Hebrew does not have a neuter case, but unlikely. If Jephthah had never intended to sacrifice a person, why not stick with an animal? The construction 'to meet' is usually applied to a person in the Old Testament. In addition, the picture of coming home victorious naturally evokes women and loved ones running out to celebrate returning warriors (Ex. 15.20; Judg. 4.18; 1 Sam. 18.6–7). Given Jephthah had only one child, a girl, it was likely she would be leading the welcoming party, surrounded by other young women. As Jephthah seemed to know what he was offering, his vow can hardly be rash or unguarded, even though his later reaction suggests he had not expected his daughter to come out first. He might, however, have expected other women, considered expendable, to do so. The vow is unusual, as there is no obvious link between what is requested and what is vowed (Block, 1999, p. 368); other vows in Scripture usually link the two (such as dedicating booty for capturing a town). However, if Jephthah is in bargaining mode, it may be offering what is most precious to him to secure a high stakes bargain (DeMaris and Leeb, 2005, p. 185).

The narrative flow resumes as if there was no interruption after the empowerment of the Spirit, moving to drawing battle

1 I will not discuss here the historicity of child sacrifice connected to Chemosh or Moloch; my concern is the theological drift of the narrative opposing the two belief systems.

lines, to battle, to victory. The placement of the vow, introduced by a disjunctive clause in 11.29 and followed by a resumptive clause going back to the expected flow, suggests a causal connection between Spirit and victory, but not between vow and victory (Chisholm, 2010, p. 411). One of the shortest battle reports in the book ensues; the terse account contrasts oddly with the long account of failed negotiations. Force and military valour are not what characterize Jephthah as a person or a leader; his style of relating, tinted by his personal experience, matter more to the narrator. Yahweh has delivered Israel, as readers expected; but this deliverance is rooted in Yahweh's compassion, rather than the people's misguided action in choosing a leader, or Jephthah's vow. To argue that victory means that Yahweh approves of the vow is to misunderstand fundamentally the nature of Yahweh's relationship with Israel, as well as the theological underpinning of the book: Yahweh is acting for, and in response to, Israel, not Jephthah; and Yahweh acts in grace, not in tit-for-tat response to human offerings.

11.34–40: Jephthah's daughter

The scene as Jephthah goes home victorious is what ancient readers would expect: his daughter leading celebratory dances, coming out to meet the successful warriors. The language of 11.34 repeats the words of the vow, she 'came out to meet him', underlining the expectability of the event. The juxtaposition of her innocent joy and the reader's knowledge of the vow heightens both pathos and irony. The narrator's emphatic note, 'she was his only child, beside her he had no son or daughter', retrospectively tells the reader that this is exactly what Jephthah should have expected – and perhaps did expect, as well as emphasizing Jephthah's plight and the combined yet separate isolation of father and daughter. Jephthah's reaction in 11.35 is one of ritual sorrow (tearing his clothes) and a recurrent feature in his reactions. He blames her for his fate: '*You* have brought me very low, *you* have become the cause of great trouble to me.' His entire focus is on the pain caused to him, rather than grief on behalf of his daughter. He then argues that his position is set in stone, his vow irrevocable. Jephthah's new-found status is entirely based on the word of the elders; for him to breach his own word, the vow, would collapse the world as he wants it to be. The faithlessness and lack of loyalty of others – his brothers and the elders – affected him profoundly, shaping his decisions and underlying beliefs and values. Jephthah additionally states that he has opened his mouth *to the Lord* – using Yahweh as guarantor and the reason why he cannot take back his vow. As leader, he is using God to justify abuse of another person and maintaining his sense of honour. Jephthah's daughter, however, is no compliant victim. Her options, in a deeply patriarchal culture where she would have nowhere safe to go as a single, unmarried girl without brothers and sisters, are very limited. But she takes what options she has, challenging her father's understanding of events. As he started with 'my daughter', she replies in kind, 'my father'. Her response stresses her father's responsibility with repeated use of 'you': 'My father, if *you* have opened your mouth to the Lord, do to me according to what has gone out of *your* mouth, now that the Lord has given *you* vengeance against *your* enemies, the Ammonites.' She repeats Jephthah's personal understanding of his conflict with the king of Ammon and emphasizes that it will be his actions that will lead to her death. She does recognize Yahweh's hand in giving victory, though she does not link victory causally to the vow. Her description of what Yahweh has done is 'given you vengeance on your enemies'. The tripartite root *nqm* is translated as vengeance, but in the OT does not have the negative connotations it has in English. It is most often used in connection with God bringing about justice. When applied to human agents, it largely denotes justice and the restoration of right order, including in connection to what is perceived as a just war (Peels, 1997, p. 156). Yet here it does not refer to Yahweh's vengeance on behalf of Israel, but to Jephthah's, with no mention of Israel. The personalization of the Ammonites as Jephthah's enemies further reinforces that Jephthah fights for himself. Human justice is ambiguous, often mixed with personal interests, yet does not prevent Yahweh from exercising his justice and deliverance

– though here Israel benefits from justice because Yahweh first extends grace. Once again, Yahweh is mentioned but not interacted with. The young woman does not plead with her father, or with Yahweh.

Whether the young woman knew of the vow is unclear. On the one hand, if she had she might not have come out. On the other hand, she responds in a calm and measured manner and does not ask for an explanation of the nature of the vow but seems to know what is involved (Greves, 2016, p. 163). Rather than exonerating her father, or asking for a way out, she holds him responsible for his own actions. Still, critics have found her obedience problematic, despite the patriarchal context. Are father and daughter equally misguided in thinking that the vow must be obeyed? Are they both beholden to inappropriate and damaging notions of obedience and respect for powerful figures, Jephthah towards Yahweh, the daughter towards her father? There is not enough in the text to answer with certainty, but there is space for questions, relevant then and relevant now. For instance, had violence been a regular feature at home, the young woman's docility may be a survival mechanism. She may have considered that dying with dignity was better than fighting a losing battle. She may have known of the vow all along and chosen to go out first to spare other members of the household, in an act of self-sacrifice and critique of a society that treats women as expendable and subordinate to men's desires. Some argue she shares in her father's guilt by not resisting and so do the young women who mourn with her (Janzen, 2005, p. 346); this completely fails to consider the realities of a deeply patriarchal setting, or the psychological impact of growing up in a violent environment surrounded by 'worthless men'. It is true, however, that both she and her father focus on the ethical obligation to fulfil the vow, rather than on whether the vow is ethical in the first place (Conway, 2019, p. 170). There are many possible explanations for the daughter's acceptance, but ultimately, none matter. She is a victim and her father, the most powerful man in Gilead, should have known better. Just as the wider community failed Jephthah in his youth, so they fail her now – and Jephthah repeats the cycle of abuse. Once again, the text powerfully explores the impact of one generation upon the next, and the web of complex relationships, power dynamics and psychological factors involved in assessing a leader.

After telling her father to fulfil his vow, she asks him to leave her alone/forsake her for two months. The language is strong, stressing the separation between them. For two months, they will not be father and daughter, and she will go and mourn with young women who share her precarious and dangerous social positioning and would understand her vulnerability and lack of choices. She will go into the hills with her companions, a sharp contrast from her father standing alone, who had only ever known the company of worthless men. She goes to mourn her virginity (*bətûlîm*); the term is somewhat vague, but together with the narrator's note later on that 'she had never known a man' it is clear that she is not mourning for children she will not have, as many traditional commentators argue, but lamenting a certain time in her life, now cut short, or possibly the impossibility of sexual experience. This time of life is the liminal stage between childhood and full adulthood, potentially dangerous because young women belong fully to neither, yet also potentially a safer time: nubile girls had a lot to lose in moving away from family, having to obey a new husband and fit into his family group, risking their lives in childbirth. Virginity forms a small subtext in Judges, as women specifically said to be virgins are all subjected to violence: Jephthah's daughter is killed, the virgins of Jabesh-Gilead are forcibly taken and married after their families are killed and towns destroyed, and the daughters of Shiloh are abducted and forced to marry Benjaminites. Virginity, in Judges 21, is used to determine life or death. Jephthah's daughter's virginity has kept her in the house of her father so far and possibly contributes to her being seen as an 'acceptable' sacrifice, because of associations between virginity and purity. In all three examples, virgins are used by the men of Israel and specifically associated with the passage in and out of war. Jephthah grants her wish, with no indication that he is wrestling with his vow or its consequences, and no one else raises objections.

The story of Jephthah's daughter inevitably echoes another child sacrifice story: Abraham and Isaac, a sacrifice that never happened (Gen. 22). Both texts emphasize that the (potential) victim is an only child; both fathers are military leaders, with a record of both battle and negotiation. Yet the two stories could not be more different. Abraham was chosen by God, blessed, wealthy, respected, the recipient of a personal promise; Jephthah was rejected, exiled and chosen by men. Abraham's dynamic relationship with God is recounted in some detail; Jephthah's only prayer is his fateful vow; Isaac is a boy, whose mother, Sarah, is known and respected; he is repeatedly said to be 'beloved'. Jephthah's daughter is a girl, whose mother never appears and whose father is of questionable parentage; she is never said to be loved. In Genesis, it is God who initiated the sequence of events and no vow is mentioned. Here, it is Jephthah who volunteers a sacrifice. In Genesis, God intervenes; here, he remains silent. Abraham thought he had to go through with the sacrifice and God teaches him that God provides and his child need not die. Jephthah, who unlike Abraham supposedly has access to the Torah, should know the Abraham story and the strong prohibitions on human sacrifice, yet ignores them all. In Genesis, Abraham goes up the mountain with his son and proffers reassuring words of faith; in Judges, the girl goes to the mountain with her friends while Jephthah stays behind, silent. Why did Yahweh not intervene this time? Was it because Abraham had no law, no revelation to shape his actions, whereas Jephthah had been given ample instructions to guard against his actions? Is it about human free will, with a story of interaction with Abraham, but Jephthah refusing to interact? Divine silence is problematic, yet fits within the pattern of increased divine withdrawal in response to the people's choice to break the covenant.

Jephthah lets his daughter go, and when she returns he makes good on his word. She is the first woman in Judges to be killed by one who should protect her, the first of three domestic murders. The narrator refrains from depicting the sacrifice, simply stating that Jephthah did as he had promised. The narrator's restraint contrasts sharply with the previous delight in the murders of Eglon or Sisera. Where powerless victims are involved – here, with Samson's first wife, and the woman of chapter 19 – the narrator withdraws and shields the women from a voyeuristic reader gaze. The narrator's return to the theme of virginity in 39b may be a way to emphasize her purity and innocence as a victim, or reassure anxious patriarchal readers that the girls' time in the hills had been entirely proper. It may also be the narrator pointing to all the possibilities that have been erased. There are no accounts of great celebrations for Jephthah or plans to cherish his memory. Instead, we are given a rare window into relations between women. While the term 'the sons of Israel' is used innumerable times in the OT, this is one of only two instances of the expression 'the daughters of Israel' (the other, 2 Sam. 1.24, exhorts women to mourn the death of Saul, also a context of lament). The celebration uncovers the importance of women's relationships, of memory and of rituals – here, rituals keep alive and voice the reality of domestic and child abuse, but they also create safe women-only spaces where the truth of their lives can be told and given wider meaning. The community of women gather around Jephthah's daughter in a way that the men failed to do around young Jephthah. In their gathering and remembering, there is the possibility of lamenting injustice and oppression, imagining a better world. Without the women's determination to remember Jephthah's daughter, would the whole of who he was have been remembered? Or would he have been remembered simply as a wonderful war hero? Biblical writers (men) did record the story, but the following chapter simply shows Jephthah living his life with no apparent regrets or deep sorrow. It is the women, those who are at risk too, who bear the memory of Jephthah's crimes and make it impossible for him to be presented unambiguously. The story does not end with silence, but with an appeal to the community. It is a community of powerlessness, exhibiting the solidarity of the oppressed. Violence and death may be unavoidable, but there are nevertheless things the women can do. They can gather, support, lament and shape what is remembered, in hope of reshaping the future. It is an appeal to testimony and witness rather than denial of the reality of domestic abuse and of the misuse of power within a broken social structure. The daughter's name may not be recorded, unlike her powerful father's. But she emerges as a courageous woman who, in contrast to Jephthah, gathers community, rather than seek to dominate it and as a result destroy it.

The legitimacy of Jephthah's vow

Jephthah's vow has been the source of much puzzlement over the years, and numerous interpretations. Those keen to maintain Jephthah as a 'hero' have tended to explain it, either arguing the girl was not put to death but dedicated as a perpetual virgin, or that Jephthah doing as he promised was a sign of integrity (e.g. Boling, 1975, p. 210). These readings, however, fail to consider the wider canonical background, specifically other narrative and legal texts dealing with human sacrifice, and the deteriorating spiral of Judges, within which Jephthah exemplifies how moving away from covenantal life endangers the most vulnerable. Jephthah's daughter is the first, but not the last, woman wrongfully killed. She is the most vulnerable of the three, as a young daughter living at home; Samson's first wife will be next, only just married; the concubine of chapter 19, within an established relationship, is the third. All three are nameless, their fate possible for every woman in Israel. We will now explore whether Jephthah's vow was rash, accommodating political norms (Webb, 1987, p. 74), the result of an abusive deity making impossible demands (Exum, 1993, p. 139), or profoundly wrong theologically and revealing Israel's Canaanization (Janzen, 2005, p. 341). Human sacrifice is seen with horror in the OT (Lev. 18.21, 20.1–5; Deut. 12.31, 18.10; 2 Kings 3.27, 16.3, 17.17, 21.6), often termed an 'abomination' or 'abhorrent' – *tô'ēbāh* – and is therefore hardly a contested issue, but one that goes to the core of Israel's covenantal identity. Jephthah is not the only father sacrificing his child: a pagan ruler, king Mesha of Moab, sacrifices his first-born in 2 Kings 3 to ensure victory. Two kings of Israel followed suit, both declared profoundly evil. Ahaz of Judah 'did not do what was right in the eyes of the Lord' and made his son 'pass through fire', an action termed abominable (*tôʿēbāh*) and linked to pagan nations (2 Kings 16.1–4). Manasseh 'did evil in the eyes of Yahweh' and followed the abominable (*tôʿēbāh*) practices of pagan nations, making his son pass through fire (2 Kings 21.1–6). For both Israelite kings, it was an active religious ritual rather than a burnt offering for battle. The closest parallel to Jephthah is therefore a king of Moab, and sacrificing one's child is associated with evil pagan practices. It is difficult to see how Jephthah's example could be taken as a positive one in Scripture. Nor is it possible, as feminist critics sometimes argue, to hold that the girl is sacrificed because she is a girl. Other canonical examples suggest that she is sacrificed because she is his child, his eldest, and there are no others available – suggesting that Jephthah's vow was conscious and deliberate. The intertext points to the Canaanization of Israel and its forgetting Yahweh as primary meaning. This interpretation ties in with Yahweh's doubts about the depth of Israel's repentance in chapter 10. It also highlights the relationship between worship and the social order. When foreign gods are followed, injustice, brutality and oppression take root within Israel itself.

A minority interpretation argues that the sacrifice is acceptable as a *ḥerēm* sacrifice (Kamrada, 2010, p. 27); this is highly unlikely, given that *ḥerēm* applies to war enemies and is performed following battle, rather than promised to Yahweh in a pre-battle bargain. In addition, the sacrifice is clearly described as a burnt offering (*ʿôlāh*), not *ḥerēm*. Jephthah's bargaining with Yahweh is more akin to a bribe offered to a judge; Jephthah had just appealed to Yahweh to be judge between him and the Ammonite king. To offer him a sacrifice to bend the outcome is to behave against clear Torah instructions against the bribing of judges (Deut. 16.19). Because this made the vow illegal, there would have been no expectation of fulfilment. Jephthah's vow, in ritual terms, fails to follow the rules for a burnt offering: it is not processed by a priest who assesses its suitability (Lev. 22.17–30); all instructions for sacrifices in fulfilment of a vow speak of animal offerings, and within this only certain animals were deemed fit for sacrifice; acceptable species for a burnt offering were cows, sheep, goats and pigeons, and the first three should be male and without blemish (Lev. 1.3, 10). The vow fails on every count. Vowed animals unfit for sacrifice would be used by the priests, sold for profit or redeemed for monetary value plus 20 per cent (Lev. 27.11–13). Leviticus 27 details how to commute vows into financial offerings, with discretion for those who cannot afford the fixed scale. Had these instructions been followed, Jephthah's daughter could never have been sacrificed. 1 Samuel 13 and 15 include stories in which Yahweh rejects improper sacrifices, because following Yahweh's instructions matters infinitely more than ritual actions in themselves. In between these two chapters of the life of Saul comes another story, a rash vow that would endanger Saul's son. Saul had made a vow that the army should not eat until they got victory (1 Sam. 14.24); his son Jonathan broke the vow and his father was faced with putting him to death. It was not a sacrifice, but the story speaks to how tightly a vow binds its maker. The people speak up in defence of Jonathan and pay the price to 'ransom' him. Leviticus 27.2–8 makes specific provision for the redemption of human beings 'when a person makes an equivalent vow to the Lord concerning a human being'. From all these examples, it is clear that the law made ample provision for Jephthah not to sacrifice his daughter, and narrative examples underscore the force of the law. When Jephthah says in 11.35 that he cannot take his vow back, he is factually wrong in terms of law and theology. Why did he not consider other options?

Jephthah may not have known the law. Even then, he could have not fulfilled the vow, taking the consequences upon himself. Eager as he is to sacrifice another, he is not willing to sacrifice his life, his honour or his word to save another. Ultimately, Jephthah values his honour, and the power associated with his word being fulfilled, more highly than following the Law or the life of his child. The rejected child who wanted to prove himself is single-minded in his pursuit of power and achieving his own aims. The young girl is the first victim of Jephthah's ruthlessness in pursuit of power; she will be followed by many Ephraimites. Just like Gideon, and worse,

Jephthah showed himself incapable of handling power well. And just like Abimelech, his personal life, and the way it shaped his character, overshadowed his every action. Yet as with Abimelech, Jephthah is not the only guilty party. He was rejected then elected by the people of Gilead who, unlike Saul's troops, remained silent as Jephthah spiralled out of control. The fulfilment of the vow has no explicit impact on Jephthah's relationship with Gilead and Israel, apart from, maybe, portraying him as ruthless and not to be trifled with. The community who failed to speak up and appeal to the law of the covenant stands in complicity with the leader they chose for themselves.

12.1–7: Conflict with Ephraim

Chapter 12 moves to the post-deliverance period, yet not into peace for the land but into larger scale internecine conflict than occurred with either Gideon or Abimelech. As in 8.1–3, the Ephraimites take issue with not being invited to fight. The conflict is tenser from the outset, with the men of Ephraim being summoned, a word often used for a summons to armed conflict, against Jephthah rather than external enemies. The Ephraimites are clearly targeting him personally, challenging his leadership. They are not saying they would have wanted to join in battle in any case, but it is Jephthah's 'crossing over' into their territory without including them that is at issue. The Ephraimites threaten to burn down his house, a sadly ironic threat given that Jephthah offered his only child as a burnt offering. All he has left is the shell of the house of the father (*bêt āb*), its physical building now at threat too. 12.2–3 repeats the pattern of Jephthah's negotiating tactics: everything is personalized; he claims the moral high ground, accuses his opponents of rejecting/harming him, and uses Yahweh as guarantor of his right to leadership. The beginning of his speech is slightly unclear, seeming to start with 'I was a man of contention', but then adding 'and my people', leading most translators to assume the statement refers to the conflict between Israel and Ammon. The term 'man of contention' is, however, quite apt to describe Jephthah. The Hebrew root, *rîb*, refers to contending, taking to court, and reflects Jephthah's fraught relationships with his brothers, the elders, his daughter and, now, wider Israel. The root was part of Jerubaal's name (6.31–32) and used for Ephraim contending with Gideon (8.1). Israel's leaders, increasingly, are men of war who struggle to bring peace, sources of conflict as much as deliverers. Jephthah again makes the conflict personal. He does not try to appease Ephraim as Gideon had done. Once again he fails at negotiations. The incident highlights the failure of epic models of leadership, focused on one main leader who relies on force and valour in battle. Jephthah does not behave as a deliverer, but as a local warlord trying to assert his power.

Sharp delineations of identity emerge in this episode, with increasing ethnographic difference within Israel itself. The focus on the identity and boundaries of specific sub-groups does not lead to greater interdependence but to fragmentation into ever-smaller units, a fragmentation that will reach its devastating fullness in chapters 20—21. When Israel shifts away from its common covenantal identity, competing internal identities come into conflict, each fighting for what it sees as being its rights and rightful place within the configuration of tribes. Jephthah has followed the same trajectory as Gideon, growing in confidence and confidence leading to less effort to avoid conflict. There were fewer details of the war with Ammon than of the conflict with Ephraim, while negotiations with Ammon are far more extensive. 12.4 sheds light on the intensity of Jephthah's reaction: an apparent slur on Gilead, calling them 'fugitives from Ephraim'. Given Jephthah's past as a fugitive in Tov, the taunt may have sharpened his need to assert his own value and honour. More widely, Ephraim's taunt is another symptom of increasing fragmentation coming from ethnic-based pride and misplaced nationalism, each tribe claiming a positive identity over and against a negatively portrayed other. The Gileadites respond in kind, choosing who to kill based on pronunciation. The mindless slaughter that Jephthah had begun within his own household now spreads to the nation, from one daughter to 42,000 Ephraimites slaughtered. Gideon had healed the rift with Ephraim,

Jephthah deepens it. Gideon and Ephraim had cooperated to guard the crossings, Jephthah uses the crossings to capture and kill Ephraim. Neither side is portrayed positively. Ephraim insults the deliverer, has no sense of national unity, insults the Gileadites, makes empty threats, fails on the battlefield, stupidly tries to cross the Jordan where the Gileadites are in control, and is persecuted for not speaking properly. Jephthah (and his followers) is incapable of looking beyond his own interests to the welfare of the entire nation, even less to the welfare of its more vulnerable members. Ultimately, it is the people of Israel who suffer for their independent choice of a leader.

Jephthah only judges Israel for six years; he dies in Gilead and is buried there, a sign of the acceptance he has craved his entire life. 12.7 has often been separated from the main Jephthah account and grouped with the minor judges that follow. There is no obvious literary reason to do so. The other accounts contain details of the life of the judge, all at a time of apparent peace, whereas Jephthah's story has been told at great length. The verse reads as a framework conclusion to the whole account, giving the length of judging and chronicling death and burial. The land is not said to have peace, as indeed it did not after Abimelech and will not after Samson, a marker of the degeneration of the nation and its leaders. The placement of Jephthah, sandwiched between Jair and Ibzan, each with 30 sons, enhances the pathos of the story. Jephthah is alone, isolated, with no past and no future. His efforts in the present have taken away any possibility of a future, either as a father or as the leader of a prosperous, united Israel. Jephthah stands somewhere between Gideon and Abimelech. Like Gideon, he is empowered by the Spirit, rallies troops, struggles with doubt, leads Israel to spectacular victory only to then misuse leadership and turn against fellow Israelites. Yet he also reflects Abimelech, with questionable parentage, a painful family rift, association with worthless men, negotiating his way to leadership, ruling brutally and killing his own family. Leadership in Israel is on a downward trajectory.

12.8–15: Minor judges

The next cluster of minor judges mirrors the beginning of chapter 10. Details are sketchy: mention of judging (but no substance to illustrate the term) and length of rule, death and burial, filiation and geography. What stands out is the display of prosperity, and the emphasis on Ibzan and Abdon's children. Ibzan sponsors exogamic marriages (outside the tribe, potentially outside of Israel), which could indicate either an attempt to mend bridges with other tribes/nations, or aggressive expansionist tactics, using women to seal alliances that extend territory and power. There is no detail of Elon beyond the framework and Abdon closely parallels Jair (10.3–5), their many children riding on donkeys, indicating an accumulation of wealth and potential pretence to dynastic rule. Abdon is buried in non-Israelite territory, which ends the series on a dark note. None of the three are said to have delivered Israel, and their rule seems to have repeated the excesses of Gideon's.

Reflections

An important feature of the story of Jephthah is that of words and speech. The different sections are articulated around, and progress through, dialogue. The theme is common in the Hebrew Bible, particularly in wisdom literature. Jephthah's words reveal his character, alienating him from others. The elders' words and those of the Ammonite king reveal their unwillingness to compromise or be self-critical; the Ephraimites' words prompt violence and deepen divisions. The daughter's words, in contrast, challenge violence and gather community, but separate her from her father. The Psalms regularly link violent speech with violent action, speech enabling the articulation between thoughts and deeds (Lynch, 2020, p. 131). Arrogant speech, deceitful speech, taunts, scheming, prideful speech contribute to the portrayal of the speech of the wicked (Ps. 12.4; 52.4; 59.7, 12; 73.6–8). Speech is presented as powerful and intimately linked to character as worked out in actions. Speech is a major strand of the book of Proverbs, with sharp contrast established between wise and foolish speech (14.3; 15.2, 7; 16.23; 18.6–7; 19.1; 23.15–16), righteous versus wicked speech (10.20–21, 31–32; 11.11; 12.13–14; 13.2; 15.28; 17.4) and an exploration of appropriate speech (apt and timely, 15.23; 25.11; sweet and intelligent, 16.21; sweet and healing, 12.18; 16.24), restraint in speech (10.19; 11.12; 12.23; 13.3; 15.1; 17.28; 18.13; 21.23; 25.15), the negative impact of flattery, slander and gossip (10.18; 11.13; 16.18; 17.9; 18.8; 20.19; 26.20, 28; 28.23; 29.5). The right type of speech marks out wisdom and righteousness, speech that is restrained, truthful, matches actions and brings about peace, healing and reconciliation rather than strife and violence. Assessing Jephthah's words against wisdom literature makes for grim reading. He prefers angry words that yield conflict and violence. His vow is typical of foolish speech, showing his ignorance of the Law and lack of forethought, while his exchange with Ephraim typifies wicked speech that leads to death and destruction. Words come into sharp focus at the Jordan; the right word means life, the wrong one death. Yet the distinction is not based on wise/righteous or foolish/wicked speech, but arbitrarily on the words themselves, so that words become instruments of separation rather than communication. Jephthah's words opened the way to status and power, but in the end words fail him and betray his lack of wisdom and self-control.

Jephthah emerges as a leader with feet of clay. He could have been a great leader, a figure of hope, transcending a traumatic beginning to gain a new place in his community. Knowing the pain of rejection, he could have focused his leadership on fostering better community relationships to create safety for the marginalized – just as Israel is told repeatedly to treat strangers well because they were once strangers. Instead, Jephthah repeats the pattern of rejection and division. He seems to regard every interlocutor as an enemy he must better, and the isolation of his beginnings is matched by his isolation at the end. The skilful interweaving of the personal and the political, public and private, shows how Jephthah the leader is shaped by Jephthah the man – the rejected child of dubious parentage.

The paradox of the introduction in 11.1 remains – he is a mighty warrior and the son of a prostitute; he delivers Israel and oppresses fellow Israelites. The genius of the narrator is to portray him as a complex figure who invites both compassion and judgement, and who shares responsibility for his actions with the community that shaped and elected him. The contrast with the story of Abraham reveals not only different decisions, but how life experience shapes different characters. Abraham had prosperity, promise and numerous experiences of God's faithfulness. He was wealthy and loved. He had family and relations, was well-established. Jephthah had no material blessings, no standing, no history of promise. He wasn't even first choice as leader. Readers are left to ask, what would be a just measure for Jephthah's life? How can it be assessed with justice and compassion? In the hall of faith of Hebrews 11, he appears in continuity with Abraham. Abraham was not unblemished either, and also visited injustice and trauma on those around him who were most vulnerable– his wife, by passing her off as his sister and allowing her to be taken into another man's household (Gen. 12, 20); a slave, Hagar, by sleeping with her on his wife's request and later banishing her to the desert with their young son Ishmael (Gen. 16, 21). Hebrews is not looking for perfection but for direction. Jephthah's hesitant and misguided steps were enough for Yahweh to work with him and bring liberation. On that count, he stands together with other leaders. In his deep humanity he stands with them as fallen, yet not beyond Yahweh's grace. Jephthah's faith is inchoate, syncretistic, at times misguided. There is no exchange with Yahweh apart from the vow which seeks to bind Yahweh to an outcome Yahweh had already committed to; Jephthah knows Israel's story but not its deeper meaning, and seeks to perform religious rituals without understanding the nature of their symbolism or place in the covenant. There is no indication that the wider community had better knowledge of Yahweh, and Israel is faithless in choosing leaders, in intertribal solidarity, or in protecting the vulnerable. Intergenerational transmission of faith and covenantal life is continuing to wane, with tragic consequences.

One of the first stories in Judges, that of Achsah, had tied together the political and the domestic as a high point at the very beginning. With Gideon, cracks start to appear in public life, and with Abimelech, obvious cracks in the life of the house of the father (*bêt āb*), the basic building block of Israelite social organization. In Jephthah, the correspondence between public and private deterioration is brought out more obviously, preparing the way for the excesses of Samson. The strain is obvious in the failure of the 'principle of protective association' (Oeste, 2011, p. 308). First, Jephthah's brothers fail to protect him and turn against him, a move supported by the elders of Gilead and, by extension, the entire town. Jephthah then violates a deeper bond of protective association towards his daughter, choosing his honour and status above fatherhood; he not only sacrifices her, he sacrifices himself as father in any meaningful way, destroying the very concept of a 'house of the father'. Jephthah then widens his dereliction of duty to fellow Israelites. Every level of Israelite society is affected, and the public and private worlds mirror each other (as far as a public/private distinction is meaningful in an ancient agrarian context[2]). Within a system dominated by martial and hypermasculine values, men may survive, as Jephthah does, though hardly unscathed; women, on the other hand, are voiceless victims. Jephthah's daughter is the first, but not the last, female victim of a toxic blend of hypermasculinity and war ideology. Hence her story is not an isolated event, but part of a developing pattern and sustained critique in Judges. Early stories in the book showcased strong women who held their place within a patriarchal culture. When Jael went out to meet a warrior, it was the warrior who ended up dead. Now roles are reversed. Women gradually lose their voices and their names. Throughout the book, women only become visible when they intersect with the male world of the story – Achsah, Jael, Jephthah's daughter, Samson's love interests, Delilah, the Levite's concubine, the daughters of Jabesh-Gilead and Shiloh. As women become nameless, they are identified solely through

2 For a discussion of public and private in an ancient context, see Hamley, 2019, pp. 109, 122–3.

the men they are attached to: Jephthah's daughter, Manoah's wife, Samson's bride, Micah's mother, the Levite's concubine. Women's agency and personhood are gradually eroded. However, the text, by linking public and private, highlights that this erosion of the personhood of the 'other' is never limited to just one group, but spreads, as it does here, to Ephraim and later to the Benjaminites and Jabesh-Gilead. The logic of violence ends in self-destruction. The book as a whole, far from condoning the violence depicted, offers a deep critique of the societal movements that have made it possible. If Israel worships foreign gods, it will start acting as the Canaanites do, which is defined by injustice, oppression and violence (in the text's own world of meaning), thereby justifying Yahweh's judgement. Ironically, Jephthah thinks he is acting justly in standing by his word, while Yahweh, having said he would not deliver, breaks his word to reach out to a troubled Israel. Yahweh acts in complete freedom, choosing to be gracious and deliver, yet also choosing not to override human choices and allowing Israel to experience the consequences of its own slide into violence. The story of Jephthah graphically depicts the futility of deliverance unless Israel first addresses the enemy within.

6

Samson (13—16)

Chapters 13—16 are some of the better-known chapters of Judges; Samson catches the imagination, with his extraordinary strength, irreverent wit and tragic end. The stories are told in the epic style of campfire stories, ridiculing an enemy defeated by a larger-than-life hero. At a deeper level, Samson is the last leader to judge Israel in Judges, last of a downward spiral, with no interest in liberation. The four chapters weave intricate thematic and semantic threads: the many forms of power – political, physical, sexual, linguistic, intellectual; unfulfilled expectations; focus on what is seen or unseen, known or unknown, told or untold. The story follows Samson's life from conception until death, a more detailed character study than any other.

13: Birth narrative

13.1–7: Annunciation

The episode opens with the framework statement, 'Israel continued to do evil in the eyes of Yahweh', and was handed over to the Philistine. This time, however, there is no statement of pain at being handed over, no crying out, and no statement of divine pathos in response to their plight. The reciprocal relationship between Israel and Yahweh has almost completely crumbled. Liberation is initiated by Yahweh only, in a movement of grace towards a nation about to disappear into Canaan. 13.2 takes the story in an unexpected turn, with a seemingly traditional birth narrative. As finding a leader out of the adults in the nation has not proved successful, choosing a leader before birth and shaping his growing years is a logical progression, though not in the dynastic style of kings. An ordinary couple are tasked with raising the deliverer-to-be. Manoah enters first, but his introduction is unusual: gender/geography/tribe/name, reversing the normal order. Geography is foregrounded rather than tribal and family affiliations. Manoah is named, but his wife is not, which is odd for an annunciation scene, leading readers to expect that Manoah will be the main character.

The traditional statement of barrenness, attributing cause to the woman, is not followed by a statement of how hard this was, or petitioning Yahweh for a child. It is a world with no promise and no expectations and, as with Israel, Yahweh's intervention is purely down to his gracious initiative. The arrival of the angel/messenger of Yahweh in 13.2 suggests that a reversal of the family's, and Israel's, situation is imminent. Narratives of barrenness and childbirth usually focus on women, such as Rachel and Hannah (Abraham being an exception), the child given always a boy. Bringing life out of the desert, a child out of barrenness, is typical of the presence of Yahweh (Gen. 21.5–7; 25.21; 30.22–23; 1 Sam. 2.5; Ps. 68.6; 113.9; Isa. 54.1, a pattern that extends into the New Testament with Elizabeth and John the Baptist, Luke 1.13–15). The angel 'is seen' (*wayērā'*) by the woman (i.e. appeared); the expressions begins a lexical chain associated with sight and its connection to right and wrong (13.3, 10, 21–23; 14.1–2, 8, 11; 16.1, 5, 18, 24, 27). The announcement that the woman's barrenness has been reversed is quickly followed by lengthy instructions about the boy and how she must care for him. While the directions are in keeping with Nazirite vows, two features stand out. First, the *unborn* child is dedicated as a Nazirite, without choice, and for life rather than a limited time; second, the mother herself must abide by the vow with regards to food and drink; the child is set apart within the womb already, as he is fed by what she consumes (this is underlined by the angel's use of 'from the womb', rather than the NRSV's, 'from birth'). These instructions set up expectations of the child's life to come in terms of dedication to Yahweh and covenantal living. If he is to follow Nazirite principles, readers may expect him to display an understanding of and follow the Law, as the command to keep away from unclean foods implies, since it applies to all Israelites, not just Nazirites. Numbers 6.1–21 records detailed prescriptions for Nazirites: abstaining from wine/intoxicating drinks, not cutting hair, not having contact with a corpse. It was seen as a temporary form of holiness (Niditch, 2008, p. 143). Given Israel's struggle to maintain its distinctive identity and relationship to Yahweh, it makes sense to have a leader symbolically and ritually set apart in Yahweh's service (Johnson, 2010, p. 277); readers are invited to judge Samson against the Nazirite principles that bookend the account, mentioned here at conception and in chapter 16 at his death. The Nazirite status prompts a wider parallel, with another judge who will be a Nazirite from birth, another promised child, Samuel (1 Sam. 1.11). The boy Samson's destiny is lofty yet ambiguous: he will *begin to* deliver. This may reflect the fact that no judge has delivered Israel properly yet, as they all limited their efforts to the political and military sphere; or it may be an indication of the deteriorating spiral, as Samson won't even be able to achieve full victory over Israel's enemies. At this point, readers are left to wonder.

The woman runs to her husband to share the news. She focuses less on the content of the message than on the identity of the messenger and the awesomeness of the event. She calls him 'a man of God' (Elohim, not Yahweh). What she has not asked, and the man has not told, will shape the rest of the story, rather than keep the focus on the child and the hope of deliverance. Her report is only faithful to a point and perhaps reflects her own priorities. She refers to her barrenness, the command to guard herself, the food and hair instructions, but does not mention deliverance, and ominously adds 'a Nazirite from the womb *to the day of his death*'. She does not mention hair, possibly because it is the better-known sign of a Nazirite. However, the omission, together with the mention of death, foreshadows the events of chapter 16. Why not mention deliverance? It seems that her son's special status matters more than his task on behalf of Israel. Yahweh's desire to deliver is marginalized in the particular story as it is in the national one.

13.8–14: Repeat annunciation

Manoah reappears, seemingly unhappy that it was his wife who received a message from God. He prays and ask Yahweh (not just 'Elohim') for directions. Manoah's prayer suggests that he does not think his wife's instructions are trustworthy enough, or possibly that he, as head of the household, should have received the revelation. It may be that he is pious and wants to get things absolutely right. He includes his wife in his prayer, asking that the 'man' (he does not call him angel or messenger, whereas the narrator does, highlighting his lack of recognition) would come to 'us' and teach 'us' what to do. It is unclear from the previous message that there would be much more to say in the way of specific instructions, given the specific Torah provisions for Nazirites. By asking for a second revelation, he marginalizes his wife's place in the story, attempting to replace her. Her namelessness may reflect focalization through Manoah's eyes and the diminishing status of women in Israel. God does hear, but only half answers, which confirms that Manoah's prayer was somehow misguided. The angel comes to his wife again, reinforcing that the initial revelation was entirely proper and Manoah not its main recipient – it is, after all, the woman who will be most affected. Ideas of male pre-eminence are undermined by the narrative. The angel comes to the woman 'in the field', a public area outside of domestic spaces; fields could be dangerous places for women on their own (as Deut. 22.25 shows, if a woman is attacked in a field, she may not be heard as she cries out, therefore a charge of forcible rape is possible), though depending on the time of year, fields may be sites of busy communal activity. Meeting her in a field protects the woman's reputation, since there would either be witnesses, or she would be protected by law. She fetches her husband, not trying to keep the revelation to herself. Manoah follows her quickly and the wording of his question suggests that he now believes his wife, 'when your words come true ...' (13.12). The couple is exhibiting faith and the ability to recognize Yahweh at work, which implies that they may provide the right environment for the new deliverer to be raised. Yet Manoah's question is ambiguous. Is he asking for clarification on how to bring up the boy, what commandments to follow, what way of life is suitable, how the Nazirite vow will work? Or is he asking for clarification on the boy's destiny, what he will do, what his overall task before Yahweh is – the part of the message that the woman does not appear to have shared? The use of *mišpāt* for way or commandments, based on the same root as 'judge', subtly reminds the reader of the boy's destiny as a leader supposed to bring justice. The angel is gracious but firm, making it clear that what he told the woman is sufficient, and he repeats the instructions she had already shared, but does not add information that she had withheld. In this way he does not undermine her credibility or importance and keeps it clear that the revelation was meant for her; she now needs to handle it appropriately. The angel does, however, add a tightening of the drink instructions by prohibiting 'anything that comes from the vine', a detail relevant to the next chapter. Manoah's reaction is more proactive than other fathers-to-be in annunciation-type scenes: partners' reactions include doubt and joy (Abraham and Sarah, Hannah and Elkanah, Zechariah and Elizabeth, Joseph and Mary), but Manoah alone tries to get a parallel revelation and gain the favour and confidence of the messenger (Johnson, 2010, p. 279).

13.15–23: Revelation

The narrator has consistently described the envoy as an angel/messenger (*mal'āk*) of Yahweh, whereas Manoah consistently refers to him as 'the man' (*ha 'îš*), sometimes 'the man of God' (Elohim rather than Yahweh). The woman called him a man but said he had the appearance of an angel. The discrepancy between Manoah's (lack of) perception and the reality of the angel's provenance propels the rest of the passage and creates an increasing ironic distance with his wife's superior understanding. The narrator labours the point, with five references to 'the angel of Yahweh' in just four verses. Manoah takes charge and he alone speaks to the angel. He offers hospitality – as a good host does, in a way similar, though less profuse, to Abraham (Gen. 18.3–5) or Gideon. Commentators disagree on whether Manoah is trying to obligate his guest to ensure his favour (Butler, 2009, p. 329), or simply following normal conventions on hospitality (Webb, 2012, p. 356); the text leaves the question open. Ambiguity about characters' motives is a defining feature of the poetics of Judges. The messenger's refusal of a meal is a clue to his identity, as he directs their focus to Yahweh. He invites them to prepare a burnt-offering (*'ōlāh*), appropriate and offered in the correct way, unlike Jephthah's. The narrator is again prompting readers to expect a positive turn in Israel's life, with Yahweh worshipped rightly. The sacrifice is like Gideon's, though the couple have not offered as much – which could reflect a lack of generosity or a lower social status with less attendant wealth. The narrator stressed that Manoah did not understand who the messenger was – yet says nothing of the woman's deeper perception. Manoah shows his lack of understanding with a further question in 13.17, asking for the angel's name. The angel had not offered it upon meeting, which set up an asymmetric relationship. Just like the woman, he remains nameless, though apparently for opposite reasons: she is not given a name by others, making her appear unimportant, whereas he refuses to share his name because it is too important. By wanting to honour the angel Manoah shows he has not understood what is happening; he still thinks it is the angel as a discrete entity who has power, rather than Yahweh, whom the angel has specifically told him to worship. The angel's refusal to share his name places Israel in a pre-Sinai position again, parallel to Jacob's wrestling with the angel, asking for a name but rebuffed (Gen. 32.22–32), rather than Moses receiving the answer 'I am' to his request for a name (Ex. 3.1–15). Symbolically, Israel has regressed to a precovenantal relationship with a God whose identity she has forgotten. They do not recognize God when God appears. The angel's reply is terse, questioning Manoah's motives and asserting that his name is too 'wonderful' (*peli'y*); the root denotes something extraordinary, if judged by normal standards, which evokes a response of awe and wonder (Kruger, 1997, pp. 615–17). It is mostly used in a religious context, and often applied to Yahweh's acts of salvation. It appears particularly prominently in hymnic contexts, in relation to specific acts towards individuals (Ps. 9.1; 40.5; 71.17; 107.15, 21, 24, 31), or in recounting Yahweh's salvation, such as in the Exodus (Ps. 78.12; Micah 7.15). It is specifically applied to Yahweh as the only one who does wonders (Neh. 9.17; Job 5.9; 9.10; Ps. 72.18; 86.10; 98.1; 105.5; 106.22; 136.4). If doing wonders is intrinsic to the character of Yahweh, then the angel's allusion to the wonder of his name is a clue to his divine identity, one that Manoah should – but does not – recognize. Manoah keeps trying to take a grasp on the encounter, but control escapes him and he is consistently wrong-footed.

13.19 has been variously translated, either stating that Yahweh performed wonders while Manoah and his wife watched (KJV, NAS), or that Manoah offered a sacrifice 'to the Lord, to him who works wonders' (NRSV). Linguistically, the first option is a more likely translation of both MT and LXX, which both have the conjunction 'and' linking the two clauses. In addition, this rendering then explains why the moment of recognition only occurs in 13.21, after the explanation of what they witnessed. The NRSV translation makes less sense narratively as it would either mean Manoah had already recognized the visitor or be a narratorial intrusion uncharacteristic of Judges. The angel going up in the flames is reminiscent of theophanies and explains the couple's falling to the ground, averting their faces from the dangerous glory of God – though, ironically, it is only once he disappears that they do so. 13.21 caps the encounter somewhat abruptly with a proleptic narratorial statement that the angel never appeared again. Manoah and his wife have been given enough supernatural guidance and are expected now to rely on the Law. The theophany occurred to highlight the miraculous birth of the deliverer, not to give specific instructions that Israel had already been given. Manoah's failing was to focus on experiencing a new revelation rather than recognizing the One who had already revealed himself to Israel. The narrator makes it clear that Manoah now understands something that his wife had sensed in her very first meeting with the angel. The motif of sight and recognition work hand-in-hand: Manoah and his wife 'looked on' (*rā'āh*, participle) in 13.20; the angel did not 'appear' again (*rā'āh*, infinitive construct) in 13.21; we have 'seen' (*rā'āh*, *Qal* perfect) God in 13.22; 'he would not have shown us' (*rā'āh*, *hiphil* perfect) in 13.23. What they see and fail to see characterizes their spiritual progression. 13.22 reveals Manoah's thoughts, that he had seen 'God', though he fails to use the covenantal name. He is aware of the tradition that talks of death for those who see Yahweh or Yahweh's glory but, like Gideon, he only knows of the generalized fear of seeing Yahweh rather than the many stories of theophany that do not lead to death. Once again, the Israelites only remember partially, and have heard about Yahweh but do not know him. Manoah's wife shows herself as more perceptive and more logical. She does not assume Yahweh (she uses the covenantal name, unlike Manoah) to be a capricious or mechanical deity. Her view of Yahweh is not based on blind terror but on a knowable God and belief in an ordered universe. Manoah tried to take control of the revelation, but his wife began and ended the episode and showed herself more sensitive to the ways of Yahweh throughout, undermining reader expectations about Manoah as principal character or spiritual head of the household.

*13.24–25: **Promise fulfilled***

Focus remains on the woman as she gives birth and it is the nameless woman who names the future deliverer (13.24). Samson (little sun) is an unusual choice, not a traditional Hebrew name; it may refer to Yahweh bringing light at a dark time in Israel, the diminutive appropriate given that Samson will only 'begin to deliver'; however, the name has strong resonances of Canaanite nature worship and its sun god Shemesh (Butler, 2009, p. 330). The name was not given by the messenger and no aetiology is given, an unusual omission in birth narratives.

The ambiguity invites the reader to wonder what kind of person Samson will be, and the degree to which he will deliver Israel from Canaan. By the end of the story, the name will be darkly ironic, as Samson, the sun, is blinded and lives in a darkness largely of his own making.

As promised, the boy grows up blessed by Yahweh. 13.25 returns to a modified framework element, 'the Spirit of Yahweh began to stir in him'. Just as Samson will only *begin* to deliver, the Spirit of Yahweh only '*begins* to stir' in him; there is a sense of incompleteness, as if either Samson needs to grow into his leadership, which would be positive, or somehow the work of Yahweh is limited by his people's rejection. The manner of the Spirit's arrival is also unusual; the verb *pāʿam*, 'stir', is unusual, closer to 'impel' or 'disturb', and often refers to inner turmoil (Webb, 2012, p. 359). There is almost a sense of Samson fighting against the Spirit and the turbulence that will characterize his life. Samson embodies the situation of Israel as Yahweh seeks to disturb them from their comfortable accommodation with the Philistines. Overall, despite some discordant notes, chapter 16 sets up expectations of change; Manoah and his wife may not be perfect, but they are loving parents who pray and are attentive to Yahweh, open to his work in their life, even inquisitive about it, in contrast to the disastrous parenting of chapters 9—12, so that hope for change is kindled.

More than a birth narrative

Chapter 14 is almost always called a 'birth narrative' for its parallels with many others (Abraham and Sarah; Isaac and Rebecca; Jacob, Rachel and Leah; Hannah and Elkanah; Elizabeth and Zechariah; Mary and Joseph). Johnson (2010, p. 272) identifies typical elements as: indication of the woman's barrenness; attempt to obtain children; promise of a son; information about the promised child; parental reaction; conception and birth; naming; and statement of the child's blessing or prosperity. As always, it is where the episode diverges from the 'norm' that most of the meaning resides. Using a type-scene sets up expectations and leads readers to fill in blanks with typical information that may later prove wrong, and enhances suspense and drama. Some typical expectations are fulfilled, such as barrenness and divine intervention. As is often the case, the woman receives the revelation, showing that women's lives are of equal importance to God and that while men may carry the sign of the covenant in their bodies through circumcision, women carry the key to the future of their households (since they are always the ones charged with 'barrenness') and can just as successfully interact with Yahweh over their part in the future of Israel. As Havrelock points out, birth narratives are the place where we see women wrestling with God (2008, p. 157). Given the scarcity of accounts of women's experience of God, birth narratives give precious glimpses of life largely ignored by male narrators and editors. Yet here, Manoah interposes himself between the woman and Yahweh, forcing himself into what is traditionally a female space; it is highly significant that Yahweh's response emphasizes the appropriateness of the earlier announcement, because it undermines the patriarchal assumption that it is men who relate to God and control women's bodies. Manoah and his wife are not said to long for a child or to have prayed for one. It may be a simple omission, or erasure of the women's thoughts, but it is unusual, and suggests that either the couple are at odds with the surrounding culture, or that Yahweh is largely absent and they do not think to cry out.

Unusually, Samson's mother is not named and no direction is given to name the child, feeding into a subtext about names and namelessness and a reversal of expectations about how meaningful names are. The dissonant notes create space for readers to wonder about Samson's destiny. The unusual instructions about the Nazirite status stand out and point to wider meaning. Block (1999, p. 399) argues that the scene is actually a call narrative. This stretches the story too far; a number of similar scenes set up the child to be born as a deliverer or a prophet (Samuel; John the Baptist; Jesus). Block's caution, however, rightly points to the danger of overfocusing on the birth and forgetting call or vocation. Samson is not an answer to individual prayer, but a child being prepared for the role he will later play. The mother's failure to tell the father of his destiny as a deliverer is significant. She focuses on the fact that he will be special, but not on the reason for it. Samson will indeed be blessed, but he will revel in his specialness without linking it to specific responsibilities. By using a type scene, the narrator skilfully manoeuvres readers to expect much, so as to highlight how far Samson fails to fulfil his destiny.

Chapters 14 and 15: The Timnite cycle

14.1–9: What Samson wants, Samson gets

Following the birth narrative, one would expect the story to move to Samson's rise to leadership. Instead, readers get their first glimpse of the man Samson. He 'went down to Timnah', in Philistine territory. The casual tone suggests that this is something Samson does often, without cause for tension or worry. The two nations' lives are closely interwoven, with no obvious friction. The lexical chain around sight continues, as Samson 'saw a daughter of the Philistines'. Just as in Chapter 13, what is seen propels the story forward. Given that the cycle opened with the framework 'the Israelites did what was evil in the eyes of Yahweh', followed by a story where sight brings about revelation, the mention of sight here prompts readers to ask whether Samson will do what is right in the eyes of Yahweh, or in his own. The question underlies much of the Samson narrative and enables the move from the framework refrain to the epilogue refrain of 'every man did what was right in their own eyes'. Instead of seeing the things of God, as his mother did, Samson fixes his eyes on physical things and satisfying his physical appetites. Being lead astray by one's eyes, especially in connection to lust, is a frequent motif in the biblical corpus, whether narratively (e.g. Judah and Tamar, also set in Timnah, also treating a woman wrongly, Gen. 38; Hamor's rape of Dinah, Gen. 34; David and Bathsheba, 2 Sam. 11) or in teaching and parenetic material (Job 31.1; Ps. 101.3; Prov. 6.25). Jesus picks up the theme forcefully in the

Gospels (Matt. 5.27–30), a theme carried through to the epistles (2 Peter 2.14; 1 John 2.16). Narrative texts exploring lust of the eyes do not simply focus on the wrong an individual might do, but on the harm he causes another and how this then threatens Israel's social fabric. Parenetic material is consistent in condemning lust, although, especially in Proverbs, the woman is often cast negatively as a seductress; in contrast, the teaching of Jesus in the Sermon on the Mount challenges any move to blame the object seen, and places responsibility on the seer for controlling their own response. Samson here, lured by his eyes and lust, is starting out on a path unwise at best and at worst dangerous for him and those around him. Samson shows little awareness of Israel's national situation, or of Torah regulations on exomarriage; what he sees and wants, he must get. There is no indication that he has spoken to the young woman, or that there is anything more to his attraction than physical desire (unless, perhaps, as a Philistine she is 'forbidden fruit', hence more attractive). The young woman's wishes are never considered. Samson nods to propriety and wants to marry her, so he orders his parents to get her for him. His speech is abrupt, without the kind of respect Achsah paid her father in chapter 1. Instead he shows impatience, wants things done 'now' (*'attāh*), and uses the imperative, with no modifier to indicate a polite request or 'please' (14.2).

His parents present a united front, encouraging him to seek a suitable match within the kinship system or wider Israel, with a preference for close endomarriage. They sharply delineate between Israel and the Philistines, not based on the commandment not to intermarry, or by appealing to the covenant, or Samson's Nazirite status, but by calling the Philistines 'uncircumcised'. Given that Hebrews were not alone in practising circumcision, the comment goes beyond intermarriage and reflects that the Philistines' cultural difference from other surrounding nations consigned them to the bottom of the social ladder (Block, 1999, p. 425). Their response is therefore right in principle, but ambiguous as to motive. Gideon and Jephthah's father both had intimate contact with women of ambiguous status, but Samson is the first to want a formal union clearly in contravention of Yahweh's instructions. Samson had initially spoken to his parents and they had replied together. Now he turns to his father only and repeats his demand. It suggests he dismisses his mother's contribution much as his father had done, or that Manoah is a softer touch, in continuity with his slower and less perceptive response in chapter 13. Samson lacks respect for his parents and, by extension, for Yahweh and the covenant. He repeats his order, but adds 'for she is right in my eyes'. The word right (*yāšar*) is emptied of any moral content, now solely an outworking of sexual desire. What is right in Samson's eyes is precisely what was decreed evil in the eyes of Yahweh in 3.6–7. Samson is making explicit Israel's slide into deep individualism, as everyone does what is right in their own judgement rather than refer to values and beliefs held by all Israel, and the God of the covenant. The inversion of right and wrong in Israel is almost complete, and taking root within the very person supposed to deliver them.

14.4 switches perspective and the omniscient narrator brings in double causality, by stating that Yahweh was using Samson's misdirected desire as part of Israel's deliverance. The focus is on what Samson's parents did not know, rather than on Samson himself, picking up on the motif of knowledge and ignorance and inviting readers into a divine, rather than human, perspective. The comment does not suggest that Yahweh is using Samson as a puppet for his own ends, but rather, much as with Ehud, human desires and planning can be used and made to dovetail with a God who is completely free to work in whatever way he chooses, even with less-than-ideal human partners. Had Samson been an ideal human partner, he would have taken a lead in resisting the Philistines. As it is, he seeks opportunities to get closer to them and Yahweh finds opportunities to push him to act, even unwittingly, in the right direction. The human–divine partnership is increasingly strained and relies on wider providence rather than the close relationship at work with Deborah or Gideon. The second half of 14.4 chronicles how far Israel has fallen: it is the only time in the book that a foreign nation rules Israel; the verb, *māšal*, is the one used in Israel's offer to Gideon (8.22–23) and Abimelech's negotiations with Shechem (9.2). Israel not only does not have Yahweh as king but is content with being ruled by outsiders to the covenant. Samson, who should be judging rather than ruling Israel, seems oblivious to his people's absorption by the Philistines. There is no hint of Israel's distress or desire for deliverance, so that Yahweh is freely and unilaterally looking for unexpected and marginal ways to preserve his people.

The next episode starts with Samson going to Timnah with his parents, following his demand to marry. He comes across as very young, repeatedly accompanied by both his parents, the wedding a chance to graduate into full adulthood. Given that they are initially together, it is odd that he finds himself alone in a vineyard; 14.8 will clarify that the vineyard represents a detour from the normal route between Zorah and Timnah. Why would Samson, a Nazirite whose vow specifically states he should avoid grapes in all their forms, go to a vineyard? The roaring lion's arrival is dramatized with *hinnēh*, the expression of surprise and emphasis. The lion is young, but still probably dangerous, and focused on Samson: 'See! A young lion, a lion, to meet him.' The use of 'to meet him' applied to an animal, particularly a non-domestic one, is unusual. The lion, unclean to eat, often appears as a quintessential symbol of fear and danger (Prov. 22.13; 26.13; 28.15; Isa. 38.13; Jer. 50.17; 51.38; Lam. 3.10) as well as exemplifying strength, so that fighting a lion was a way to prove valour (1 Sam. 17.34, 36–37; 2 Sam. 1.23; 23.20; 1 Chron. 11.22). The lion's appearance comes as a test of Samson's strength and valour as a man. Yet Samson does not fight the lion alone – Yahweh sends the Spirit to empower him. The Spirit 'rushes' on him, giving a sense of urgency and matching Samson's turbulent nature. As with Jephthah, it is unclear whether Samson is aware of the presence of the Spirit. He will never attribute his victory over the lion to Yahweh, unlike king David, who equally proves his valour by fighting lions yet recognizes Yahweh's part (1 Sam. 17.37). Samson's physicality is consistently ambiguous in value, leading him to weakness and power in equal measure. He has great physical strength, but does not reflect on its provenance or how it should be used.

Slaying the lion brought him into contact with an unclean animal, doubly so as it is now dead. Yet this does not trouble him and he does not follow the purification rituals set out for Nazirites (Num. 6.9–12). Samson does not tell his parents: keeping secrets may give him power; alternatively, or in addition, he may know that he should not have been in the vineyard and that he is ritually unclean. Keeping quiet means that he potentially contaminates them too, showing his disrespect and carelessness towards others. As they get to Timnah, he speaks to the Philistine woman, seemingly for the first time, and 'she was right in his eyes'. The reference to eyes is slightly ironic given that it follows 'talk', reminding the reader that Samson's reaction is primarily about lust, and reinforcing Samson's lack of understanding of right and wrong.

The narrator compresses the narrative and skips several days or weeks to Samson's journey to marry the Philistine woman (14.8). He again makes a detour by the vineyard, where he knows the dead lion lies: he intentionally imperils his Nazirite status in two separate ways, through the grapes and through potential contact with a carcass. Why? Is the lion a trophy he is proud of? Does he want to check it really happened? Is it fascination with death and killing? Readers may expect him to keep his distance and voice his thanks to Yahweh for deliverance. But Samson wants to 'see' the lion. As he approaches, he sees bees and honey. The collective word used for the bees is a 'community' or 'assembly' (*'ēdâ*), a word normally used for the people of Israel. Symbolically, the bees are bringing sweetness out of death and decay, just as Israel are a people or community called to bring light in darkness (Block, 1999, p. 429; Beldman, 2020, p. 164). Samson, however, does not ponder metaphors, nor wonder at the sight. Instead, he is led by his body and chooses to eat the honey out of the unclean carcass of an unclean animal, deliberately breaking covenantal regulations (Lev. 11.24–25, 39 specify that carcasses themselves are unclean and cause uncleanness, and what animals are unclean) and his Nazirite vow. Once again, he shows complete disregard for others as he shares the honey with his parents without acknowledging its provenance. Instead of the deliverer delivering Israel from their (unclean, uncircumcised) enemies the Philistines, Samson the deliverer spreads uncleanness around him.

14.10–20: Wedding, riddle and brawl

Samson's father now takes a lead in arranging the wedding. His mother disappears from the story, a woman with spiritual discernment replaced by a series of increasingly questionable choices of sexual partners for Samson. His move into adulthood, separating from parents, is not portrayed particularly positively. The bride, like his mother, is nameless, 'the woman', the object of Samson's eyes, and a victim of bargaining between the men. While his father is busy, Samson makes a feast, '*mišteh*', a word derived from the root for drinking. Once again, Samson places himself in a situation where he will be tempted to breach Nazirite regulations. He chooses to go with the customs of the young men of Philistia, rather than the deep distinctiveness of his Israelite Nazirite status. He seems to identify much more easily with the practices and people of the Philistines. So far, we have not seen him relate to any other Israelites apart from his parents; as the story progresses, his only such interaction will be an antagonistic one with Judah.

Samson, who sees what he wants and goes for it, is now seen by the people of Timnah, and their seeing leads to 30 'companions/friends' being brought for him. It is unclear who these men are. Are they friends Samson already has among the Philistines? Or are they guards, to keep an eye on him? The verb *lāqaḥ*, means they were 'taken', possibly conscripted for the task, rather than volunteering. Samson cuts a lonely figure, needing the people of Timnah to bring him friends so that he does not stand alone at his own wedding. There is no mention of Israelite guests, so that Samson celebrates with the Philistines, in the style of a Philistine. The Nazirite, supposed to be set aside as holy and distinctive, behaves in ways indistinguishable from that of the surrounding people.

Samson initiates a game with high stakes, not an unusual event at a wedding feast, but he does so unfairly, with an unsolvable riddle. The riddle is based on his encounter with the lion, and the contradiction in terms between eater and food and strong and sweet. A riddle is normally based on logic and can be answered through ingeniosity and wit (Bal, 1988b, p. 6). A riddle is a way of safely acting out power struggles; here, Samson is trying to prove that he has power that exceeds his physical strength and, as a member of an oppressed minority, assert a position of dominance over a subset of the Philistines in a relatively safe context. Since the riddle is not fair, the Philistines do not play fair, and Samson is caught at his own game.

Time indicators in the story are confusing. 14.14 states that on the first three days of the feast the men are trying to work out the riddle. In 14.15, LXX has the men approach the bride on the fourth day, whereas MT has it on the seventh. Given the narrative's uneven use of time and the absence of any indication of when Samson actually set the riddle, either is possible. In 14.17, we are told that the bride cried for seven days, which does not tally with either indicator, if we attribute her crying to the men's threat. It is, however, possible that she was worried about the riddle all along or, indeed, wise enough to be anxious about marrying Samson. Samson's wife is used as a pawn in more negotiations between men. She is caught between two families, two ethnicities, both sides claiming higher loyalty. The men's threat echoes Ephraim's threat to Jephthah, though they do not limit their threat to property but threaten her personally too – and anyone else in her father's house. Their motivation, on the surface, is financial – the stakes of the riddle are high, though much higher for Samson. The bride is made to choose between the family she already knows and loves, and Samson, whom she barely knows and who has so far only treated her as an object of desire. She is the only woman mentioned in the wedding scene, surrounded by men all wanting something from her. Her presence tarnishes the picture of all-male companionship and turns a contest of wits into a real, embodied power struggle. Neither Samson nor the men treat her as a subject or show any empathy. They all use her as a conduit to satisfy their personal desires – for power, sex, or both. The threat to burn her and her house is grimly ironic, as it is precisely in trying to avoid this outcome that she will bring it upon herself in 15.6. The woman portrayed is stereotypical, crying and using emotional blackmail. Samson is initially impervious to his wife's demands and oblivious to her split loyalties and liminality, as she is not fully part of her father's house anymore, but not yet fully part of his. Samson does not seem torn in the way she is; he suggests that his parents come before her, but his reference to his keeping secrets from his parents shows that he is not really torn between parental loyalty and loyalty to his new wife but makes his own decisions and takes his own counsel. In this, his psychological development seems poised between childhood and adulthood, with the self-centredness of adolescence. Loyalties are confused throughout: the men ask her to betray her husband by being loyal to them; she betrays Samson by asking him to be loyal to her; he states his loyalty to his parents is even stronger, yet he has disrespected them by making them ritually unclean and not telling them. His loyalty appears to be only to himself, especially as he caves in, not because he thinks it is right or because he wants to show her love, but because he gets tired of her questions. The verb in 14.17, *ṣôq* (constrain, oppress, distress), is often used for a nation greatly distressed by another's oppression (Deut. 28.53, 55, 57; Job 32.18; Isa. 26.16; 29.2, 7; 51.13; Jer. 19.9; Dan. 9.25). Samson, the deliverer, is not exercised by Israel's situation; instead, he feels oppressed by a woman seeking to save her life and those she loves, a pattern repeated in 16.16. Samson may be physically strong but he is emotionally and ethically weak. The bride overpowers his resistance and he tells her the answer, which she promptly passes on to 'her people'. Clearly, *his* people have not become *her* people yet. This window onto the wedding shows a new aspect of mixed marriages: rather than religious compromise, the text explores the complexity of intermarriage; how it can easily put the most vulnerable partner into a dangerous position so that concerns about intermarriage are not reduced to religious or cultic concerns but widened to their social consequences, particularly when one group is a minority and the other in power. Readers are unexpectedly drawn into sympathy for the young bride, and to the realization that intermarriage can be negative not just for Israel but for powerless Philistines too.

Now they have the answer, the Philistines underscore their triumph by phrasing the answer in the form of a question, implying that it is rather obvious. Of course, the answer is not obvious; an answer to the initial riddle, as well as the Philistines' answer, in the context of a wedding feast would probably be 'love' or the act of love. Samson's replies pick up on the theme of sexuality, with a crass sexual innuendo in 14.18. He accuses them of cheating at the riddle, and simultaneously accuses his wife of cheating on him and the Philistines of sleeping with her. Calling his wife 'my heifer' casts her as his property, primarily a sexual object. Samson reacts with ill grace, shocked at the implication of his loss – a financial loss, but also a loss of honour and face and of his bride's loyalty. He is a sore loser – after all, he had cheated too, but he never acknowledges his own part in his fate. The Spirit rushes on him again, an odd detail at this point if we think of Samson as behaving badly and being in the wrong. It does make sense, however, considering the wider narrative of Yahweh being secretly at work to deliver Israel. Samson is potentially in danger now (as much from himself and the way he may react) so that the Spirit provides protection; more than that, it is part of Yahweh's plan to disrupt the easy accommodation of Israel with the Philistines. It is unclear how much is *directed* by Yahweh, and how much is *used* by Yahweh for his providential purposes, but not condoned. Samson receives the Spirit, but it is Samson who decides what to do with the power it confers. We are not told what the Spirit was meant to do, and Samson does not ask Yahweh for wisdom or direction. The picture of Yahweh therefore is not of an all-powerful deity pulling the strings, but rather of a self-limiting God who makes himself vulnerable by choosing to work with human beings. The very self-limiting of power is what makes it possible to talk about a relationship of love and freedom between Yahweh and Israel.

What Samson chooses to do is to take out his anger on random Philistine men, rather than fight the men who have ostensibly shamed him. In a twisted version of honour, he murders and robs Philistines to repay his debt to the wedding companions. To admit that he could not repay them, or bankrupt his family in trying to do so, would be to admit defeat, a lower position, and bring shame. By committing murder he procures payment and proves his power. The attack on other Philistines widens his personal conflict to an ethnic dimension and drives the ongoing feud of the rest of the story. As Samson not only kills but takes the garments of the dead, he brings himself yet again in contact with dead bodies but shows no concern for his Nazirite status. He then goes back to his parents, as a child after an argument with a friend, with a note from the narrator, 'in hot/burning anger'. Anger can be a righteous emotion in the face of injustice, but here, linked to Samson's humiliation through his own foolishness, it ties in with consistent warnings about anger leading to sin (Job 5.2; Ps. 37.8; Prov. 12.16; 14.29; 14.17; 15.18; 19.11; 22.24–25; 29.11, 22; Eccles. 7.9). In wisdom literature, human anger is often associated with foolishness, especially when anger is quick and leads to immediate action. As Jephthah was foolish with respect to speech, so Samson is foolish with respect to anger.

Meanwhile, Samson's 'woman' (it is unclear whether she was formally his wife, since the feast had not ended; the Hebrew word could mean either) is used in the affairs of men again and given, without agency, to 'Samson's friend'. The word friend is the one used for the 30 Philistine young men in 14.11, and he is therefore unlikely to be a 'friend'; giving one of them his wife is a calculated insult, telling Samson he does not belong with the Philistines and that he has not just lost a riddle, but lost his status among them.

15.1–8: The foxes and the hound

Chapter 15 continues the story of Samson's attempted marriage, as he tries to patch things up. An unspecified length of time has elapsed but there is no sense of urgency. The detail of the wheat harvest will be relevant in the latter part of the episode as Samson sets fire to the fields about to be harvested. He takes a young goat with him, presumably as a peace offering, a gift to pacify her and her family. The only other times a goat was offered to another in Judges, the 'other' was the angel of Yahweh and the goat was sacrificed to Yahweh (Gideon and Manoah). Samson, in contrast, offers a kid to his wife and father-in-law, with no mention of Yahweh. Once again, Samson comes across as naive and immature – a gift can hardly compensate for his behaviour. The scene portrays his remarried wife staying in her father's house, indicating a patrilocal rather than virilocal marriage. Samson intends to go to his wife's room, implying a sexual motive for the visit consistent with his treatment of her so far, but also suggesting that he had embraced the concept of patrilocal marriage in another sign of accommodation (there is no evidence of patrilocal customs in Israel). He makes no apology to her father and does not say he wants to speak to her. Samson does not consider her safety or the impact of his actions upon her. He intends to pick up the relationship where he left off, and thinks he is fully married, hence the woman is still available. It is unclear from either the text or ethnographic material at what point a couple would be considered officially married, and whether customs differed between Israel and Philistia. The woman is therefore trapped again in a liminal state, disputed by those around her. Her father stands up to Samson, showing considerable courage, and tries to reason with him; first, by reminding him of his actions; second, by offering a substitute, his younger daughter, which could be considered an insult and of less value. The man is attempting to bargain using women at his disposal. The scene foreshadows the horror of chapter 19, when a young woman is discarded by her husband, offered as bargaining chip and brutalized by local men and used as a pretext for war. The events of Samson prepare the reader for what is to come; just as women were not safe in Philistia, so Israel will follow suit. Samson once again widens the scope of his personal quarrel and makes threats towards all Philistines (16.3). He consistently escalates quarrels and blames others for the violence that ensues. Samson plans vengeance, which he considers to be proportionate and reasonable. In his mind it is justice, and he administers it. The escalation of the violence, and its ultimate consequences, causes readers to question again what 'justice' is, and how it may be decided upon. Samson intends to do 'evil' (*rāʿâ*) to the Philistines. The word echoes the framework 'doing evil in the eyes of Yahweh', and stands in opposition to what is right; but of course Samson decides for himself what is right (*yāšar*) as he did in 14.3. Samson is again making himself judge of what is right or wrong, good and evil, without reference to Yahweh. Doing evil to the Philistines is what he implies is right for him to do at the moment; ironically, it may serve Yahweh's purposes, but Samson is doing the right thing for the wrong reasons, which underscores the irony of the entire passage and the depth of God's providence for Israel.

Samson is resourceful in his revenge and uses unclean wild animals to wreak havoc on the Philistines' crops. Catching 300 foxes looks like a typical exaggeration of epic literature but implies purposeful, planned action, unlike his hot anger of the previous chapter. The foxes' rampage across the fields echoes the Midianites' oppression of Israel in chapter 6, destroying what makes life possible. The year's wheat crop would have been lost, but with the destruction of vineyards and olive groves it is years, if not decades, of work that are lost. Just like the Midianites, Samson attacks ordinary people and destroys their livelihood, so that the entire land is affected through the destruction of its produce and its animals. Samson seems to sow death in his wake wherever he goes. There is no mention of the Spirit of Yahweh in this sequence, and Samson is portrayed in the way foreign oppressors have previously been portrayed. Previous judges went after the leaders of oppressive nations and fought their invading armies. Here, Samson never seems to care about attacking leaders who ultimately are responsible for oppression, but simply undermines from below a nation's ability to survive, for purely personal reasons. Nor does he follow this attack by leading an army to challenge the Philistines, thereby opening up the possibility of reprisals for his selfish actions against Israel as a whole. He is much more similar to Abimelech than to other judges. The psychological portrait of Samson is fascinating and believable: a man-child, impulsive, without control over his emotions, unable to consider others' feelings and oblivious to the consequences of his actions. The addition of cruelty to animals and playing with fire adds two details consistently picked up today as signs of deep psychological disturbance. While ancient authors did not use contemporary psychological categories, they nevertheless accurately observed patterns of behaviour, and the pattern here suggests that Samson is increasingly likely to behave in unstable and violent ways. And yet ... Yahweh is still able to work to deliver Israel, not casting Samson away because of his struggles.

15.6 is chilling in its terseness. The cycle of revenge takes its course, escalating from damage to the earth to the burning of Samson's wife and her father. It had all started with Samson's provocative riddle, leading the men to threaten the young woman. The threat is now actualized, even though she had given in to them. Their use of fire matches Samson's, reminding readers of the nameless young woman murdered in the previous cycle in a burnt offering. Israel and Canaan mirror one another in how they treat young women. Her father is also killed, like many other men as part of the cycle of revenge in the Samson saga. By attacking the woman, the Philistines are attacking Samson, who still regards her as his property, and his honour, since he is unable to protect her and therefore fails as a head of household. Samson had killed random Philistines in 14.19, rather than confronting the young men at the wedding; the Philistines kill Samson's wife and family, rather than confronting Samson himself. In a world where characters decide on what is right and wrong for themselves, human lives are increasingly expendable in support of the powerful.

15.7 gives a glimpse of Samson's thought processes. In 14.19, he had considered that attacking strangers to procure what he needed to repay his debt was sufficient. In 15.3 he decides to do evil to the Philistines and considers that he will be blameless for it, as if destroying the crops of dozens of families was an equivalent to the loss of his wife to another man. Now here, he sets himself a revenge target that he again sees as justified in response to the Philistines' murder of his wife (though there is no mention of his mourning her). He is working with an idea of proportionality, given that he wants to take revenge, and then stops. How the proportionality is worked out is unclear, and given the level of escalation so far readers are left to wonder at his – and the Philistines' – idea of retribution. Samson bases his own actions on the Philistines': 'if this is what you do, then I will take revenge, then I will stop' (my translation). Samson does not consult Yahweh, or cast his own actions in covenantal terms. He defines his sense of justice with respect to non-Israelite conduct, with a sentence constructed as a grammatical parallel between two clauses each introduced by 'if' (*'im*). The verb Samson uses for taking revenge is *nāqam*, the same word Jephthah's daughter had used to describe her father's war on the Ammonites. Samson, however, is not fighting an external threat on behalf of Israel, but taking revenge for himself. The notion of justice implied in the root *nqm* is problematized even further than it had been with Jephthah: is this justice, revenge, or a feud? Webb argues that the root here refers to the 'principle of justice recognized in Genesis 9.5–6, and given formal expression in the law of Moses' (2012, p. 379) and Samson deciding what is reasonable and when to stop is a sign of considered thinking and maturity. I find this argument rather dubious. The law of Moses does not permit escalating violence in revenge, but seeks to limit it through the *lex talionis*. If the maximum prescription in law is 'an eye for an eye', then Samson's campaign against the Philistines vastly exceeds what is permitted. Samson's thoughts are also deeply naive. Nothing has stopped the escalating cycle of violence so far; the point of the law of Moses is to interpose a third party as referee in a dispute, so that the penalty is constituted as justice and does not incur revenge. What Samson does is bypass justice and engage in revenge, which will inevitably cause the Philistines to retaliate. Besides, Samson's own actions started the cycle; justice would have to be served against him. Samson has shown a complete inability to control his urges, whether for sex or violence, and the assertion that he will stop is not entirely believable. Samson has not actually set a specific definition for what would be 'enough', so how would he, or the readers, know when the limit has been reached? Finally, his statement may not reflect justice achieved but his desire to have the final word and hold the position of power at the end of the altercation. The Timnite cycle exposes the futility of thinking that it is possible to end violence with one more act of violence. The only possibility for an end to the cycle is likely to rest not in justice or revenge, but mercy, since each side's justice will always form the other's grievance.

Samson carries out his killing mission. The expression 'he struck them down hip and thigh' conveys with an image what the rest of the verse states, 'a great slaughter'. The number of dead is undefined, but likely greater than in his last killing spree (30). The indeterminacy undermines the notion of proportional justice evoked in the previous verse. The indeterminacy also applies to the identity of the victims: Samson does not seek out the men responsible for his wife's death. The Spirit of Yahweh is nowhere mentioned: Samson's strength may still be God-given, but there is no sense of special endowment or divine direction. Samson now flees and hides in caves, a typical image of a runaway. In the time of Gideon, the Israelites hid in caves because of Midianite oppression. Here, it is self-inflicted. In chapter 21, the Benjaminites will have to live in caves because Israel turned against them.

15.9–17: Battle at Lehi

Violence now broadens to wider Israel as other Israelites are mentioned for the first time, and with them the possibility of Samson finally stepping up as deliverer. The Philistines now take the initiative in the cycle of revenge, though their focus is Samson alone. The Philistines display a stronger notion of proportionality and justice than Samson and de-escalate the conflict by focusing on its source. They deploy their troops in Judah, so a new tribe is affected. Whenever foreign troops have 'encamped' in Israel before, the people cried out to Yahweh so that a leader could be raised. This time, the pattern is broken because neither Judah nor the deliverer are interested. Judah's question, 'Why have you come up against us?', could potentially lead to dialogue similar to Jephthah's with the king of Ammon, starting with 'What is there between you and me?' The Philistines' reply shows that they have no interest in Judah but are focused on Samson only. The logic of retribution in their answer in 15.10, 'to do to him as he did to us', echoes Samson's 'if this is what you do ...' in 15.7, and will be repeated by Samson in 15.11, 'as they did to me, I have done to them', which reveals a shared ethical framework based on retribution and violence, failing to see each side as an agent with the power to change course. Each side sees its actions as necessary and legitimate, and neither refers to a wider framework of meaning or the impact of conflict on wider communities. This highly individualistic outlook feeds into the impossibility of leadership for Samson. If he only considers his own desires, welfare and battles, and Israel frame their life in terms of personal needs, it is difficult to see how they can come together under one legitimate leader for the sake of the entire nation. Their shared ethic with the Philistines undermines Israel's distinctiveness and therefore its need for deliverance.

The men of Judah show no desire to protect another Israelite; their motivation in handing over Samson is not justice but self-preservation. They are afraid of the Philistines, accept the status quo and resent Samson for risking it. Their wording picks up on Samson's and the Philistines' 'What then have you done to us?' (15.11). The dialogue is marked by reflectivity and concern for what the other has done to the self. Samson shows no empathy or concern for Israel as a whole; it is his revenge that matters, regardless of consequences. He continues the trend of leaders failing to love Israel as Yahweh does and using power for their own ends rather than the common good. Despite his lofty beginning, Samson is failing. Even Israel does not treat him as kin but as the enemy. Samson does not treat them as kin either and makes their lives harder rather than leading them to freedom. There is no sense in which Samson is perceived or recognized as either a leader or deliverer. 15.12–13 is heavy with irony, as twice the men of Judah say that they will bind Samson and give him into the hands of the Philistines, a reversal of the usual motif: normally, Yahweh gives the enemy into the hands of the deliverer. Here, Judah gives the deliverer into the hands of the enemy. The irony deepens the gap between human and divine perspectives, which then underscores the motif of gracious divine providence over against sinful human action. Samson's negotiations show that though he does not want to fight fellow-Israelites, he nevertheless does not trust them. The binding motif foreshadows chapter 16. Samson has not yet emerged as an invincible man of strength. He has accomplished great feats, but it is unclear whether he could overpower the men of Judah and whether the ropes would truly bind him. Once he does, the stage is set for his increasing recklessness and belief in invincibility. His choice not to fight Judah may be a surprising sign of new self-restraint, an acknowledgement of kinship, or simply a ploy to take the Philistines by surprise. Samson's negotiation with Judah had been an opportunity: he could have used it to cast a vision for freedom, rally troops and take a lead in delivering Israel. Instead, he chose to reaffirm his right to vengeance and disregard for other Israelites.

Samson, with the troops guarding rather than following him, meets the Philistines. Now Yahweh intervenes through the giving of the Spirit; with the same urgency as before, 'the Spirit rushed on him'. The exact action of the Spirit is unclear: is the Spirit mostly in the fire that melts the bonds, or is it empowering Samson himself? The positive use of fire here, melting bonds, freeing Samson without hurting him, contrasts with Samson's and the Philistines' own use of fire. Symbolically, the action of Yahweh is highly significant, reminding Israel that he is the God who delivers those who are bound: that is his nature and how Israel most consistently remember him – the God 'who brought you out of Egypt'. The giving of the Spirit in the presence of enemy troops normally signals anointing for battle as Yahweh blesses the leader's endeavours. Here, Judah stay behind and are never mentioned again. Yahweh will give the enemy into the hand of Samson to deliver Israel, but neither Samson nor Judah frame the events in these terms. In Lehi, a place whose name means 'jawbone', Samson providentially finds the jawbone of a donkey (15.15). The narrator notes that the jawbone was fresh, which would make it stronger but highlights that it therefore belongs to the category of carcass and Samson, a Nazirite, should refrain from touching it. Samson, attracted to death and decay, does not stop to think and picks it up to use as a weapon. Does the man empowered by the Spirit who tore a lion apart with his bare hands (14.6) need the bone to fight the Philistines? Every time Samson faces a test of his Nazirite status, he fails. The battle report has typically large numbers, as always in Judges, enhancing the mystique of the character and consistent with epic literature. The report is followed by a song, but this is no song to Yahweh. Samson makes up a witty ditty, in the style of his earlier riddle. In the wake of a massacre, surrounded by dead bodies, Samson is experimenting with words, playing with homonyms: the word for 'heap' is the same as for 'donkey' (*ḥămôr*), so that he sings of turning the Philistines simultaneously into a heap of dead bodies and a heap of male asses. Samson takes complete credit for the victory, 'I have slain a thousand men'. There is no sharing of glory with Yahweh, no acknowledgement of divine empowerment, and no setting of victory into theological context for new generations to be formed in the ways of Yahweh, as with the song of Deborah. Samson seeks to go down in history on his own merits, alone and separated from either human or divine help.

15.18–20: Samson prays

In keeping with Samson's character, the next episode is prompted by his physical need, this time thirst. Physical need prompts him to utter the first prayer he offers, though it may be closer to tantrum than prayer. It is the first proactive calling on Yahweh in the cycle, but not phrased as a polite request. In battle, Samson would have touched many dead bodies as well as the jawbone, yet he does not acknowledge his unclean status, in sharp contrast to his father's fear at the angel of Yahweh. Samson's tone is closer to that he used with his parents in 14.2–3 rather than that of a supplicant or grateful warrior after a miraculous victory. He does start by acknowledging that Yahweh had a part in his success, 'you gave in/by the hand of your servant this great deliverance'. This is an improvement on his earlier ditty and shows that he is at least familiar with the conventions of prayer. He describes himself as 'your servant': it is unclear whether this is more than an honorific form of address, given that Samson has not proactively tried to serve Yahweh so far but rather sought to fulfil his own desires – as he is now. He talks of the battle as 'deliverance' but this is disconnected from Israel or his own role as deliverer. Rather, he is focused on himself and his own deliverance from enemy hands. Readers, however, know that Yahweh is at work to deliver Israel. Just as with Jephthah, it is unclear how far Samson's god-speech arises out of lived faith and covenantal understanding, or out of cultural traditions that he is struggling to appropriate for the present. The second half of his 'prayer' accuses Yahweh of being ridiculous in delivering him but then letting him die of thirst. There is a certain amount of exaggeration and petulance in his statement: he has not precisely been wandering in the desert, as in other passages of miraculous provision of water. His words sound closer to emotional blackmail than a lament or cry to Yahweh for help. They betray a feeling of entitlement in Samson, that after he has battled and won he should be looked after physically, as if victory was not enough and he had been blameless throughout the conflict. His description of the Philistines as 'uncircumcised' rings hollow, given his own disregard for his Nazirite status and his dismissal of his parents' concern about him marrying a Philistine, expressed in precisely these terms (14.3). The description therefore seems to be more of an ethnic slur than a reflection of covenantal identity and points to the arrogant exceptionalism that shapes his self-perception. The turning of the covenant into a sign of exceptionalism rather than grace and an appropriation of blessing for the few rather than blessing for the nations is a recurrent misunderstanding and a perversion of Yahweh's promise to Abraham. Israel's destiny is to be a blessing to others, refracting the divine presence and enabling other nations to see Yahweh at work (see Gen. 12.2–3; 18.18; 22.18; Micah 4.1–7; Isa. 2.2–4), in line with the countermovement of foreigners being incorporated into the covenant. As an individual, Samson sees deliverance as his personal gain rather than a calling on behalf of Israel, just as Israel sees deliverance in terms of their own political freedom rather than a calling to bless all nations.

Samson asks for water, as if he were another Moses. Moses, however, had asked for water for the people he led, rather than for himself (Ex. 17.6; Num. 20.10–13). Yahweh responds with the same patience as he had with Gideon's recurrent doubts or the people's hardness of heart in the desert. Yahweh is the God who brings water out of the rock, life out of wilderness and death, whose character is displayed despite Samson's inadequacy. Yahweh's response, a typical wilderness miracle, leads to Samson's 'spirit' returning once he is no longer in need, Yahweh disappears from his sight. Samson names the spring En-hakkore, spring 'of the caller'. When Yahweh had provided water for all Israel in the wilderness, the springs were named Massah and Meribah (test and strife) in witness to their grumbling and lack of faith. The name of Samson's new spring memorializes the one who called, as if the most important, but does not acknowledge Yahweh's response, and certainly not Samson's own impatience towards Yahweh. 15.20 returns to the framework with the length of Samson's judging, though his judging is not marked primarily in relation to Israel, but against the presence of the Philistines, drawing attention to the fact that he had only begun to deliver. The nature of Samson's 'judging' is unclear; there is no indication that anyone in Israel ever recognized him as a leader, nor that he sought to lead. His actions have not followed the deliverer pattern; though he may have helped prevent the Philistines from encroaching upon Israelite life to a greater degree, he never drove them out. Previously, the framework elements reflected the joint action of Yahweh and his human partner; now, the partnership is almost sundered and the reach of Yahweh's action is limited by the character and unwillingness of the deliverer. Yahweh persists in working for his people, even when they least deserve it. The framework is not quite complete; as there is no notice of death, but the story continues, readers expect a death story to follow.

By the end of the Timnite cycle, Samson is alone in the desert, with no wife, no children, no friends, no kin. The desert in OT symbolism is a place of testing, of purification, where character is laid bare and idols shattered. Samson did turn to Yahweh in the desert, for the first time; but he does not stay there or learn from it. The desert is a tipping point. Until now, Samson had been getting increasingly stronger and aggressive; from now on, he will grow increasingly weaker, yet in weakness he will in the end achieve more than at any other time. At this apex point, Samson has not yet learnt war in the way of Yahweh; he claims victory for himself and confuses Yahweh's power with his own. Out of all the judges, Samson, the last, seems to know the least. The second part of the cycle will focus on Samson's harsh realization that his strength was never his own.

16: The Gazite cycle

16.1–3: The Gazite prostitute

The narrative moves geographically from Timnah to Gaza. This new set of stories begins in a similar way; Samson had gone down to Timnah for no obvious reason, and seen a Philistine woman (14.1). In 16.1, he goes to Gaza for no obvious reason, and sees a Philistine prostitute. It appears nothing has changed: Samson still roams the country, attracted to Philistine areas, is still led by his eyes, making no effort to restrain his lust. This time, the woman is a prostitute or loose woman (as with Jephthah's mother, the term could refer to either a sex worker or a woman living in ways not sanctioned by the patriarchal framework that controlled women's sexuality). He no longer strives for 'respectable' relationships and his association with a woman who is both foreign and described as morally questionable moves him further away from the covenantal notions of cleanness and purity associated with Nazirites. Visiting prostitutes is another sign of foolishness in wisdom literature (Prov. 6.26; 7.10; 23.27), continuing the portrayal of Samson as failing to show wisdom or maturity. There is no specific time marker following the length of Samson's judgeship, so that this may be 20 years later, or just shortly after Lehi. The effect, however, is to suggest that Samson never really grows up, or moves out of adolescent impulsiveness, not learning from the past. The Philistines still fear him and it becomes clear that they have a sustained focus on Samson, while Samson himself is oblivious and gets distracted by his eyes. His trespassing into Philistine territory is reported immediately and an ambush is laid, men encircling the house, hoping for the element of surprise. It is easy to see an Israelite storyteller delighting in the story, showing how clever the Philistines think they are, only to find that it is Samson, the Israelite hero, who surprises them by rising half-way through the night. In a time without artificial light, it would have been unusual, and reckless, to leave the safety of a house and journey in the dark. The ambush is set at the gates of the city; Canaanite city gates usually had six guardposts, three on each side, with a passage leading to the gate, making it impossible to pass undetected (Webb, 2012, p. 395). Samson would have had to fight guards and ambushers, albeit in darkness or simple torchlight. The idea that he could simply pick up the city gates and carry them all the way up a hill at a fair distance is extraordinary, and begs some questions (beyond the miraculous element). There is no mention of the Spirit, but Samson's strength is still probably supernatural. Does this mean it is linked to his Nazirite status, or simply inherent, rather than to the empowering of the Spirit? Is the Spirit not mentioned because Samson is oblivious to its presence, or because it is absent? How much of Samson's strength is innate, and how much conferred by the Spirit at specific times? If his strength is God-given, he grossly misuses an attribute meant for deliverance for his own ends. Samson does not seem to ask himself questions, but as the narrative develops the source, nature and purpose of his strength will become increasingly central to the plot.

Removing the gates is a powerful symbol at multiple levels. First, it takes away the safety of the city and enables Samson to prove himself superior to the Philistines by a considerable margin. Simply fighting his way out would not have made quite the same point. Setting them at the top of the hill is a reminder to the Philistines that he is alive and fighting. Second, it reinforces the portrayal of Samson as turning life into death, civilized places into ruin. He turned fields and crops to ashes: now he destroys part of the city. Finally, gates have special symbolism – they enable passage from one state to another and serve as boundaries. Samson has been transgressing barriers and smashing boundaries his entire life: between Israel and Philistia, between nature and civilization, between clean and unclean. As a Nazirite, his life is supposed to be ruled by boundaries that set him apart as holy. Yet his entire story has focused on ignoring or crossing the boundaries set for him.

16.4–22: Samson and Delilah

Two narrative arcs now converge: Samson seeking out Philistine women and the Philistines going after Samson. The introduction of a new woman breaks the pattern so far. Samson does not 'see' her first. Instead, he 'loved a woman'. It is highly unusual for a man to be said to love a woman in the Hebrew Bible; this is one of only three instances outside of the Song of Songs, the other two in 1 Samuel 18.20, 28. What Samson considered to be love is unclear, but the use of the term contrasts sharply with the pure lust of previous encounters; as the narrative develops it is clear they have some sort of ongoing relationship. The narrator is signalling a qualitatively different relationship and this difference will enhance the pathos of the betrayal (as opposed to Samson's bride, whom he barely knew). Like Manoah in 13.2, the woman's introduction is conducted in the reverse order to convention: first, 'a woman', then geography, finally name, but without family ties. She is from the valley of Sorek, on the boundary between Israel and Philistia, and her ethnicity is not specified. 'Sorek' was the name of a choice wine grape, an area known for its vineyards (Klein, 1993, p. 61), hence a hint about Samson's ongoing disregard for his Nazirite status. Her name, Delilah, is of indeterminate origin. It could be Philistine, drawing on the Arabic cognate for 'flirting' (Block, 1999, p. 454), but could just as easily be based on the Hebrew for night, drawing a contrast between light (Samson, little sun) and dark. Delilah is ambiguous and ultimately as unknown to the reader as she is to Samson. Her motives are never explained. No filiation is recorded, she stands alone, with no family, no ethnicity, no man looking after her, and she looks after her own well-being. In this respect, she is the opposite of Achsah, whose story had set an idealized picture of healthy relationships within the culture of the time, embedded into protective, reciprocal, thick networks of kinship. Everything about Delilah is different, designed to prompt questions. The undecidability of her ethnicity works as a deliberate narrative ploy, first to enable suspense, second to parallel Judah's rejection of Samson. If she is Israelite, her actions are more reprehensible and provide a deeper commentary on Samson's judgeship. If she is a Philistine, then Samson's own proclivity for forbidden relationships is the root of his downfall. If it is not possible to know, then her character reflects how far Israel has become indistinguishable from the surrounding nations.

The Philistines are still after Samson, with a difference. Now it is 'the lords of the Philistines'. The conflict has escalated from guerrilla warfare between Samson and locals to an official bounty placed on his head by the ruling class. They have learnt that they cannot overpower Samson through brute strength, so they exploit his weakest point, his relationship to women. They use their considerable economic power to achieve their ends and offer Delilah an exorbitant sum in exchange for the key to defeating Samson (1,100 shekels per governor, three times the weight of the gold taken by Gideon; in Ex. 21.32 it costs 30 shekels to redeem a slave). Unlike the men at the wedding, they make no threats. Delilah is not an impressionable young girl and her lack of kinship and community ties make her more difficult to blackmail. Instead, they offer what is most valuable to a lone woman in a patriarchal society: financial independence and security. Delilah is expected to use her sexual power to get Samson to yield his secret. The wording of the lords' request turns the table on Samson: they ask her to 'open' him so that she can 'see' what makes his strength great. Samson used to 'see' women and take them; now Delilah will 'see' him so that others can take him. Delilah shows no obvious reluctance to take part in the plot and no hint of any feelings towards Samson.

Delilah has often been portrayed as deceitful, but she is remarkably straightforward in her dialogue with Samson. In her first attempt (16.6–9), she simply asks him what his secret is and how he can be bound, with no coaxing or deception, relying solely on the power of his love for her and the safety of an intimate context. We are never told she loves him or makes him think that she does, and there is no record of a pledge or commitment between them. Samson appears to understand exactly what she is asking in 16.7 – 'if they bind me'. Presumably, 'they' is the Philistines, the men that are after his life. If Samson understands what lies beneath her question then he is the architect of his own downfall. She is the first woman he loves; if she is as unique in his life as the narrator implies, sharing his secret with her would be a proof of his love, growing into new intimacy, a chance for Samson, who counts on himself alone, to grow up and learn interdependence. His immaturity and impulsiveness, however, have made him reach for the wrong person to share with. Asking for his secret is also an invitation to play with fire; Samson loves danger and provocation, so that he and Delilah may be playing a dangerous game together which he finds arousing. Unlike in the wedding scene, he does not refuse to answer, but lies. Speech has never been his way to power, and it is obvious that the lie cannot hold. Samson's words may betray his longing for a different life. First, he tells her he should be bound with 'undried sinews' (i.e. from a freshly killed animal), something which would again make him unclean and negate his Nazirite status. Then he would become 'like another man'. His words work at two levels. As a lie, he says that being bound in this way would make him no stronger than other men. But as a truth, the removal of his Nazirite status would make him like other men. Samson's failure is not to connect the two more closely or understand that the outward signs of his Nazirite status are merely signs of a deeper reality. Delilah and the Philistines appear to have set a better trap than others, so that none of them are killed by an enraged Samson. Delilah binds him and tests whether the bonds will hold, thereby revealing to Samson that she meant to use the knowledge he shared; yet, given that no Philistines were seen, it could still have been an elaborate sex/bondage game.

Delilah makes two more attempts, constructed in parallel with the first. Now she uses emotional talk: he is not taking her seriously by deceiving her, an ironic statement given her own behaviour. Their relationship is not based on truth or honesty, it is only a pastiche of real intimacy. The incidents proceed predictably, a predictability that suggests that either Samson is a bit dim, or he is enjoying an elaborate power game. Delilah plays on the stereotype of women in a patriarchal society, wheedling and coaxing, using emotional blackmail and sexuality. It is precisely because she does not fit the stereotype but uses it for her own ends that she is dangerous and powerful. She uses the weapons of patriarchy and male ego against them. Every time, Samson's answers point to external objects as able to master him, in traditional magical thinking. Samson's lack of reference to Yahweh in earlier episodes creates doubt as to whether he understands the source of his power, or whether he sees it as a given, something he possesses by nature. Delilah and the Philistines' easy acceptance suggests that this type of magical thinking is widely known and accepted. The third interaction, in 16.13–14, comes closer to Samson sharing his understanding of himself, with a mention of his hair. The readers expect Samson to eventually give in, as in the wedding episode when he gave in to a woman he was never said to love. This scene also harks back to Jael and her peg; Samson the hero is caught in a domestic, womanly space. Put to sleep by a woman who then takes a pin from the loom (the language in unclear, but the word for 'pin' is the same as Jael's peg, *yātēr*). Readers familiar with the earlier story will inevitably wonder whether Delilah will now drive the peg through his skull. Delilah does not, although presumably she could have done. Why not? Delilah could have killed Samson any time he was asleep on her lap, without having to resort to the elaborate plan to find out his secret. Her motives are never revealed. She may have been unwilling to deal the final blow. The Philistines may have wanted him alive, so that they could humiliate him. She remains shrouded in mystery, faithful to the night implied in her name.

Samson finally gives in in 16.16, after Delilah wears down his resistance in the same way his wife had done at the wedding. Until now, she had accused him of 'mocking her', and simply asked for his secret. In this final episode, she plays on his love for her and links the sharing of his deepest secret with the truth of his love. 16.16 picks up the language of 14.17, Delilah 'oppressing' (*ṣûq*) him for several days. Little has changed since then: Samson is still lured by women, still feels oppressed by them yet is oblivious to the Philistines. While the description is reminiscent of his wife, Delilah is a much more confident, powerful figure, in control of the process. Samson's feelings in 16.16 are hyperbolic – his soul/life is 'wearied to death'; questions from his lover bring him to a similar state as his fight with the Philistines at Lehi! Grim irony underlies the narration, as it is Samson's capitulation to being 'wearied to death' that will lead him to his physical death, much as his wife's yielding to the blackmail of the Philistines eventually led to the outcome she was seeking to avoid. Delilah had told him that his heart was not with her in 16.15, and now Samson tells her 'his whole heart' (16.17). The heart in Hebrew is not primarily the seat of emotion, but the noetic centre of the self, the place for thinking, rationality, volition. Delilah therefore accuses him of knowingly and voluntarily failing to love her – perhaps implying that while he lusted after her, he had not given the whole of his person. Now Samson does give her everything, that is, his best reasonable explanation for his strength. He tells her the truth as he sees it, but it is not the truth as the narrator has told it. He does acknowledge his Nazirite status, but not in terms of holiness, commitment and relationship to Yahweh, or as a calling. Instead, he treats it as something he possesses, rooted in his own body – his hair. He does not use the covenantal name, but simply says he has been a Nazirite to God (Elohim), treating his strength as a permanent gift rather than the ongoing activity of Yahweh in his life. The association of the gift with his hair makes his status paradoxically fragile: if his strength is in his body, rather than in a relationship with Yahweh, it can be easily taken away. It is significant that Samson goes to his hair, and his body, as his imagined source of strength. It is the only part of his Nazirite status that he has not violated so far. It is unclear whether his words are another symptom of magical thinking, or whether, because he has broken every other Nazirite rule, he does not think that breaking this one would result in negative consequences. Either way, he seems to think himself invincible.

In response to Delilah's first two questions, Samson had told her that telling her his secret would make him 'like another man' (16.7, 11); it was the essence of the Nazarite status that it made its bearer 'other', in reflection of Yahweh's otherness. To become like an 'other' man, for Samson, would be to rejoin the ranks of ordinary Israelites. In the third exchange (16.13), there is no mention of other men in MT, though LXX restores the parallel. The omission is significant: as Samson comes closer to the truth, he is more reluctant, perhaps afraid of what being like any other would be. In the fourth and final exchange, Samson ends with a variation on his statement, 'I will be like all other men'. Otherness is not something that Samson had desired or cherished in terms of his Nazirite status. His dalliances with Philistine women suggest that he was magnetically attracted to the life of all men as he saw them, rather than the life of holiness he had been called to – just as Israel preferred to cohabit with and imitate the surrounding nations rather than embody the distinctiveness of the covenant. We are not privy to Samson's thought processes. He may be stupid and arrogant and think his strength will never leave him. But he may also think that in breaking the final Nazirite command he will finally have a chance at normality, however naive that thought may be. Samson does not realize that he had been moving away from Yahweh for most of his life, but Yahweh had stayed with him out of mercy and faithfulness towards Israel. Instead, he enjoyed and misused the power entrusted to him. As an immature leader, Samson never considered that power comes with ties and responsibilities, and that to ignore these usually leads to an eventual loss of power. His hair was the symbol not of his commitment – after all he never made a vow, he was given his Nazirite status – but the symbol of Yahweh's commitment to saving Israel. As the symbol goes, readers are left with the question, will Yahweh still save?

Delilah now 'sees that he has told her his whole heart'; the man who saw is now seen fully by another and his being known makes him weaker and more vulnerable than ever. The narrator does not explain how Delilah knows he has been truthful; she may have picked up the difference in his pattern of speech and manner; she may be Jewish, or familiar with Hebrew traditions, and know about Nazirite vows. Delilah this time does not call 'men' but the 'lords of the Philistines', and collects payment before Samson is taken. The bargain was about the secret of his strength, but Philistine warriors make the actual capture. However, the strong, powerful man is depicted in ways that do not show him as dangerous, falling asleep on Delilah and not even waking up when another man shaves his head. His braids were the last vestige of his Nazirite identity. He had let go of anything distinctively linking him to Yahweh. Symbolically, giving Delilah what he thought was the secret of his strength was a complete rejection of his calling as deliverer, a choice to walk away from Yahweh. It is his forsaking of Yahweh, symbolized in the cutting of the hair, that causes the loss of his strength. Delilah is the active subject of the verbs in the sentence: she got him to sleep, she called a man, and she 'began to afflict/humiliate him'. The use of *'ānah* in the *Piel* is intriguing; as the story progresses it will become clear that the Philistines want to humiliate Samson, and Delilah here begins the process. The semantic range of the verb includes active affliction or torment and is consistently used in biblical rape narratives (Gen. 34.2, 13; Judg. 19.24; 2 Sam. 13.12, 14, 22, 32). In a scene similar to Jael overpowering Sisera, Samson is presented as a warrior overpowered by a woman and, symbolically, feminized, as his strength, a key to his masculinity, leaves his body. The Jael scene is now reversed: Jael had lured the enemy general to sleep to hand him over to the deliverer of Israel. Delilah has lured the deliverer of Israel to sleep to hand him over to the enemy. Israel's position in the Promised Land has been completely reversed. The scene proceeds along the pattern set in 16.6–14, and Delilah wakes him in the same way. Why wake him? The Philistines could have killed him while asleep; it seems that they wanted to capture him alive and get credit for the capture. Readers are told that Samson's strength has gone, but Samson does not know. The dramatic irony enhances suspense, but also draws attention to how little Samson understands the ways of Yahweh. It seems he did not really think his hair was linked to his strength, but that his strength was inherent. The narrator's comment, 'for he did not know Yahweh had left him', makes clear that this was never about hair. Samson's power lay in the presence of Yahweh. Samson was so spiritually insensitive that he did not sense a change, nor did he understand that ultimately his consistent breaking of the covenant and moving away from Yahweh would result in the withdrawal of divine presence, so he would be left weak, like any other man, just as Israel had moved away and was left weak like any other nation.

Samson is taken (16.21) but not killed: the Philistines' hubris and thirst for revenge will ironically be their downfall too. They torture and humiliate Samson: they gouge out the eyes that had consistently sought out their women; bind the arms that had fought them; and put the ultimate alpha male to the humble, womanly task of grinding grain in the prison. Grinding was a task normally done by women, slaves or fettered animals, hence Samson is turned into the ultimate 'other' by the Philistines, a slave in the Promised Land. Narratively, the Philistines' treatment of Samson reinforce the themes of the entire episode. Samson had always been led by his body, with no spiritual awareness, doing what was right in his own eyes; the emphasis on sight ends in physical blindness, cutting off Samson's way into sin while symbolizing his failure to see beyond physicality. He had spent his life living in Israel but roaming the land as he wanted, constantly attracted to Philistine territory; but now he is tied to a stone, in Philistine territory, and they make it clear he is not one of them. Samson had spent his life taunting, humiliating and hurting others, oblivious to the consequences of his actions, and he is now the one upon whom abuse and hurt are heaped, suffering the consequences of his lifelong misbehaviour. He was a lone man, looking after only himself, but he is now tied to others physically, grinding grain for others to use, dependent on others to guide him where he needs to go. The warning of Proverbs, about foolish men who lack self-restraint, who let themselves be guided by lust, who prefer anger to wise words, comes grimly true and Samson embodies exactly what a man should not be. While there is a sense of poetic justice, the cruelty of the Philistines rankles, with torture and ongoing humiliation, once again prompting the question, is this justice? Even if it is deserved, is it right? Canaanite war practices, such as those of Adoni-Bezek in 1.5–7 or the Philistines here, keeping captives alive to humiliate them and enhance the ruling power's hold over the public imagination, contrast sharply with the covenantal order to kill enemy rulers. 16.22 interrupts the descent into death as Samson's hair grows again. A broken Nazirite vow could be renewed; Numbers 6.9–12 makes provision for cleansing and re-dedication. First, the head is shaved, before a new commitment is made. Samson's hair growing again symbolizes the possibility of a new beginning and a second chance. It would be easy for readers to be drawn into magical thinking that sees Samson's hair as the source of strength. But the narrator does not say that Samson's strength is returning – this will only occur when Samson cries out to Yahweh. The narrator is, instead, signalling the possibility of hope.

16.23–27: Samson's humiliation

In sharp contrast with the narrator's hint of hope, Philistine dignitaries celebrate the fall of Samson and cast their victory in theological terms: their statement, 'our god has given Samson our enemy into our hands' is normally a typical Israelite statement before or after battle. In the Samson narrative it is only ever uttered by the Philistines. Samson and the Philistines have similar faith configurations, their god not truly Other or free, but tribal gods, bound to give them victory. The pattern of divine withdrawal and subsequent re-engagement with Samson will show that Yahweh is no such God: beyond manipulation or tribal affiliation, Yahweh will bring justice to bear on both Samson and the Philistines, as he had with Abimelech and Shechem.

What was true of the ruling class in 16.23 is true of 'the people' in 16.24 – all rejoice, all attribute victory to a tribal god, all join in humiliating Samson. They, however, voice the pain of Samson's actions more forcefully, reversing the pole of previous narratives: it is they, the ordinary Philistines, that have been oppressed by Samson, 'who devastated/dried up our land'. They may recall Samson destroying the crops, his impact not just on the people but on the entire local ecosystem. The line between oppressed and oppressors is increasingly blurred. Israel has not heeded the warning to not become oppressors themselves. The use of victim/oppressor identity reinforces a dualistic view of self and other, as both sides claim legitimacy for their own actions, seeing themselves as victims, and demonize the other, seen as the aggressor. Readers are caught between colliding perspectives – Israel was given to the Philistines in 13.1, and Yahweh is acting to deliver. Yet there is little to praise in Samson, and at times 'justice' seems to be on the Philistines' side. A discrepancy is created between the discrete acts of human agents and Yahweh's working at a macro-level to achieve justice and liberation not just for Israel but for the blessing of nations. The Philistines do not simply rejoice, but use Samson as entertainment and a symbol of their own strength and power. Samson had revealed his heart to Delilah, the Philistines now reveal theirs in 16.25: with the feast in full swing 'their hearts were good'. The image of making the heart good/merry, usually through wine, is often a precursor of disaster (e.g. Judges 19; Esther 6—7). 16.26 paints a tragic picture of Samson, led by a youth, jeered at by the crowd, which reinforces the sense of complete powerlessness and defeat, setting the scene for Yahweh's intervention. Great (hyperbolic?) numbers of Philistines were there, and the narrator carefully highlights that they represent the Philistines as a whole – men and women, lords and ordinary people, 'seeing as Samson amused them'. They are drawn in by their eyes, as Samson had been drawn to Philistine women, and their careless delight leads to their downfall.

16.28–31: The last laugh

16.28 relates the first and only covenantal prayer that Samson prays. He addresses Yahweh by his covenantal name, calling on him to 'remember him' (*zākar*). The verb is a crucial covenantal term, often used of Yahweh turning to his people after judgement or when they are in great distress, and linked to covenant promises (Gen. 8.1; 9.15–16; 19.29; 30.22; Ex. 2.24; 6.5; Lev. 26.42, 45; 1 Sam. 1.19; Ps. 9.13; 98.3; 106.45; 111.5; Jer. 31.20; Ezek. 16.60; Jonah 2.7). It is repeatedly used in commands for the people to remember in ways that form their identity as the people of Yahweh (Ex. 13.3; 20.8, 24; Deut. 5.15; 7.18; 8.2, 18; 9.7; 15.15; 16.3, 12; 24.9, 18, 22; Ps. 103.18; 105.5; 136.23; Isa. 44.21; Mal. 3.22) or when the people call on Yahweh to act on his promises (Ex. 32.13; Deut. 9.27; 1 Sam. 1.11; 2 Kings 20.3; 1 Chron. 16.12, 15; 2 Chron. 6.42; Neh. 5.19; 13.14; Job 14.13; Ps. 25.6; 106.4; 137.7; Isa. 38.3; Jer. 15.15; Lam. 5.1; Hab. 3.2). Conversely, failure in covenantal faithfulness is often described as a failure to remember, remembering being a thick concept that goes beyond cognitive knowledge to encompass active embodiment of what is remembered (Judg. 8.34; Ps. 78.42; 106.7; 119.55; Is. 17.10; Jer. 23.36; Ezek. 16.43). Samson confess his own unfaithfulness, but by asking Yahweh to remember him he acknowledges the reality of fracture and begs for the restoration of a covenantal relationship. Samson's tone is radically different from the entitled arrogance of his other prayer in 15.18. He has been brought much lower than at Lehi, and he makes his request from a position of weakness rather than power, with repeated use of the particle of entreaty, *nā'*, to enhance politeness. Samson has finally learnt that it was Yahweh who was the source of his power. His strength had not returned as his hair had grown; the words 'strengthen me just this once' acknowledge that strength is not his personal attribute but a gracious gift from Yahweh every time that it is given. Samson is not a completely changed man, however. His prayer may show a new-found humility, but it is still self-centred and motivated by a desire for personal retribution. He does not ask for strength so that he can free Israel, or lead it, or become free himself. He asks for strength so that he can 'get revenge for [my] two eyes'. It is justice and repayment for the very organs that led him astray that he is seeking. The petition for 'revenge' may be one for the justice inherent in *nqm*; whether it is justice or revenge will be left to readers to judge.

Samson's plan to collapse the temple becomes clear in 16.29: he targets the 'lords of the Philistines' in the 'house of their god' – a chilling parallel to Abimelech targeting the lords of Shechem and, just as with Abimelech, the only attack on a foreign god in his story, and an incidental one. Neither man cared much about pagan worship; for both, the real target was those they wanted revenge on. Double causality, however, inscribes these events onto a broader canvas. Samson's final words welcome death. It is clear that his plan could only mean his own death, the second suicide of a leader in Judges and another parallel with the bramble king Abimelech, who also liked to play with fire. The assessment of Samson in the broad sweep of Judges is not particularly positive. Samson asks to die with the Philistines, united with them in death as he wished to be in life. His fate and theirs were so intricately interwoven that to kill one is to kill the other.

The meaning of his final act is ambiguous: is it revenge, suicide or sacrifice? In Samson's eyes, his life is not worth living anymore; bringing together suicide and revenge is his way to go out in a blaze of glory, regaining the honour of a warrior. Does this make Yahweh complicit in his death? By granting Samson his wish, Yahweh hastened Samson's death and was an accessory to suicide. It shows that Yahweh's respect for human freedom runs very deep; it also fits within a framework of thought in which death is not the worst fate that human beings can face. There is no condemnation of Samson in the text for wishing death, and Yahweh's cooperation further takes away any hint of suicide as being morally reprehensible.

There is a further dimension to Samson's death, however: he sacrifices his own life (in the temple of another god …) to bring down the Philistines. Samson himself would not have framed his wish in these words, since he was focused on his own gains, not Israel's. However, in the wider context, his death enables Israel to have a new beginning. The local Philistine hierarchy was all present, together with many ordinary people; the decimation of leadership will inevitably weaken the Philistines. In this final act, Samson has unknowingly acted for the first time as deliverer. This is no noble act of sacrifice, however; the revenge subtext prompts readers to question whether 3,000 lives for his two eyes is a fair price, and the end of multiple cycles of revenge is the destruction of all involved. The story as a whole graphically chronicles the futility of violence, exposing the need for the type of justice that can only be possible when individuals choose not to do what is right in their own eyes but agree on a framework for social relations such as the covenant to regulate individual action. The narrator's final verdict on Samson is damning: he achieved more in death than he ever did in life. Samson's life had had no discernible impact on the health and prosperity of Israel, let alone their partnership with Yahweh. Despite all of this, Yahweh accomplishes what he had promised, and Samson begins to deliver Israel from the Philistines. Once dead, Samson is gathered into Israel, with family and kin. In life he had consistently refused to associate with Israel or follow the covenant. In death he is made into everything he had resisted, buried in Israel in the tomb of his father. A restatement of the length of his judging follows, yet with no peace for Israel.

Final reflections

The Samson cycle paints Yahweh as a God who works to preserve his people even when they are bent on self-destruction. The gap widens between Israel's and Yahweh's perspectives. At a micro level, the stories are unsettling and ethically dubious; at the macro level, Yahweh works with his people even when they appear to be working against him and against themselves. As the gap widens even further in the final chapters, there will not even be a flawed deliverer like Samson to work with, exemplifying further Yahweh's self-limiting in response to human freedom.

The story of Samson is puzzling in its apparent drive towards the self-annihilation of Israel through assimilation with the Philistines. It is not, however, an unusual story: migrant people living as minorities have always been under pressure to assimilate and lose their distinctiveness. The pressure can be external, as in the books of Esther or Daniel. The Samson saga, however, names the reality of the pressure to assimilate becoming internal and tearing apart a man and a nation, between their historically-rooted identity and their need to survive in the present. Samson's ambivalence is shared with all Israel, but it is strengthened for him as he is called to embody a distinctiveness that separates him from both Israel and Philistines, possibly underlying his wish to be 'like any other man'. The Judahites reinforce the tension by wanting to be seen as what is often called the 'model minority' (Bonfiglio, 2013, p. 169): not only is the minority pressured to imitate the language and customs of the majority or dominant group so they can take part in daily living (such as Samson adopting the marriage customs of the Philistines in chapter 14); there is in addition a cultural construction of what the good minority will behave like, over and against a 'problem minority' that disrupts power relations and exposes the pressure points. This 'problem minority' is then resented by the majority for being disruptive, and by the model minority – such as the Judahites – for undermining their efforts at prosperity within the boundaries of their world. Strange as the Samson saga may be, it exposes a site of tension and difficulty, of unbearable psychological pressure, and the real human dilemma of being called to deliver a people who want to assimilate.

At one level, the story works as a typical set of stories told by an oppressed people, wishing for a strong man, making fun of oppressors in ways remote enough not to warrant too much hope, yet reflecting the difficult situation listeners would be in.

It is the kind of story told to keep alive a sense of identity for the minority group, and a safety valve in imagining possibilities for change. At a deeper level, the stories preserve the memory of the ambivalence and political reality of being a minority group, with less economic and technological capital (Israel is presented as agrarian over against the city-dwelling Philistines). Retold at a later stage, the stories contribute to shaping memory in forming national identity. In their final form, they are problematized and fit within a wider questioning of what kind of leadership could be sustainable and constructive for Israel in the long term, and what kind of character and underlying values leader and people need in order to prosper.

The wider narrative also problematizes simple dichotomies such as powerful/powerless or oppressor/oppressed through a careful and nuanced exploration of different types of power and powerlessness, and how different perspectives yield radically different perceptions. While Samson is presented as the strongest of the Judges physically, he is also the weakest in self-control; Delilah, a woman unattached to any man, would have been considered particularly powerless, yet she emerges as one of the most powerful characters in the story; the Philistines look powerful to Judah, yet feel powerless before Samson. The story showcases physical power, intellectual power (riddles), knowledge as power (what Samson's parents know or do not know, the secret Samson refuses to divulge), sexual power, economic power (the Philistines' payment to Delilah), spiritual power. The different types of power overlay and interweave so that power relations are never one-dimensional but multifaceted and complex. The most complex – and dangerous – positions are the liminal ones: Samson's bride, caught between two cultures, a woman between childhood and adulthood, between father and husband; Samson himself, called to embody one culture yet inexorably attracted to the other. Samson is liminal in many ways: a child-man who never fully matures, someone who constantly crosses the boundaries between the two cultures, who is part of Israel yet set apart for Yahweh, who is part of the constructed human world yet often wild, living in a cave and dealing with the natural world (lion, bees, foxes, donkey). Samson refracts all the ambivalence and tensions of Israel's life at that particular time. In the end, notions of power are not just blurred but completely subverted in the narrative. Samson and those around him thought of him as most powerful when he was at his strongest physically and able to trade witty riddles, yet the larger narrative places him at his most powerful when he is at his weakest and made foolish in the eyes of the Philistines. Therefore the narrative does not exalt force and violence but works to undermine the idea that force will produce any lasting solution for either Israel or the Philistines. This undermining of notions of power is deeply consonant with the shape of the canon as a whole. Time and again, Yahweh chooses to work with younger brothers, with women, with those who are oppressed and enslaved, rather than with the powerful of the world. The subversion of power blooms to its fullness in the narrative of Jesus, from birth in humble and hidden circumstances to a shameful death on the cross. The entire biblical narrative focuses on this point of God's voluntary relinquishing of power in order to transform the world at its deepest. As Jesus is said to be 'the image of the invisible God ... in him the fulness of God was pleased to dwell' (Col. 1.15, 19), this reconfiguring of the meaning of power is central to any definition of the nature of God. Hence the epistles regularly reaffirm humility and a reconfiguration of power as central, with passages such as Phil. 2.6–11 associating the very power and glory of God with the voluntary relinquishing of both, or Paul's insistence that God chooses the foolish things of the world to shame the wise (1 Cor. 1.27). Samson's tragic story is predicated on his, and Israel's, failure to see the world through a divine lens, so that they deem the covenant and its demands foolish, or less powerful than the possibilities offered by other gods; Samson only comes close to fulfilling his calling once he realizes that it is partnership with Yahweh that is the key to true power.

7

Micah and the Danites (17–18)

The story of Micah ushers in a different mood in Judges; the framework has now dissolved completely, though the main cycles are echoed throughout the epilogue. The final judge, Samson, had prepared the way for the Israel of the last five chapters, with a widening gulf between Israel and Yahweh, increased divine withdrawal, and a move from acknowledgement of evil in Israel, 'they did evil in the eyes of the Lord', now replaced by an individualistic assessment of right and wrong without reference to Yahweh, the epilogue's refrain now, 'every man did what was right in his own eyes'. The first half of the refrain, 'in those days there was no king in Israel' aptly describes the political situation. Samson's judging had been an empty judging at a time when the Philistines ruled, by a judge with no interest in Israel. Now, leadership has completely broken down and Israel has neither human nor divine ruler. The epilogue widens the narrative lens from Israel's leadership to Israel's 'every man', revisiting the theme of communal responsibility and the interplay between people and leaders. The epilogue is structured around two main episodes which chronicle the deterioration in Israel from two different but interrelated angles, as the prologue had done. Chapters 17—18 consider the degeneration of cultic and religious expression, while 19—21 explores the social and political aspects of deterioration. The refrain punctuates both episodes and underscores a common underlying factor, the rejection of Yahweh as king and the individualization of morality and ethics. The unity of the epilogue is strengthened through common motifs: they are both situated in Israel's heartland, between Judah and Ephraim; events in both are set in motion by a nameless Levite connected to Bethlehem/Judah and the hill country of Ephraim; both refer to Shiloh; both have a subtext about displacement.

Despite the epilogue's unity in tone, motif and refrain, and its links to the main narrative, making it a suitable conclusion to the spiralling deterioration of Israel, it has often been treated as a separate part of the book and sometimes dismissed completely as an appendix rather than a conclusion (Biddle, 2012, p. 11; Boling, 1975, p. 37; Moore, 1985, p. 40; Soggin, 1981, p. 5). These views mostly rest on a redactional analysis that attributes different sections to different redactors, tying together prologue and epilogue. Resonances between prologue and epilogue include the role of Jebus, oracular consultations, weeping at Bochim and Bethel, a focus on women and family arrangements, and links to Joshua. Some commentators dismiss the epilogue precisely because it focuses on 'every man' and uses specific stories as an illustration of all Israel. Traditional commentators with an overarching interest in politics and war have often failed to attend to the multi-vocal nature of the narrative and its windows onto different but interrelated aspects of Israel's life. More recently, the weight of scholarly writing has shifted towards understanding the book as a deteriorating spiral which culminates with 19—21 (Bal, 1988a; Klein, 1989; Schneider, 1999; Webb, 1987; Wong, 2006) and in which the epilogue acts as full conclusion by echoing motifs from the major sections: Micah's mother's money echoes the sum paid to Delilah; the Levite's treatment of his wife, Samson's treatment of his; the left-handed Benjaminites, Ehud; Israel's dealings with Benjamin echo Gideon's and Jephthah's stories; women are used as money of exchange and doorways in and out of war; the murder of the concubine echoes the sacrifice of Jephthah's daughter; the motif of rash oaths and their consequences on young women, the Jephthah narrative. In addition, the civil war of chapter 20 magnifies the troubles incipient in the stories of Deborah, Gideon, Abimelech and Jephthath; close connections with other biblical texts – Genesis, Deuteronomy and Joshua – are as rife in the epilogue as in the main cycles. These echoes weave a tight net between different parts of the narrative and suggest that the final episode is an indictment of all the judges and that all Israel shares in the flaws and weaknesses of each individual judge. Reading the epilogue in continuity with the rest of the book is crucial in discerning the theological emphases and nuances of Judges as a whole.

Chapter 17: Micah

17.1–5: Thieving and idolatry

A new chapter opens on 'a man', an introduction similar to Manoah's in 13.2, but with no framework assessment of Israel at the time, either religiously or politically, preceding the introduction of the character, leaving readers to wonder whether he will be a leader, connected to a leader, or a minor character. Just like Manoah, we find out his gender first, followed by his geographical location, the hill country of Ephraim. Given the role of Ephraim so far, the location rings alarm bells. No lineage is given, which is highly unusual for a named man and extends further the pattern of Samson's individualism and disconnection, making him a cipher for any man in Israel. His name, given last, is used in full only here in 17.1 and in 17.4: Micaiah (*mîkāyəhû*), meaning, 'Who is like Yahweh?' The name will function ironically, given that no one seems to know the answer to the question, and the Yahweh suffix will drop out early on, his name being given as 'Micah' for most of the narrative. The change in name problematizes his understanding of Yahweh and symbolizes the turn away from Yahweh in all Israel (García Bachman, 2018, p. 198). At the outset, however, readers are led to think that this is a Yahwistic household. The impression does not last, and 17.2 immediately shatters the hope for covenantal living. A spontaneous confession to his mother (another woman who remains nameless) reveals that he has stolen from her. The confession is slow and gradual, phrased to avoid using the word 'I'; Micah seems to confess mostly in response to a curse his mother has uttered, rather than from a guilty conscience. The sum stolen is the same as what each governor had paid Delilah in 16.5, showing Micah's mother to be a woman of considerable means, and establishing a less-than-favourable parallel. In this short introduction, three out ten commandments are broken: Micah does not honour his parents, he steals, and his mother curses/swears, using the name of Yahweh in vain. Micah's confession does not lead to bad consequences but to a blessing as his mother turns her curse into 'May my son be blessed by Yahweh!' The mother uses Yahweh in line with her whims, not bothered by her son's actions. Instead of holding him accountable, she treats him as if he had done good to her. She dedicates some of the silver to Yahweh in thankfulness, yet immediately undermines the dedication by specifying it is to be turned into an idol (*pesel*), in contravention of another commandment. A picture emerges of highly syncretistic worship, if not mostly pagan. Micah and his mother are colluding in their cavalier treatment of the covenantal god, ignoring the law and the consequences of one's actions. Leviticus 6.1–7 makes provision for atonement for stealing or defrauding a neighbour; here, Micah has stolen from his mother, which compounds his crime. Following an acknowledgement of guilt, Leviticus 6 prescribes not just restoration of what was taken, but the addition of a fifth of the value and seeking atonement through the ministry of a priest in order to be 'forgiven from any of the things that one may do and incur guilt thereby' (6.7). The mother's blessing cannot erase her curse or the guilt that Micah has incurred before Yahweh. Their relationship, rather than recognizing guilt and dealing with it, tries to deny it. The interaction exemplifies cheap grace, the grace that bypasses acknowledgement of the harm done and the need for repentance and to deal with the underlying causes of actions. It is fundamentally different from divine grace, where Yahweh holds his people accountable, yet forgives and walks with them through the consequences of their actions. Cheap grace does not enable the relationship to be properly restored because the deeper wound, the underlying evil, is left unchallenged.

The configuration of household at this end of Judges contrasts negatively with that explored in the story of Achsah.

There, Caleb, a father, intentionally blessed a daughter who respects him, while here, at the other end of Judges, a mother inadvertently curses a son who treats her disgracefully. Micah and his mother do things in the name of Yahweh but the substance of what they do is antithetical to the covenant. The picture worsens in 17.5, with the information that Micah has a household shrine, with idols and an ephod (like Gideon), and has installed his son as priest. The description of his shrine emphasizes the depth of his idolatry: the teraphim, small religious figures meant to bind generations together (Butler, 2009, p. 382), are an ironic icon given Micah's treatment of his mother; having one's own shrine is in violation of the command of Deuteronomy 12.5 to worship 'in the place your God will choose'; the consecration of his son undermines the Levitical/Aaronic priesthood. Micah and his mother may be sincere in their religion, but they are misdirected and neither understand nor follow the covenant. Either they have not learnt the ways of Yahweh, or they have chosen not to follow; establishing a rogue priest compounds the problem since one of the roles of Levites and priests was to shape the community of faith by teaching its stories. In addition, there are dangers inherent in a clan leader choosing a religious leader out of his own family, as opposed to the more detached system of a priestly tribe offering service to all of Israel. Micah is acting like a Canaanite leader. It is in the sentence that details Micah's pagan religious paraphernalia that his name first drops its Yahwist suffix. Who is like Yahweh? The answer will not be found in the house of Micah.

17.6: The refrain

17.6 concludes the introduction with the refrain, which summarizes everything that the story has exemplified so far: there is no sense of a central authority around which worship and social life coalesce, nor is there a sense of justice or law and order as Micah is absolved from, and even rewarded for, his dishonest actions. 'What is right' is defined by characters themselves, to the detriment of truth and justice. The entire epilogue is structured around the refrain and its four occurrences (17.6; 18.1; 19.1; 21.25) and unified by its underlying theological theme. The epilogue refrain is the counterpoint of the framework's 'Israel did what was evil in the eyes of Yahweh'. By now, 'the eyes of Yahweh' are no longer a criterion for judgement within Israel. Human beings are focused on making their own ways, meeting their own needs, serving their own desires and making their own decisions as to right or wrong, with no sense of responsibility or accountability to a higher authority or to the common good. It is the practical working out of the desire of Adam and Eve in Genesis to know good and evil for themselves, rather than being taught good and evil by Yahweh.

Commentators have often argued that the refrain is a pro-monarchic statement aimed at drawing attention to what happens in a leadership vacuum (Butler, 2009, p. 417; Frolov, 2012, p. 322), preparing the way for the arrival of the monarchy in Samuel. Given that the final edition of Judges is most likely exilic or post-exilic, it is doubtful that monarchy would have been seen as an unqualified success. The sexual behaviour of David with Bath-Sheba, his condoning of Amnon's rape of Tamar, to name but a few, suggest that the type of stories recounted in the epilogue were just as likely to occur under the monarchy and were as poorly dealt with. As to the complete disarray of cultic life, a cursory read through Kings undermines the hope that human kings would tackle the root of Israel's sin. What the refrain does point to is that the lack of a central authority is problematic. Whether this central authority is a human king is debatable: looking back, the judges as central authorities have not fared particularly well, and looking forward, neither will kings. The problem is deeper than political systems: as Gideon stated, only Yahweh is the true king. If Yahweh is no longer king in Israel, then Israel has lost its distinctiveness and the covenantal life with the power to shape a different society. What Judges has shown so far is that people and leaders often mirror each other. The main section of the book showed the leaders' gradual abandoning of Yahweh as king; the epilogue shows that the people abandon Yahweh as easily as leaders do.

17.7–13: A Levite for hire

The refrain slices chapter 17 in two. Just as Micah had been introduced somewhat abruptly, with no explicit link to what had come before, so now another character is introduced, again in unusual order. He is a 'young man' (*na'ar*), a word that suggests he is not quite fully adult, or not fully independent. His geographical provenance comes next, Bethlehem in Judah, but he no longer resides there, and he is given neither lineage nor name for now. Now comes the most important piece of information: he is a Levite, who had been residing (*gûr* in the *qal* participle) in Bethlehem. Levites were not allotted land and lived with other tribes; within each tribal territory, cities were set apart as Levitical cities and apportioned to Levites according to clan. Bethlehem was not a Levitical city and later information in 18.30 will reveal that the Levite is from the line of Gershom, who were assigned cities in Asher, Issachar, Manasseh and Naphtali. The young man is therefore doubly displaced: away from the place his family/clan was assigned and away from his choice of residence in Bethlehem. Levites were given responsibility for spiritual leadership by Moses (Ex. 32.25–29); some were consecrated for priestly service in the sanctuary designated by Yahweh, others lived out their calling amidst other tribes (Butler 2009, p. 387). There is no explanation of the young man's decision to leave Bethlehem; he does not go to a place Yahweh had chosen as sanctuary (Deut. 18.6–9), does not join other Levites, and will negotiate a salary for serving Micah rather than drawing the allowance set in the Torah for Levitical service (Deut. 18.1–5), which suggests that he may have been seeking a better or wealthier life. Just as Samson had been separated from birth as a Nazirite, as a Levite he was separated and given a calling he had no chance to refuse.

The youth wandered in search of somewhere to settle, looking to make his own way according to his own judgement, rather than walk in the path set by the covenant. The end of 17.8 is ambiguous, 'he came to the house of Micah ... to carry on his way'. Does 'his way' refer to his wandering, with

Micah's house being a step on a journey that may carry on later, or does it hold the sense of work or way of living, and so a reference to practising his calling as a Levite, or contravening the lifestyle of a Levite? The ambiguity invites readers to assess him as the story progresses. Arriving in a house of idolatry, his task would be to set things right and teach those who may not have been taught. The dialogue with Micah again majors on geography. Micah takes the lead, as appropriate for the host and older man with higher status as head of the household. The Levite repeats the information given by the narrator, suggesting that he is transparent at this point, though he does not explain the reasons for his wandering. Micah's response shows that he understands the young man to be seeking a stable and better situation and offers him a position in his house – one he had previously given to his son, implying insecurity about that arrangement. Micah's offer is generous, designed to tempt the Levite not just to stop but to stay. No mention is made of the son he has displaced in favour of a higher model. He has not checked the young man's credentials, or whether he was part of the Levitical priesthood. Neither man consults Yahweh. Micah behaves with the Levite as he had with the silver, taking for himself what should not be taken and using it to prop up his own unorthodox shrine. Micah, the older man, asks the Levite to be to him 'a father and a priest'; the expression is honorific, but sits oddly against the description of the Levite as a youth trying to work out what to do with his life. Micah seems attracted to the superficial aspects of the Levite's identity: he wants to make his shrine appear proper through paraphernalia that he acquires, rather than by engaging with the covenant or Yahweh himself. 17.11 immediately reverses Micah's offer by saying that the youth became like a son to him. The lines between parent and child are completely blurred, which contributes to the picture of the degeneration of family life evoked in 17.1–6. The reversal of father/son language suggests that Micah never actually wanted the Levite to define the spirituality of his shrine and set the spiritual and religious rules for the household. Micah himself wants to shape the household, including its religious life, and the Levite will be expected to comply with his rules and practices, a far cry from the picture of the Levitical priesthood's independent service to all Israel.

The Levite is installed as a priest in 17.12, an idiom that literally means, 'Micah filled the hand of the Levite'; it is the usual expression for the consecration of a priest (Ex. 28.41; 29.9, 29, 33, 35; Lev. 8.33; 16.32; 21.10; Num. 3.3; 1 Kings 13.33; 2 Chron. 13.9), but here, taken literally, Micah has filled the hand of the Levite with money as a bribe to have a priest do his bidding. The Levite is not consecrated, that is, set aside, for Yahweh but for Micah, and binds himself to serve one family rather than an entire tribe or all Israel. Micah's price means a commodification of ministry now potentially available to the highest bidder. Micah's concluding statement in 17.13 again exposes him as both genuine in his belief and deeply syncretistic. Securing the Levite seems to draw half on magical thinking, as if the youth was a good luck charm, and half on a belief that Yahweh's blessing can be bought with the right objects/people. The Levite should know better, but completely fails in his calling: he does not serve Yahweh or lead Israel closer to Yahweh, but willingly participates in apostasy in exchange for money. As a nameless character, potentially representing other Levites, he makes it clear that it is not simply Israel's political leadership that has failed; those with a specific calling to make known the ways of Yahweh have fallen too.

18: The Danite migration

18.1–10: Looking for a place to settle

The new chapter is introduced by half the refrain – 'In those days there was no king in Israel'. The focus on the first half emphasizes that the story to follow has political ramifications and is linked to a lack of overall leadership; the rest of the story exemplifies the reality of the other half of the refrain. 18.1 is constructed symmetrically, with a parallel between the refrain and the Danite venture, both introduced with 'in those days', which implies that the story is an illustration of the refrain. Just as the young Levite had struck out in search of a place to live, so does the tribe of Dan: what is true of one individual is true of many from a different tribe, and thereby, implicitly, of all Israel. The place they are looking for is not just a territory (NRSV), but *naḥălāh*, an inheritance, territory graciously apportioned to Israel by Yahweh. Territory had been apportioned to Dan (Josh. 19.40–48), but they failed to take possession of it (Judg. 1.34–36). As a result, they were forced out of the lowlands by the Amorites and cut off from good agricultural land. In an agrarian economy where access to arable land means survival, their plight was dire. However, the choice to strike out and go elsewhere, rather than turn to Yahweh for help, creates an ethical dilemma. An inheritance is not something one secures for oneself. *Naḥălāh* usually refers to a grant of land from a superior power to a vassal, implying a relationship between them. It is therefore impossible to take it by force. What the Danites are planning is to depart from the Israel-wide pattern of distribution of land, meant to be equitable between tribes, just as the Levite had departed from the tribal pattern. They have moved from seeing the land as a gift that can only be received in partnership with Yahweh, to seeing the land as something to conquer through their own strength. Faced with hardship, Dan does not turn to Yahweh but to its own strong men for deliverance.

18.2 parodies the sending of the spies in Joshua 2. Men of strength are sent from Eshtaol and Zorah, where Samson, another 'strong' man supposed to deliver, had come from. Right at the outset, the parallel with Samson causes concern about their faithfulness to the covenant and ability to carry out their mission. They are meant to go and spy out the land, as in Joshua 2. In Joshua, however, the people were responding to divine command, and the spies' actions showed compassion for Rahab and faithfulness to Yahweh (Josh. 2.24), whereas here only strength is highlighted and Yahweh specifically ignored. The structural parallel seems to equate the 'house of Micah' with the 'house of Rahab' – a house of idolatry is parallel to a house of literal prostitution, frequent imagery in the Old Testament, though the different outcomes of the stories provide an interesting commentary on the way narrators view the two practices. Rahab witnesses to Yahweh, is treated with compassion and brought into the covenant, whereas Micah leads away from Yahweh and is left bereft and alone without his false gods.

The men recognize the Levite, whose youth is stressed again in 18.3. It is his voice that is clear to them. There is no explanation of how they know him, given they come from different places, though the Levite could have wandered through Dan before getting to Ephraim. The men's question shows that they are puzzled by his presence. The focus is heavy on questioning his geographical location, with three adverbs of place in three questions, reinforcing that the Levite's decision to leave and find his own place was unusual. His role is equally unclear, eliciting the question, 'What are you doing in this place', followed by a shrewd, 'What is there to you here?', as in, 'What is in it for you?' The Danites' thinking pattern parallels the Levite's, with no exploration of Yahweh's role in directing the path of individuals or groups, and a focus on material benefits. The Levite's response is vague, but he describes himself as 'hired' by Micah as his priest, a far cry from the Levites' calling to be a tribe separate for Yahweh and for the nation. His relationship with Micah is reduced to a business transaction, rather than the kinship language used by Micah himself. Somehow, the scope of his vision has been radically reduced, domesticated and commodified as priesthood is sold to the highest bidder. Just as Samson had slid further and further away from his calling as a Nazirite, so the young man slides further and further away from his calling as a Levite. Stating the nature of his arrangement with Micah opens the door to the possibility of being offered a better arrangement, since he is clearly motivated by money and ready to serve a man rather than Yahweh. The Danites recognize the potential of a Levite's skills and, like Micah, they seek to use him as a good luck charm. They want reassurance that their venture will succeed and request an oracular enquiry, from 'Elohim'. A pattern is emerging in the latter part of the book of men trying to use Yahweh as guarantor of their plans, as a tribal god looking after them mechanistically, with no sense of reciprocal obligations. The

Levite does not apparently stop to enquire, pray or consult Yahweh, but answers immediately with what the Danites want to hear, reinforcing the sense of his willingness to mould himself to whoever asks his services. He simply answers that their 'path' is 'before Yahweh'. The word for path/way, *derek*, is used frequently in the OT, most often figuratively, with strong covenantal overtones. It usually refers to a way of life consonant with all that the covenant demands (Ps. 32.8; 119.2, 32, 33; 143.8; Isa. 48.7; Jer. 7.23; 42.3), and is a particularly potent metaphor in Deuteronomy, where walking in the way of Yahweh is synonymous with keeping his commands (Deut. 5.33; 8.6; 9.12, 16; 11.28; 13.5; 19.9; 26.17; 28.9; 30.16; 31.29). Conversely, the choice between two ways, one that leads to life, one to death, is a common way of speaking of the choice to either follow the covenant or not (Ps. 146.9; Prov. 2.20; 4.19; 6.23; 14.12; 15.9; 16.25; Jer. 21.8). The metaphor highlights the integrity and integration of the whole of life, so that justice and right living are intimately linked with worship. The metaphor extends into the New Testament, as the early Church was often referred to as 'The Way'. Whichever of the two paths one chooses, Yahweh watches both: 'The Lord watches over the way of the righteous, but the way of the wicked will perish' (Ps. 1.6). Considering the wider biblical use of the word, the Levite's response is tragically ironic, as he misuses the name of Yahweh to assure the Danites that their way is good, when it is not. Both the Levite and the Danites fail to differentiate between living in the way of Yahweh and success in human ventures. In this, their view of Yahweh is highly mechanical, equating success with blessing and failing to discern questions of morality and ethics. The Levite's instruction to 'go in peace' takes the irony even further, given that the venture will end in the slaughter of people of peace, the people of Laish.

As the five spies go on, they come to Laish. Joshua had only sent two ordinary men to scout out fearsome Jericho. Here, five strong men scout out peaceful Laish, whose name ironically means 'lion'. As the men get to Laish, they 'see' the nature of the city and, just as Samson did when he 'saw', immediately desire to take it for themselves. The city is described in positive terms as quiet, peaceful, prosperous, with no enemies and largely self-sufficient. From the Danites' perspective, it makes it an easy and desirable target. From the narrator's perspective, there is no spiritual judgement or negativity towards Laish; it is the picture of what Hebrew settlements could look like. The men who were told to go in peace decide to shatter peace and bring war. They are not going into battle in possession of a promise, or at Yahweh's behest, or in judgement against evil or injustice; instead, they are pursuing an aggressive expansionist policy at odds with the vision for a settled nation living within the boundaries set by Yahweh. The spies' report back to Dan stresses what they have 'seen' as motivation for swift action. The description of Laish is hyperbolic, sounding like another Promised Land, and the positive aspects of its life as quiet and trusting are twisted into a dismissal by warriors who see it as easy prey. It does not seem to occur to the Danites that the people of Laish may be prosperous precisely because they live in peace and have good relationships with others. The description is rather naive, failing to connect 'lacking nothing' with either hard work or social organization. The impression is that the men think they can simply take over and have an easy life, rather than shape their own lives in ways that will lead to prosperity and peace. Their imagination is constrained by their belief in competition and scarcity and contrasts sharply with the picture of the people of Laish. The urgency in their entreaty to the tribe is reminiscent of Samson urging his parents to get him the woman he had just seen. Dan are equally impatient, focus on taking what they see without consulting with Yahweh, and assume that what they want must be right. 18.10 has the spies argue that 'God (Elohim) has given it into your hand'. Even though the Levite had used the divine name, the spies shy away from it and simply refer to an unspecific god. To claim divine backing is a tool to manipulate the rest of the tribe to follow them. It is unclear whether the men truly believe it, in which case they are confusing their own desires and Yahweh's will, or whether it is a turn of phrase or an attempt to use a tribal god as guarantor of their plans. They do not refer to the Levite's false oracle, but locate their certainty of victory on their assessment of Laish as easy to take and so good that they simply have to take it. Like Micah and his mother, and many others before, the men have not learnt to walk in the ways of Yahweh or even recognize what is of Yahweh and what is not.

Their story is therefore an anti-spy mission. The parallels with Numbers 12.16—14.45, Deuteronomy 1.19–46 and Joshua 2 highlight how misguided their venture is: it is purely human rather than Yahweh-inspired. The reaction of the Danite scouts to what they see is radically different; they are raring for battle, rather than awed at what Yahweh is promising to do and frightened by what they saw; the land is described as easy to conquer and its people as gentle, rather than full of fearsome enemies; the men see themselves as easily able to conquer in their own strength, rather than having to rely completely on Yahweh. The story completely reverses expectations: it is now Israel that is the enemy in the land, brutal and godless. They have not just been Canaanized, they are showing themselves to be the worst of the people of the land, while foreigners are portrayed positively, victims of Dan's bloodlust.

18.11–20: Levite stealing

In contrast to the idyllic picture of peaceful Laish, 600 Danite men arm themselves with 'instruments of battle'. The description reinforces that this is a military operation, an offensive, rather than the migration of an entire people searching for a better life. Their journey through Judah and on to Ephraim is reminiscent of the Levite's wanderings, but the scouts' mission to spy out the land was wider than a simple search for a place to live. Their report about Micah's household reveals that they are after treasures and riches, as happy to rob fellow Israelites as the people of Laish. Their report focuses only on the religious artefacts; at first sight, it could be an indication of disapproval. The instruction, 'now think about/decide what to do' at the end of 18.14 could be an invitation to break down idols. The picture painted so far, of course, does not encourage this reading at the level of characters, but the phrasing invites readers to pause and ask what *should* be done, and to wonder what the men will do: do they see the artefacts merely as treasure (then why not anything else in Micah's household?) or are they attracted to the idols per se, or both? In 18.3, the men were offered hospitality at Micah's house. They now go straight to the Levite, proceeding to violate all rules of hospitality. The breakdown of rules of hospitality also features in the second half of the epilogue and symbolizes the breakdown of kinship and intertribal solidarity. The sense of belonging to Israel is shrinking as every man does what is right in his own eyes and ceases to buy into a wider social contract. Micah's prosperity is obvious in that his household is a complex of multiple houses within which the Levite, whose youth is again emphasized, has his own separate accommodation. Going to the Levite rather than the head of the household is itself an insult.

The expression of greeting at the end of 18.15 is ironic. The men, armed to the teeth, standing menacingly around the door, with a large army behind them, 'asked him about peace/welfare'. The image of the army at the gate forms an inclusio in verses 16–17, around the five scouts going in to steal the idols. The Levite stands at the gate with the men, either willingly or under duress; his options are limited, whether he is being guarded, restrained, willing or merely curious. The large force, representing an entire tribe, is an escalation from Samson's rampages: they do not distinguish in targets between Israel and Canaan, and their representative function suggests an institutionalization of brutality and oppression. The narrator skilfully presents actions first, and only elicits their meaning through dialogue in verses 19–20. The Levite now enquires about the men's motives: it may have been a challenge (which would be brave), it may have been a simple question. The men respond with an offer – partly to buy his silence but also to carry on building their 'inheritance' through whatever means they can. They replicate the offer of Micah to the Levite, that he be to them 'a father and a priest', with a higher bid – a tribe and clan rather than one man and his household, which underlines that this is about personal gain and status. The Levite should seek to minister to an entire tribe for Yahweh, but the offer is predicated on the wrong reasons, as is the Levite's acceptance. In the same way as serving Micah had forced him into a spirituality of Micah's making, serving the Danites will force him to be the priest that they want. The choice given the Levite is one that resonates strangely across the centuries: serving a large congregation as preferable to a humbler assignment. The definition of 'success' for the Levite has been reconfigured, away from the heart of his calling to be consecrated to Yahweh and lead others in knowing the way of the Lord, towards practical measures – numbers, prosperity and pleasing those in power. The Levite is completely divorced from any structures of accountability and decision making. As everyone does what is right in their own eyes, social structures designed to protect justice and integrity have disintegrated.

18.20 finally reveals the Levite's thoughts. He is now called 'the priest' and we are told 'his heart was glad'. He welcomed the offer and had no qualms about its legitimacy, or leaving Micah behind. The motif of a 'glad heart', which had appeared in the Samson narrative, will carry on in the next chapter, with dramatic consequences: what gladdens Israel's heart has inexorably tragic consequences. The priest himself takes the cultic objects, showing both his acquiescence to the theft and his acceptance of the men's offer. He, as a priest, handles sacred objects; and he, as a priest, will sponsor idolatrous worship. He has shown neither loyalty to Micah nor personal integrity. He then takes his place amid the men; symbolically, he is one of them, though the position may be a practical one: to keep him and the idols safe and shield him from the sight of pursuers. The Levite and the Danites, who both had a God-given mandate in the Promised Land, have now joined forces to look for a land and a path of their own.

18.21–26: The robber robbed

The Danites get ready to go, preparing for Micah to pursue: they put vulnerable children and anything valuable at the front of their group, with the warriors protecting the back (18.21). Micah, who himself had stolen the money to make idols, has now had these idols taken away, while the priest he had bought through a bribe is bought by a higher bidder. This is poetic justice again, but neither side invites sympathy. The Danites are confident of their strength and do not wait to be challenged, but challenge Micah first, feigning ignorance. Micah is in a combative mood; it's ironic that he should challenge them for taking what is his when he showed so little regard for what was his mother's. The episode exposes the flaw in relative ethics decided by individuals: Micah can only appeal to justice if there is a shared framework for understanding right and wrong that applies to all, independent of power and status. In a world that does not hold in common a vision and framework for living well, 'doing what right in their own eyes' becomes no more than the law of the strongest, and victims have no recourse. Micah's complaint strikes a desperate and pathetic note, 'you took away the gods that I have made!' The admission that they are gods of his own making shows them to be empty and powerless, and indeed they do not defend him. Yet neither he, nor anyone else, sees the irony. They are all fighting for man-made gods, rather than choosing to follow Yahweh. Man-made gods had the advantage of being moulded and shaped by human hands and thoughts, to accommodate what human beings want right or wrong to be. Yahweh, as Other, is much more difficult to deal with. As an independent being, he cannot be fashioned, bent or bribed; his power and mercy may be attractive, but the covenant imposes boundaries on human beings that demand that they recognize both Yahweh and themselves for who they are and live within the boundaries of what Yahweh, rather than they, declare to be right. For Micah to fashion his own gods is for him to make himself into the ultimate authority, taking Yahweh's place. In those days, Micah, the Levite, and the Danites had no king, not even Yahweh. The loss of his idols leave Micah bereft, 'What have I got besides them?' (18.24), and highlights the futility of idols that can be stolen compared to the everlasting promises of Yahweh.

The Danites do not even intend to fight but are so sure of their superiority that simple threats suffice. They do not deny the claims that Micah makes, but silence him by implying that he would be responsible for the death and ruin of his household should he speak up. Micah 'saw' that they were too strong: in this world, nothing is ruled by right or wrong, integrity or loyalty. The law of the strongest wins, a law that Micah himself had used to gain power and now causes him to lose it. Ultimately, he falls victim to men with similar values to his own.

18.27–31: The Danite settlement

The Danites follow through with their plans, in a narrative with an unusual amount of narratorial censure. First, the narrator reinforces that the Danites have taken what was not theirs, 'what Micah had made and the priest that was his'. Their ruthlessness is juxtaposed with the third retelling of the people of Laish's ways as quiet and trusting. The impression is that the town did not even resist; the Danites could have driven them away, but instead they burn the city and kill its inhabitants, in their own version of *ḥērem*. Whereas *ḥērem* had been directed at those who worshipped other gods (Ex. 22.20), here it is the idolaters who put others to death. 18.27 further reinforces the reversal of roles between Israel and Canaan by stating that there was no deliverer for the people of Laish; the word used (*maṣîl*) is not the same as for deliverers of Israel (*môšîaʿ*), but still implies that it is the people of Laish who needed deliverance from their oppressors, the Israelites. The Danites rebuild the city for themselves, but the next verse reminds the readers that it did not belong to them. In another reversal of normal biblical practice, the narrator gives readers the name of the new city, Dan, an Israelite ancestor, followed by a restatement of the former name. Normally, a place name is given, then changed by the Israelites, followed by a statement that the new name endures to this day. The narrator here reverses the perspective and encourages reader to remember the former name, as if its history is better than its future. Then, looking forward rather than back, in 18.30, the new city will be known as the home of an idolatrous shrine 'until the time the land went into captivity', a verse that marks out the narrative at least partly as an aetiological account for the sanctuary of Jeroboam. Jeroboam, the first ruler of the northern part of the newly divided kingdom, will set up rival sanctuaries to Solomon's temple, one in Bethel and one in Dan, with a golden calf in each, as well as commissioning a new priesthood (1 Kings 12.25–33). The parallels in the narratives, with the setting up of idols and an unauthorized priesthood, provides an explanation beyond geography for the choice of Dan as a sanctuary later. Jeroboam's concerns in Kings is that the people should not keep worshipping in Jerusalem because it may prompt them to revert their loyalty to David. Establishing a formal place of worship somewhere with an existing tradition and habit of worship such as Dan is likely to be more successful because it expands existing practice rather than creating a new tradition. Linking these two episodes in the canon shows that the roots of later political and religious problems lie deep within Israel's history, further problematizing the events of chapter 18 by highlighting that the decisions of today have far-reaching consequences for generations to come. Furthermore, the linked episodes also show that establishing a monarchy is unlikely to be the answer to the problems of Judges; it is only dealing with the root causes of Israel's troubles, its departure from the covenant and inability to even want to follow Yahweh, that will yield long-term change. Within the Christian canon, the problem is tackled only by the coming of God himself in human form, in Jesus, so that humanity can learn to relate differently to the one king. The idea that socio-political change can achieve lasting results is undermined by the entire history of Israel, and will be obvious in the history of the Christian Church. The cycles of the Judges bring out sharply the need for every generation to relearn the ways of Yahweh for itself, whatever the socio-political configuration of the time.

18.30 completes the transfer of idols and priest to the Danites; both belong to the Danites and their focus is the tribe, rather than the nation or, indeed, Yahweh. The young Levite's story suggests that the degeneration of the nation has reached even those specifically entrusted with overseeing its spiritual life. He is only one Levite, but the appearance of another in chapter 19 will confirm that this is a collective indictment. The priest's name is now given, right at the end of the narrative. Keeping him nameless had been a way of universalizing his behaviour; naming him now is a way to shock the readers into realizing quite how bad things have got: he descends from Moses, showing that genetic descent from a 'good' family or tribe is no guarantee of integrity, feeding into the theme of the problematic handing down of faith across generations. His being 'son of Gershom, son of Moses' could be a chronological marker to loop the entire narrative back to its beginnings, showing that degeneration happened very early on in the history of Israel. This would tie in with the reference to 'Phineas, son of Eleazar, son of Aaron' in 20.28, making both episodes occur around the same time and forming a chronological inclusio with the prologue. Equally, the term 'son of' is a loose one that could have the wider meaning of 'descendant': the ambiguity ultimately serves the overall narrative strategy, to get readers to wonder how widespread is the behaviour described, how representative it is of Israel, and humanity as a whole, in any time. The blurring of chronology supports reading Judges as a prophetic book with the power to speak into any context. While the stories may be specific as to time and character, they have a universal quality in describing the struggles of human communities. The conclusion of the story in 18.31 once more gathers the essential threads of the story: the idol was man-made, it was stolen, and it lasted through many generations, in competition with legitimate worship centres such as Shiloh. The conclusion makes clear that it is the perversion of worship away from Yahweh and towards what is chosen by humans that underlies wider trouble in Israel, trouble about to unfold to its widest and most tragic in the final three chapters.

Reflections

The story of chapters 17—18 functions symbolically much as 19—21 will. The narrator starts with a small, focused story centred on one family, then tells a tribal/national story that progresses along the same lines. The effect is not just to generalize the patterns of behaviour, but also to expose the deep interrelatedness between family and nation, between private and public realms, between what individuals do and how the nation fares. At the level of the epilogue as a whole, the juxtaposition of two stories told in similar ways reinforces the link between their basic themes: the idolatry and perversion of worship in 17—18 works together with the socio-political breakdown of 19—21. Both episodes will focus on the destabilization of the family as an essential component of the wider breakdown of law and order.

Just as Micah and his mother subvert good family relationships by removing child-to-parent respect and obedience, replacing parent-to-child blessing with a curse, and Micah taking money he would have inherited before his mother has died, so the Levite steals from Micah who had treated him as a son, and the Danites take land for themselves rather than coming into the inheritance they had been granted by Yahweh. Patterns collapse and blur in both: Micah is both father and son to the Levite, who is both son and father to him; Micah steals his inheritance from his mother, but gives it back to her; his mother pronounces both blessing and curse upon her son; Micah has a son of his own, whom he places in an inappropriate position, then discards and replaces with the Levite, who never actually saw himself as a son but merely as an employee. Family is in a state of confusion, with no appropriate boundaries to roles and behaviours. The confusion and lack of boundaries, applied more widely, leads Dan to misunderstand the nature of its own inheritance, and ignore Yahweh who had bestowed it, and leads them to treat a host, Micah, with complete disrespect and set up their own confused father/son relationship with the Levite; this generates the lawless, unjust society that makes justice impossible (in response to theft by

Micah or the Levite or the Danites) and condones the murder of the peaceful people of Laish by the grasping, brutal Danites. Geographical confusion adds to the picture, with Levite and Danite both living where they are not supposed to live, blurring the traditional identity construction of Israel in its close relationship between people and land. The complete lack of connection to the covenant is exemplified by a systematic breaking of the ten commandments: stealing, dishonouring parents, taking Yahweh's name in vain, lying, coveting, killing and idolatry. There is neither law and nor divine king in the story, paving the way for the anarchy to come.

8

Dismemberment (19—21.24)

Judges' grand finale paints a frightful picture of a nation on the brink of anarchy, its very survival at stake. Through the small lens of one couple, we see family disintegration, geographical displacement, violence and victimization, and a challenge to any sense of interdependent identity; the story is then refracted through a wide-angle lens to show how all Israel has forgotten its identity as the people of Yahweh and turns on one another in internecine conflict. With Yahweh virtually absent from the narrative again, how can this story be read as a sacred text?

These final chapters have traditionally been neglected by interpreters, with chapter 19 in particular often dismissed as nothing more than an irrelevant 'domestic interlude' (Soggin, 1981, p. 282), and critics concentrating on the meeting of the tribes and the political dimensions of 20—21. More recently, integrated readings have consistently rehabilitated the epilogue as a fitting conclusion to Judges as a whole (Block, 1999; Klein, 1989; Schneider, 1999; Webb, 1987, 2012), while feminist readings have challenged the erasure of women's stories from interpretation (Bal, 1988a; Trible, 2002). Chapter 19 is a particularly contested space; an overfocus on politics and the stories of men have often led to the occlusion of women's perspective and Judges' focus on women's situation. Equally, feminist attention has also often led to isolated readings of 19, which preclude the possibility of reflecting on wider social and political dynamics and the concurrent violence to male identity and personhood. Reading 19—21 together and identifying key motifs and structural patterns enables each narrative to offer a commentary on the other, and readers to catch a glimpse of an implicit, but definite, narratorial judgement. Chapters 19 and 20—21 mirror each other: what happens to one is reflected in the experience of the many. Violence towards one 'young woman' is repeated in violence and forced marriage for the 'young women' of Jabesh-Gilead; those supposed to protect the vulnerable fail to do so throughout; an old man in 19 and elders of Israel in 21 peddle women's sexuality as a way to solve conflict; both narratives portray failure in self-restraint and an excess of violence; just as the body of one woman is torn apart by her husband, the body of the nation will be torn apart by its people. The continued use of the refrain links the entirety of the epilogue together, with a specific inclusio for 19—21. The structure demands that we read 19—21 as a coherent whole.

19: The Levite and the *pilegeš*

19.1–9: Levite, pilegeš *and father-in-law*

The unit opens with the refrain's temporal positioning, 'in those days'. The use of 'in those days' creates distance and invites readers to recognize the text as 'other', yet reflect on how it relates to 'now'. Following the refrain, the narrative repeatedly links backwards and forwards within the history of Israel, so that the text is distant yet deeply embedded within a shared life. The Levite's home in Ephraim evokes past stories, while the woman from Bethlehem projects us ahead into the world of Ruth and an allusion to David. The text works as bridge between canonical past, present and future. Only the first half of the refrain is used, as in 18.1. The outer uses of the refrain, in 7.6 and 21.25 use the full formula, whereas truncated inner uses let the story itself exemplify the second half.

Immediately after the negative narrative of one, mostly anonymous, young Levite, another opens with an older anonymous Levite. The difference in geography shows that this is not an older version of the Levite of 17—18, and readers are left to wonder whether this Levite will be a parallel or a contrast. The absence of names in 19—21 contrasts sharply with earlier parts of Judges such as the Gideon cycle, where virtually everyone is named and Gideon has two names. This new Levite is not a youth, *naʿar*, but a man, *ʾîš*, unlike his wife/concubine and his servant, respectively *naʿărâ* and *naʿar*. He is the head of a household within which he has no equal. Unlike in 17—18, the protagonist is not consistently called 'a Levite'. His Levitical identity only surfaces when it is useful: when asking for hospitality and appealing to the tribes. No context, family or attachments are mentioned, no sanctuary where he serves. He is as alienated from his Levitical identity as his predecessor. His only relationship is to the *pilegeš*,[1] a secondary wife – an odd relationship as no first wife is mentioned. Why would he only take a *pilegeš*? Why not a full wife? Is there one in the background? Unanswered questions abound. The Levite is introduced as a stranger, sojourning in Ephraim. Together with the old man from Ephraim sojourning in Gibeah in 19.16 and the Bethlehem *pilegeš* now living in Ephraim, displacement and unbelonging emerge as foundational themes. The *pilegeš* has no name and is identified only through the social roles she plays. She is from Judah, which sets up a loop and mirror back to the story of Achsah.

Pilegeš were not full wives with rights enshrined in law, yet they were not illegal or illegitimate, nor were they slave wives or captive brides. They have a status of their own, albeit an uncertain and precarious one, as shown in their uneven inclusion in genealogies and harem lists. Nothing outside of the biblical text exists to help define their status, but an examination of other detailed narratives that feature *pilegeš* (Bilhah, Gen. 35; Rizpah, 2 Sam. 3, 21; and David's *pilegeš*, 2 Sam. 5, 15, 16, 19, 20) reveals a troubling pattern. Every one of these texts is linked to a story of sexual violence where *pilegeš* are liminal figures through which men play out their wider political battles (Hamley, 2017, pp. 415–34). There are no 'good stories' of *pilegeš*; all are dark tales, so that the scene is set for a story of violence and abuse. The narrative shifts between calling the *pilegeš* 'young girl' (*naʿărāh*) in her father's house, and simply

1 Given there is no accurate translation for *pilegeš* in English, I will retain the transliterated Hebrew.

'woman' at other times. When she is *pilegeš*, however, after the Levite 'takes' her (19.1) she is always either 'his *pilegeš*' (19.2, 9, 24, 25, 27, 29) or 'my *pilegeš*' (20.5, 6), consistently marked out as his possession. The episode sits in sharp contrast with the story of Achsah (1.11–15), who was named, whose status was unambiguous, who negotiated with the men and thereby challenged her position as bargaining chip.

19.2 uncovers the crisis that propels the rest of the story: the woman leaves and goes back to her father. Travelling back to her father's house in uncertain times is an extraordinary feat, and strengthens the parallel with Achsah. The reason for her leaving is contested, resting on different translations of *znh* (the root used to describe Jephthah's mother) in 19.2: was she unfaithful/sexually immoral (MT)? Leave him (LXX[B])? Angry (LXX[A])? If the correct translation is 'she was unfaithful', then she is presented as a woman of independent mind, a moral agent who, like others in the story, epitomizes the moral deterioration of Israel. If she became angry or turned away from him, she is still acting as an active subject, but more likely to gain reader sympathy. There is little textual support for changing MT (Hamley, 2015, pp. 41–61), but following it is problematic. What is the nature of this alleged infidelity? There is no mention of another man, though the four months wait before he goes after her suggests that the Levite is waiting to ascertain whether she is pregnant. The woman does not leave him to cohabit with another man but goes back to her father, normally the recourse of an 'innocent' or wronged daughter. The ambiguity may be intentional, luring readers to side with the Levite, which makes his later behaviour all the more shocking and forces readers to re-examine their presuppositions. Was the *pilegeš* really guilty to start with, or was this the Levite's perspective? Was her leaving so shameful for the Levite, so countercultural, that it amounted to unfaithfulness? Even if she was guilty, does this justify the Levite's actions? If the *pilegeš* was guilty, was it because the Levite had driven her to seek safety in another? Many commentators, following the lead of the Reformers, either make a causal link between her initial behaviour and 'narrative punishment', or resist seeing her as guilty because they want to avoid the sense of narrative justice. Segal (2012, p. 102) neatly illustrates this by arguing that having the *pilegeš* commit adultery explains her death 'too neatly'. However, why should one follow from the other? Why the need to have a sinless/innocent victim? Why should she be less of a victim if she had been promiscuous? The debates are typical of victim blaming. The narrator, however, never makes such simplistic links, and tells a complex tale that reveals as much about readers' attitudes as it does about those of the characters.

Superficially, this is a traditional narrative crisis of forbidden female desire leading to chaos and death; it suddenly sets the woman as subject with choices that challenge the male view of the universe as under his control, with female sexuality belonging to the men of her household. Such an expression of desire and subjectivity (whether being unfaithful or simply leaving) constitutes a Copernican revolution for the man, who no longer occupies the position he thought he had. Whatever the woman has done is neither permissible nor fully representable in a patriarchal context, hence the need for ambiguity. At a deeper level, the word *znh* is crucial in establishing narrative continuity with the rest of Judges, where women do act independently, and their actions disintegrate into the same amorality as their male counterparts. To set up women as 'pure' or somehow occlude their ethical choices is to treat them as less human. The narrator does not simply use her as a foil, or a 'type' (victim or whore), but as a complex character in her own right who, like all Israel, does what is right in her own eyes.

The Levite finally seeks to repair his relationship in 19.3 and goes after her to get her to come back. He intends to 'speak to her heart', that is, appeal to the heart as the seat of volition and reason. He wants to persuade her to come back. The narrative, however, never records him doing so. Instead, he will make his own heart glad feasting with her father without ever speaking to her. The Levite is clearly not poor, as he has two donkeys and a boy-servant (*na'ar*) to accompany him. His going after the *pilegeš*, bringing a means of transport for her, casts him in a positive light: a wronged husband willing to forgive, thoughtful enough to think of how she can travel back comfortably (though there are three people but only two donkeys). When he arrives, the young woman brings him to her father, who rejoices to see him, presumably because a woman separated from her husband would only have very bleak prospects at that time. As they enter the house, the woman's father's presence dictates everything. He goes by two descriptions, the girl's father, *'ăbî hanahărâ* (six times) and father-in-law, *ḥōtēn* (three times). In her father's house, the *pilegeš* becomes *na'ărāh*, on a level of the boy servant, *na'ar*, who, like her, bears a recurrent possessive suffix. They are both possessions of the Levite. The term *na'ărâ* (young woman/girl) and the emphasis on the relationship to her father highlight her vulnerability, and echo the only other biblical text to use the idiom 'the young girls' father', Deuteronomy 22.13–21, a legal text exploring what parents should do if their daughter is accused of sexual immorality.

The intertextuality is significant in positioning the narrator's ethical stance. Deuteronomy 22.13–21 is part of a set of household laws. Laws shed interesting light on socio-political organization because they form an explicit 'grammar' for a society, yet one that creates discrepancy between the ideal and lived reality. By its very nature, law assumes that the ideal will not be fulfilled. The question then is, what ideal was envisaged, what 'normal' is lived with, what 'abnormal' is condemned, and what 'abnormal' is so disruptive that the normal rule of law cannot deal with it. Judges follows rather than precedes legal texts so there is an implicit canonical encouragement to bear the Law in mind as Israel's story progresses. The relationship between legal and narrative texts is problematic, however. Narrative texts usually present lax (or gracious?) responses to law-breaking compared to punishments prescribed in Leviticus or Deuteronomy. Considering them together does not presuppose that laws were consistently applied, but that the Law can offer an ethical commentary on the narrative. Deuteronomy 22.13–21 considers the case of a new wife being accused of harlotry (*zanāh*, as in Judg. 19.2), and her father ('the young girl's father') defending her. Semantic parallels with Judges 19, beyond 'the young girl's father', include 'the entrance of the house' and her dying there alone at the hands of the men of the city, outrage (*nəbālāh*) being committed, and burning evil from the midst of Israel. Several features are worth noting: the presumption of innocence of the daughter; the presumption that her parents will defend her (the means to do so is easy to contrive to save a guilty child); clear punishment threatens men who mistreat their spouses. In contrast, Judges 19 presents a picture of a girl who may well be guilty – though one must ask whether 19.2 represents the Levite's accusation rather than a fact. She then goes to her father's house where, according to Deuteronomy, she should expect her father to defend her. Yet she finds neither defence nor condemnation but indifference and eagerness to hand her back to the man to whom she is not wife but *pilegeš*. Her husband has either mistreated her or failed to hold her accountable. Later, her father and an old man will hand her over to a mob of men 'from the town' and she will die on the threshold. The Levite is never held accountable. She dies, not through justice, but as a victim of the lust and violence of men who fail to protect her. The entire episode is a travesty of Deuteronomy 22.

In Bethlehem, the father is entirely focused on his son-in-law. He greets him warmly, which suggests either that the girl has not spoken badly of him, or that he disregards her opinion, or that he is trying to win the man over. The father is master of the household. He repeatedly prevails over the Levite, and is the only one to speak. His speech is characterized by use of the imperative, though tempered by the particle of entreaty. He provides hospitality far beyond what can be expected; whether this is generous or overbearing is unclear. Assessing his behaviour is difficult: he could be held responsible for preventing the couple from setting out at a sensible time, and blamed for not protecting his daughter; or his attempts at holding the couple back may be the desperate effort of a father trying to protect his daughter from a man who has legal rights over her life. The girl disappears into the house, though the men 'making their hearts glad' remind us that this all started with the Levite's intention to speak to *her* heart. The feasting seems excessive and self-indulgent: several days of eating, drinking and making merry, with no work or activity referred to. Critics often point to the apparent weakness and indecision of the Levite. He stays longer than the customary three days, has nothing to say, and gets up to go four times, yet stays behind. When he finally decides to go, his words do not suggest an active decision but an attempt to escape. His choice of departure time is foolish, late in the day rather than in the coolness and light of early morning.

19.10–15: Journey into the open country

The normal rule in biblical narrative (and in most cultures without artificial light) is to start tasks early, continue during the day, finish in time to be home before dark, and then stay within the safety of home. The day of the Levite, who feasts first and sets out on a journey later, unmistakably signals trouble. As they journey out in 19.10, the status of the *pilegeš* falls further, a mere afterthought after the donkeys. They draw near Jebus, the location of the first battle in Judges, where the Israelites brought Adoni-Bezek to be mutilated. At this point in Judges, Jebus/Jerusalem is a liminal place, partly conquered, partly pagan. The boy-servant speaks up, unlike the silent concubine, who is ignored by the men throughout, and suggests getting shelter. The Levite, however, immediately reasserts the mastery he had lost in his father-in-law's house; described as the boy's master (*'ădōnāyw*), he dismisses the suggestion, since Jebus is 'a city of foreigners'. The boy retrospectively shows himself wiser than his master. But the master wants to be in control and this is first exerted through speech in relation to the boy, and to assert his identity as an Israelite over and against the 'others'. The 'other', here, is a negative image, the one whom the Levite is not, the Jebusite. He does not expand on his thoughts – what exactly does he expect to find in Jebus? He may be reluctant to associate with them for fear of becoming ritually unclean, or because of distaste for different customs, or because he sees Israel as superior, or for fear they may treat *him* as a stranger. The physical lay of the land functions as graphic representation: a choice between Jebus and Gibeah, between Canaan and

Israel, between paganism and Yahweh worship, a choice that turns out to be no choice as the two nations have become indistinguishable in practice. This exchange in 19.11–12 enhances the irony and horror of Gibeah. Gibeah was chosen as 'one of us': the Levite wanted a city with 'sons of Israel', who would see him not as Other, but as kin. Instead, the despised and feared Others might have been a safer option as Benjaminite kin treat the Levite as Other. A cognitive dissonance is set up between perceived and performed identity. The like-self behaves as the not-self, the opposite, the dark mirror image of Israelite identity, which threatens the perceived identity both of the ethnic Other (Jebus) and the self (Israel). The boundaries between self and Other have blurred, so that a hint of shared identity now threatens the clear demarcation between them. As they arrive in Gibeah, a city where they expect to be treated as kin, and therefore offered hospitality, things go downhill and they are treated as strangers, left uninvited in the city square.

19.16–21: The old man from Ephraim

The fourth man in the narrative enters in 19.16. Like the Levite, the old man of Gibeah is a stranger, sojourning away from home. Home is Ephraim, the place the Levite says he is from, which sets up a presumption of kinship. All the characters are away from home, journeying or sojourning, at the transitional time of sunset, in a place of passing through in Gibeah, an Israelite town on the border of Canaan. The old man is returning from *his* work in *the* field, rather work in *his* field, and is probably neither wealthy not well-established in Gibeah, which undermines his right to offer hospitality on behalf of the town. Without initial greetings, he ascertains where the strangers are from, majoring on geographical provenance and destination. The Levite is economical with the truth: he says he is from Ephraim, but not a sojourner there; he stresses his association with the House of Yahweh, presumably his Levitical identity, suggesting that this is the reason for the trip and entitles him to proper hospitality. He tries to give an image of himself as a reliable, pious man, but his speech reveals him as self-centred, because he starts with 'we are travelling' but quickly defaults to himself only, 'no man has invited *me* in'. Before any true relationship can be established the men assess each other, displaying suspicion and the need to position themselves within the wider social order. The old man does not reveal that he is a stranger in Gibeah; the narrator tells us. As fellow strangers, the men should be on an equal footing. Withholding this information gives the old man the upper hand as host and resident. The Levite's response betrays similar concerns. He seeks to establish himself as someone with a claim to respect, and to compensate for his alien status by emphasizing that he is a Levite and wealthy enough to travel with everything he needs. He subtly insults his host by implying that should the old man be unwilling to extend customary hospitality, he can provide for himself and his dependents. He shows politeness, introducing the woman as 'your maidservant' (*'āmāh*) and the entire party as 'your servants' (*'ebed*); interestingly, while he singles out the woman with a gendered term of polite abasement, he only includes himself in the plural, servants. The use of *'āmāh* as a device to express humility is normally only ever used self-referentially (Lapsley, 2005, p. 44). When used of a third party, it simply refers to a slave woman. The Levite uses his *pilegeš* to purchase humility at her expense, but also puts her down, in a subtle pattern of humiliation that reinforces her otherness as woman and *pilegeš*. The Levite is struggling to strike the right note, oscillating between being overbearing and obsequious. The old man relents from questioning in 19.20, and offers a long-delayed greeting, 'peace be with you', an indication that the relationship can proceed on a mutually understood basis. The old man mirrors the Levite's self-centredness by extending peace only to him, in the singular. The old man's plea, 'just don't spend the night in the square', may be straightforward hospitality, or a foreboding sign that he knows that strangers are at risk in Gibeah. They enter the old man's house, and donkeys are fed first. The guests then wash, eat and drink; the narrator does not specify whether they are offered food and drink or use their own, and they wash their own feet rather than be attended to. The verbs are all in the masculine singular, so that the *pilegeš* once again disappears from a house she has just entered.

19.22–26: Outrage in Gibeah

Once again, men are making their hearts 'good'; the use of the masculine plural masks the composition of the gathering. The women may be included, they may not. Men of the town surround the house, much as men of the town had surrounded the house of the Gazite prostitute in 16.2. Here, however, the men are wicked, 'sons of Belial'. The expression is used sparsely in the OT, always associated with extreme wickedness: in Deuteronomy 13.13 to describe those who lead Israelites into idolatry; in 1 Samuel 2.12 applied to the sons of Eli, who misused their status as priest for material gain and sexual favours; in 1 Kings 21.10, 13 for men who bear false witness to prop up the king's oppression, and in 2 Chronicles 13.7 of the men surrounding Jeroboam. The qualifier enhances suspense and the sense of danger. The ensuing dialogue is a contest between men. While the men undoubtedly know the Levite is a stranger, they do not highlight the fact in their words, nor do they highlight the old man's alien status, unlike the men of Sodom in the similar story in Genesis 19. Xenophobia may be a factor in their behaviour, but this is not explicit. The men only speak once, demanding that the Levite be given to them for sex. Their language is direct and graphic, using the usual euphemism, to know (*yāda'*), for sexual intercourse. 'Knowing' as a euphemism for sex points to the shared intimacy presupposed in the act and the attending possibility for self-disclosure of personal identity; here, 'knowing' the Levite would violate his identity and what should only be self-disclosed. The old man's earlier insistence at not spending the night in the square turns retrospectively ominous.

The old man comes out to speak to the men of the town, addressing them as 'my brothers' in 19.23. He is seeking identification with them, inviting them to see him not as 'other' but kin, someone to listen to. At first glance it is quite clear he is not kin, as we have been told pointedly by the narrator. He is a sojourning alien. As the story progresses, however, men gradually bond over their agreed abuse of women – first with the old man's offer, then the Levite's actions, and finally in Israel procuring brides for Benjamin. The old man may not be that different from the ruffians of Gibeah after all. He enjoins them not to do evil (*rāʿaʿ*), then expands to say, do not do *nəbālāh* (outrage, wicked thing). The word appears to refer to homosexual rape in this particular case, with the attendant abuse of a stranger and breaking the laws of hospitality. The word will appear again in 20.6, 10, by which time the meaning will have shifted significantly. The old man is the first to suggest offering women as substitutes – his guest's *pilegeš* and his own virgin daughter. The implication of the offer is that in his eyes the man is his guest (singular, 19.23) and therefore cannot be harmed. The woman, absent from the drinking scene, is not his guest in the same way, not worthy of protection. His daughter is his to use. He is fully aware that to hand them over will lead to the men doing 'what is good in their own eyes' (19.24), in a chilling echo of the refrain.

The offer itself illustrates the respective value of women and men, and the added value of virginity. Twice he contrasts the acceptability of abusing women to the evil and outrage of abusing the man. The use of *nəbālāh* is applied to what would be done to the man, but not the women. This suggests it is not sexual violence *per se* that is disgraceful and unthinkable, nor simply violence against a guest, since the woman is one as well. It is sexual violence against a *man* that is the problem. Gender expectations and value judgements lie at the heart of his offer. The offer of another man's *pilegeš* may transgress against another man's property, but also shows the two men united in fighting a common enemy – men who threaten their sense of self as *men*. The old man does not shy from graphic details of what the men can do to the women he offers, using the biblical word closest to the contemporary meaning of rape, *ʿānāh* in the *Piel*. This could be interpreted as callousness, or a hint of titillation; or it could be an attempt to shame the men by naming what they are proposing. The old man does not consult the Levite; he expects his offer to be acceptable both to the men of Gibeah and to the Levite, which implicitly comments on the state of Israel's social fabric. Consequently, he shows that he is no different from either the men he calls his 'brothers' (19.23), nor from the Levite who stays safely inside with him, but rather shares their disregard for women and the lives of others. His daughter, meanwhile, only ever appears as a possibility in speech rather than as a character. She is invisible and unspoken for.

Many (male) critics seek to explain and justify the old man's offer. Most of these rest on honour and shame interpretations: the old man is caught out by circumstance, his honour at stake; homosexual rape is taboo and shameful but heterosexual rape a less shameful, acceptable substitute. Hence his sense of duty towards his male guest supersedes his obligation to his daughter and female guest (Block, 1999, p. 537); McCann agrees emphatically, and describes the old man as the only righteous person in the story, offering 'right' hospitality (2002, p. 130); Kawashima (2011, pp. 14–15) sees his action as a legitimate use of his power of consent over women's sexuality, while Morschauser (2003, p. 482) states that the old man reminds the crowd of their duty and (bizarrely) that his use of 'do what is good in your own eyes' is an invitation to self-restraint through ethical reflection. A number of faultlines underlie these arguments: first, there is no evidence from ancient texts that hosts would have no obligations towards female guests; second, the old man has no legal power over the sexuality of another man's wife, his offer trespasses on the Levite's rights; while the argument about the taboo of homosexual rape is powerful, it is unclear how two women could be a suitable substitute; his speech does not invite restraint, it gives permission. The echo of the refrain and its judgement over a degenerate Israel is unlikely to be a positive narratorial comment, and instead picks up on the shocking nature of the old man's offer and his sudden transformation from model host to abusive father and accomplice in the gang rape of another man's partner.

Following the old man's offer, the Levite throws the *pilegeš* out without a word. Critics have disagreed vociferously in assessing his actions. A strand of thought seeks to justify both the old man and the Levite's actions by arguing that it is not unusual for men of the OT to use their wives to save their own lives, as Abraham and Isaac did (Gen. 12.10–20; 20.1–16; 26.1–33), or as Lot offered his daughters (Gen. 19), and that both are acting legally by exercising their power of consent over their women's sexuality. Penchansky (1992, p. 82) reads the incident as a contest of hospitality with host and guest both trying to protect the other, which the Levite wins by disposing of his *pilegeš* (Penchansky does not comment that doing so he saves himself). Auld (1984, p. 238) seeks to exonerate the Levite by suggesting that he was so horrified at a virgin daughter being thrown out that he put out his *pilegeš* himself (but surely such an altruistic man could have given himself up first, as the intended target – but just like Jephthah, the men do not consider sacrificing themselves). It is difficult to exonerate the Levite, and indeed, one wonders why one should. Why show so little regard for the woman he had crossed the country to retrieve? The man who had until now been 'her husband' (*'îšāh*), is now simply 'the man' (*hā'îš*). The relationship is revealed as one of rule and power as he later becomes 'her lord/master' (*'ădônêhā*) in 19.26. The door is shut, and readers may wonder fleetingly whether the man sits in safety, relieved, or distressed and ashamed.

However, there is no search party. The Levite is not anxiously waiting, but just goes to bed. Even the old man's daughter, who nearly shared the fate of the concubine, fails to wait and open the door when she collapses on the doorstep in the morning, her hands stretched out towards the door. The abundance of time markers in 25–27 stretches out the horror of the night and quite how long it was for someone to come out to her: 'All through the night', 'until the morning', 'as dawn started to break', 'as morning appeared', 'until it was light', 'in the morning'. The narrator skilfully tells a story in economic, terse terms that both bring out horror and force readers into a voyeuristic and powerless position, complicit with those safe inside.

The parallel with Genesis 19

Judges 19 is not a unique story; it closely matches Genesis 19 and Lot offering his daughters to the men of Sodom to protect two angelic visitors. The parallels are obvious; at a structural level, this is a story of antithetic hospitality which helps justify judgement against a city and leads to a crisis about future progeny, solved through dubious means (Edenburg, 2016, p. 186). The plots move in parallel fashion: a small group of travellers arrives in a city at a late hour; they consider spending the night in the square; someone, themselves a stranger, sees them and insists they should come indoors; the host attends to the guests and they share a meal; worthless men from the city surround the house and demand the guests be handed over for homosexual gang rape, the host protests, tries to establish a sense of common values but fails; two women are offered as substitutes, a virgin daughter mentioned in each case; in both cases the host invites the men to 'do what is good in their own eyes'. The parallel sustains Israel's reaction to Benjamin: the war against Benjamin is possible only because the story of Judges19 has cast them as so 'other' that they can be treated in the same way as an external threat, deserving the same annihilation as the town of Sodom. Both texts comment on anxieties to do with masculinity, power, fear of the stranger, with the use of sexuality to assert or undermine identity. Both are cast within a wider political context that demands a good enough justification to explain an appalling loss of life.

Divergences between the accounts are equally revealing about the narrator's intentions in crafting such a closely linked account. Lot is sitting in the square and rises when the guests arrive, whereas the Levite, the guest, is sitting, unwelcome, when the host arrives. Because Lot is proactive, there is no delay in hospitality. The contrast between the men of the town and Lot is therefore heightened in Genesis, and lessened in Judges. Lot does not ask questions, whereas the old man's hospitality appears reluctant. Lot himself 'prepares a feast' whereas in Gibeah they just eat and drink. No drink is mentioned in Genesis, whereas Judges specifically mentions drinking and making merry. While women are offered in both, Lot offers only his own daughters, whereas the old man offers the Levite's *pilegeš*, which further undermines the quality of his hospitality. While both permit the men to do 'what is good in their own eyes', the old man's suggestion is more forceful and verbalizes the possibility of rape. Lot actively argues and shuts the door against the Sodomites, and the men of Sodom protest; in Judges, the door is not said to be shut and there is no protest against the old man. In Sodom, the visitors bring Lot in to keep him safe; in Gibeah, the Levite throws out his *pilegeš*, a visitor, to keep himself safe. In Genesis, all manner of men come, therefore justifying judgement on the entire city; in Gibeah, only 'worthless men' surround the house, so that judgement on the entire city is suspect. Finally, Sodom is judged by Yahweh and destroyed through nature, whereas Gibeah is judged by men and destroyed by men (Klein, 1989, p. 166). In Genesis, the visitors tell Lot and his family to get up and go, and they are saved; in Judges, the Levite orders the woman to get up, and she dies.

Close attention to the pattern of divergence shows a carefully constructed account designed to highlight the actions of the Levite and the old man as significantly falling short of Lot's already flawed behaviour. More than anything, the parallels prompt readers to expect a supernatural rescue that never comes, and therefore enhances the picture of Israel as having cut itself off from divine presence and help, as with the Jephthah/Abraham parallel. In Judges, intertextual echoes set up expectations that are consistently disappointed. In the process, the narrator amplifies the difference between the stories of the patriarchs, flawed but willing to enter into creative dialogue with Yahweh, and the people of Judges, who have forgotten Yahweh, do not bargain with him to save the righteous as Abraham does over Sodom, but simply do what is right in their own eyes – and are left with the outcome they asked for: divine absence that leads the nation to self-destruct.

19.27–30: Dismemberment

Daybreak, another liminal time, could herald relief and safety, yet as the narrative picks up pace, and time accelerates again, the *pilegeš* is trapped in the aftermath of a night of terror. Readers get a glimpse of the woman collapsed across the threshold as those safely inside would have seen her, her hands stretched out towards them. The woman who had independently left her husband is brought back into submission to male values. She had trespassed into the public domain by leaving the marital home, and had later come out of her father's house to greet her husband, but meets disaster precisely within the public space onto which she had trespassed – and is never allowed back into the safety of the private world. The door that the Levite had opened to throw her out, opens again – to let him out and escape from a town of horror. He had just got up, which implies that he had slept and was ready to start the day as if nothing had happened. The graphic picture of the woman, laid across the entrance reaching out for safety, evokes emotion, yet the Levite displays none. The detail of the hands suggests that she had tried to enter the house, perhaps beating on the door, crying out for help that never came. As she bars his way out, he utters the first words addressed to her in the entire chapter – 'get up', but no answer comes. The terseness of the narrative magnifies his callousness. MT does not specify when the woman dies, hence at this point (19.28) she may still be alive, too traumatized or injured to answer. Many commentators either *assume* she is dead already, or follow LXX which adds, 'for she was dead'. MT, however, is silent on the moment of death, and the ambiguity powerfully enhances the narrative. The Levite does not ascertain whether his *pilegeš* is alive or dead, but slings her on a donkey, takes her home and dismembers her. The man's status as a Levite matters here, as it would have prevented him from contact with a corpse (Ex. 32.25–29; Num. 8.10–18; Deut. 18.1–8). Just like Samson, the Levite cares little for his distinctive calling. Not checking could imply that he thought she was alive – then he likely is her murderer. Dismembering her could imply that he thought she was dead

– in which case he shows no concern for Levitical laws. The ambiguity enhances the sense of shared responsibility for her death.

The most violent act committed against the *pilegeš* occurs within the marital home in 19.29: 'the place that is expected to serve as the secure centre of a woman's life (and the locus of whatever authority she may have), becomes for this woman, the site where her husband finally, and most horrifically, destroys her' (Bohmbach, 1999, p. 96). The loss of the home as safe space illustrates how all space has become unsafe for women as Israel's descent into amorality pervades every aspect of its life. The dismembering is puzzling and unexplained. The Levite desecrates her corpse in a way that denies her dignity in death as surely as he had denied her dignity in Gibeah. The Levite prevents her burial, and sends out body parts in a grotesque call to arms. There is some evidence in the royal archives of Mari that human dismemberment was used in this way (Webb, 2012, p. 474), another indication that Israel has adopted the practices of surrounding nations. The OT refers consistently to the proper treatment of bodies following death and the expectations of kin in protecting the integrity of the corpse (Olyan, 2013, p. 257); allowing a body to be desecrated was a paradigmatic covenant curse, inverting normal expectations of burial with one's kin. That the act is directed to the body of the *pilegeš* suggests that she is the bearer of the covenant curse – yet parallels to other corpse desecration stories (Saul's body, Jezebel's) illustrate the disproportion of the Levite's actions and its misdirectedness (there is no explicit or legitimate link between breaking of the covenant and the desecration of her corpse). Furthermore, the fact that the Levite may have murdered her *in order to* use her body parts makes this story very different from that of a corpse *allowed* to be desecrated as a symbol.

The picture of a Levite, poised with a knife, inevitably suggests ritual sacrifice, but one that stands in continuity with Jephthah's in its inappropriateness. Jephthah did not recognize what sacrifices were appropriate, but Levites were supposed to guide Israel in their cultic life, so that this Levite's actions epitomize the complete collapse of Yahwistic worship. The use of intertextual references enables the narrator to provide an ethical commentary. First, the motif of human sacrifice and two specific vocabulary parallels suggest an intentional allusion to Genesis 22. Both texts use 'the two of them together', *šənêhĕm yaḥdāw* (Judg. 19.6 and Gen. 22.6, 8), the only two passages in Scripture to do so in reference to human companions. Even more saliently, an unusual word for knife occurs in both texts: *ma'ăkelet*. Both texts state, 'he took *the* knife'; while the definite article makes sense in Genesis as it had already been mentioned, there is no antecedent in Judges, and the combination of unusual word and definite article suggests a deliberate echo. The echo may suggest the woman is alive at this point, just as Isaac was. Yet there is no divine intervention. In Genesis the episode was initiated by Yahweh; here the Levite takes action on his own and conducts a human sacrifice, forbidden by laws not available to Abraham, carried out by a rogue Levite who never seeks divine direction: the indictment is searing. The narrator's oblique judgement is further reinforced by an echo to another sacrifice–dismemberment text, 1 Samuel 11: Saul dismembering the oxen and sending out the pieces as a call to arms. The texts share specific language normally used for animal sacrifices, the ritualized method for a call to arms, the emotional response and parallel locations (Gibeah, Benjamin, Jabesh-Gilead). Saul's action, however, is appropriate and leads to the deliverance of Jabesh-Gilead, whereas the Levite's is inappropriate and leads to its destruction. The use of 1 Samuel 11 as a positive example against which to judge Israel rather undermines a blanket argument on Judges as anti-Saulide. Saul is driven both by anger (unlike the Levite's cold, impenetrable actions) and by the Spirit of the Lord (as earlier judges were); the parallel sets up a contrast between the Levite and both Saul as a later leader and the Spirit-led leaders earlier in Judges, and paints the Levite as a parody of rightful leadership. In Samuel, we are told the pieces are distributed by messengers, and they are given a specific message to accompany the physical sign; in Judges (in the MT), the message is cryptic and does not explain the call to gather, what led to it, nor what would happen should the people fail to respond. In Samuel, the threat is external, in Judges, internal. And, of course, the main contrasting detail, the sacrifice is human rather than an animal. Every detail contributes to the portrayal of the Levite as misguided and abhorrent.

The Levite's actions read as an intensely personal attack on the *pilegeš*, denying her personhood even beyond death. He asserts his mastery over her by manhandling her body, finally tearing it to pieces – at which point she comes to 'signify' independently, in ways that escape the Levite's full mastery, with ambiguity, uncertainty, and a call for sympathy on her behalf. Her body parts speak of her story and bear witness, albeit partially, to her ordeal. In some bizarre reversal, she is more loquacious in death than in life and arouses horror and compassion in death in a way that should have been forthcoming in life. The sending out of the body parts is unclear in its message, and the Levite interprets them a posteriori in his speech (20.4–7). At this point, in 19.29–30, her corpse is meant to signify something to Israel, something that, on the one hand, is the lie of the Levite, in one final betrayal and rape, yet also something that escapes the Levite's attempt to contain her, as she graphically embodies the fragmentation and destruction of the entire nation. The Levite's words say little and are curiously ambiguous: 'Has such a thing ever happened since the day when the Israelites came up from the land of Egypt?' (19.30) What is 'such a thing'? The events of Gibeah? The dismemberment? Something too terrible to put into words? The Levite's use of the history of Israel draws attention to the erasing of Yahweh; he does not say, 'since Yahweh brought Israel out of Egypt', the usual formula, but 'since Israel came out of Egypt', so that Yahweh is erased from past as well as present. The end of his message, 'Consider her, take counsel, speak out' is equally ambiguous. 'Her' could refer equally to the *pilegeš* or to her corpse (normally a female noun). What is Israel meant to ponder?

As chapter 19 closes, it is worth observing the disappearance of another character, the boy-servant, also young, associated to the Levite, his master, via a possessive suffix. Just like the woman, he disappears from every house. Unlike her, and despite being a servant, he is oddly safe in Gibeah: if the men of the city were after male rape, why not offer the boy, who also belonged to the Levite? His status would not have precluded it; only his gender might, which may suggest that homosexual rape was so taboo that offering him would have been too close to acknowledging the full horror of the situation. Offering the *pilegeš* instead enables the Levite to reassert the 'normal' order of sexual activity and avoid thinking of himself, a male, as a potential victim of sexual violation. The boy then disappears from the narrative, perhaps too embarrassing a witness to acknowledge.

20: Things fall apart

20.1–7: Summoning Israel

Chapter 20 opens onto Israel acting as an entire people for the first time since chapters 1—2; pan-Israelite expressions abound in 19—21 (all Israel, all the men/children of Israel, as one, as one man) yet with no clear overall leadership. The only exception is 20.2, which refers to the chiefs of Israel (*pinôt*), a new word for leaders in Judges. Israel assembles for war without having heard clear reasons for it. Rather than sending a delegation, or assembling leaders, or investigating, they assume that violence and war are the solution to a problem still undefined. There is no recourse to law or due process, even less to Yahweh. The parenthetical statement of 20.3 qualifies the earlier description of 'all the Israelites came out'; Benjamin is already excluded from 'all Israel'. Might there be others? The people ask, 'how did this evil happen?' in 20.3; just as with the Levite's message, it is unclear what 'this evil' refers to. The question may be a sincere request for information, or looking for a pretext to attack Benjamin.

For the first time since 19.1, the Levite is called 'the Levite' in 20.4, but the narrator qualifies it with 'the man, the Levite, the husband of the murdered woman'. He is not a Levite, a spiritual leader, but a 'man' among the men of Israel. The use of 'murdered' (*nirəṣāḥāh*) is significant, as *rāṣah* normally denotes premeditated murder. Since the men of Gibeah had let her go, and she had made it back to the house, they clearly had not intended to kill her, which the narrator could reflect by saying she had died (as the Levite will). The choice of 'murdered' suggests it is down to someone's specific, intentional action, possibly a condemnation of the Levite's direct killing of her through dismemberment, or indirect killing through throwing her to the crowd.

The Levite presents his grievance in a speech designed to present himself as the main victim. He gives no detail of his journey or the reasons for it. He correctly identifies himself as the initial target yet modifies the story to gain sympathy and detract from his actions. He widens the incident by stressing that Gibeah is from Benjamin, appealing to tribal loyalties, prejudices and past grievances against Benjamin. He then changes a group of wicked men into 'the lords of Gibeah', making the conflict sound legitimized by local rulers and thereby the city as a whole, a normal state of affairs. This elevates him to the rank of someone worthy of the enmity of the lords of Gibeah. He distorts facts by alleging attempted murder against him. The shift from sexual violence to murder implies that male rape was something he could not bring himself to acknowledge publicly, though it is possible that he would have seen attempted murder as the greater crime, worthy of greater punishment. He does not explain how the woman came to be the sole victim, and his own part within it. He acknowledges her ordeal, but keeps his own predicament central: what will Israel actually be responding to – the attempted murder of a man, or rape and actual murder of a woman? He calmly recounts the *pilegeš*' abuse, death and dismemberment and carefully avoids saying she was murdered, but simply states, 'she died', with no time frame.

The discrepancies between his story and the narrator's make him unreliable. He presents the dismemberment as a logical outcome, the obvious thing to do in response to such events – now termed *nəbālāh* (outrage). The word is often used for deep, sexually-based evil, identified as un-Israelite, so that offenders must be eradicated (Gen. 34.7; Deut. 22.21; 2 Sam.

13.12; Jer. 29.23). Israel is baited into a self-righteous response of self-defence against the enemy within, those who have compromised the integrity of the nation through such un-Israelite action. The Levite is positioning himself in solidarity with the rest of Israel, over and against Benjamin, now cast as quintessential others, who have done something never seen since the Exodus. Yet *nəbālāh* is ambiguous: does it refer to attempted murder? To the abuse and death of the young woman? Or both? For the Levite, the repressed threat of homosexual rape may be *nəbālāh*. For Israel, it may be the attempted murder, though murder is not normally termed *nəbālāh*. For the readers, who know the entire story, it is the fate of the woman that is the greater crime. The same ambiguity is repeated in 20.10, yet amplified as Israel now takes up the word. A narratorial hint, a word play on *nəbālāh*, nudges us to see the woman's fate, especially her dismemberment, as the true 'disgrace': with the second syllable pointed differently, with a *tsere*, the word now means 'corpse'. *Nəbālāh* is the very body, abused, maimed and dismembered, presented to them.

The Levite, who should be a spiritual leader, had a *pilegeš* who committed some sexual sin and whom he gave to other men, in contravention of Levitical laws on sexual purity for priests; he performed a ritual sacrifice on a human subject and now leads the people, not into worship but civil war, based on false testimony and an appeal to Israelite history and identity emptied of Yahweh's presence. Just as the *pilegeš* is a focus for ambiguity, the Levite focuses irony. He asks Israel to go to war for the woman whose plight he has caused, and is willing to sacrifice the sons of Israel on the account of the woman he used to save himself – if, indeed, it is on *her* account he has asked them to go to war, rather than *his*. Many will be killed in response to his false claim of having almost been killed. The Levite is a parody of judges leading Israel into battle: this time, there is no external threat, the threat is internal and contained (a few men), yet he misrepresents the events in order to enact a personal revenge, and almost destroys Israel in the process.

The challenge of hegemonic masculinity

A thread running through Judges is that of the construction of gender identity, and how male leaders are shaped by hegemonic masculinity (as in the stories of Gideon and Abimelech). Here in the epilogue, we witness a crisis of hegemonic masculinity, challenged at both individual and national levels. Hegemonic masculinity is an idealized version of what it means to be male, which asserts itself by denying other embodiments of masculinity (Carman, 2019, p. 305), whether intentionally or not. Hegemonic masculinity is at work in the male–male bonding of chapter 19, but challenged by the threat of homosexual rape. The feminization that had been implied through innuendo in the stories of Ehud and Eglon, or Jael and Sisera, has now become an actualized threat. Given that the warrior-based picture of masculinity rests partly on the ability to defend oneself, and on controlling the sexuality of others in the household (Haddox, 2016, p. 180), the events of chapter 19 shatter the Levite's sense of self and expose the devastating consequences of such masculine ideals, as the Levite reasserts his masculinity first at the expense of his *pilegeš*, then of Benjamin and Israel as a whole.

The *pilegeš* herself had triggered the first challenge to his identity when she left. Betrayal always challenges identity and the way in which we narrate our place within relationships. Within the context of Ancient Israel, the woman's actions present specific challenges to the Levite's identity *as a man*. In a world where chastity was an indicator of social worth for a girl's family, loss of chastity (real or imagined) implies that the men have failed as men (Frymer-Kensky, 1998, pp. 84–5). In addition, identity is constructed socially, so that men need to see their masculinity affirmed and reflected in women's idea of their role, something the *pilegeš* clearly shatters, along with any sense of his being *necessary*. Gibeah precipitates the main crisis of the passage for the Levite, already vulnerable in terms of identity and social positioning. The men's demand to 'know' him constitutes not just immediate danger, but a challenge to everything he perceives himself to be – an Israelite, one of them; a man, not a woman; a Levite, someone of status who deserves respect; safe in his own country. What the men are demanding amounts to a complete erasure of identity, a complete *othering* that puts him in the sexual position normally occupied by a woman (being known), and under the threat of violence normally exerted against foreigners in war (Niditch, 2008, p. 193; Stone, 1996, p. 76). He is *othered* both as a man and as an Israelite, his identity inverted. The threat of the men of Gibeah also endangers his fundamental narrative about Israel and thereby himself: Israel is a people who do not do 'such a thing'; the men of Gibeah's demand tears apart his national sense of morality, of how Israel is known through its actions. He is then placed in the position of object of exchange and bargaining, the position women normally occupy. Hence the old man's offer is not good enough: while it rescues him from physical abuse, it does not restore his position as a man between men. Sacrificing his *pilegeš* enables him to restore himself as in control and in the position of a man, using women as money of exchange in a contest between men. This dynamic also explains why the men first refused the offer of the two women but accepted the *pilegeš*: they were not bargaining with the old man for an outcome. They were intending to humiliate the Levite. The old man's daughter was irrelevant to their purposes. The *pilegeš*, however, provided a proxy for the Levite; they may not rape him, but through her they still attack his identity as a man, albeit in a more socially acceptable way. By taking her they violate his property and mark him as ineffectual and weak as head of his household. He cannot protect his dependents and is forced to remain inside the house, the traditional domain of women. The exchange is now 'like-for-like': instead of a man being worth two women, one of them a virgin and therefore of extra worth, he is worth the same as his *pilegeš*. He had attempted to regain a sense of male identity by throwing her out and reasserting his place in the world of men, but the symbolism of the story says otherwise. The very patriarchal culture that elevates masculinity also creates the conditions that make Gibeah possible.

The profound loss of identity experienced by the Levite helps explain his anger towards the woman: anger that she dared to challenge his masculinity in the first place, and displaced anger against the men of Gibeah. The *pilegeš* and her body are a vivid embodiment of his loss, of sexuality gone awry, and he does everything he can to erase it, physically and verbally. The mutilation of the woman's body is a graphic attempt at suppressing her sexual identity. She is no longer an object of desire, his or anyone else's; he is ultimately master of her body and disposes of her as he likes, and uses her broken body to shore up his crumbling identity. In his speech to the nation, he regains control of the narrative and re-establishes himself as a man in a society that prizes war as an ultimate expression of masculinity.

The same dynamic explains the Levite's inability to witness to his own potential rape; doing so opens up the possibility of identification with his *pilegeš*, the possibility of a shared human identity. Admitting that men from Benjamin had considered othering him like this would open up an unpassable chasm: a raped man had no place within the society that Israel could imagine, whereas a raped woman could still marry. In Judges 21, the forcible marriage of women, even against their kin's wishes, nevertheless forges links between men and yields reconfigured households; a male raped by males has no place within this system of exchange but undermines the very principles – societal concepts of the household – that undergird it. Berquist (2002, p. 93) encapsulates it well:

> Because men who are heads of households control their own sexuality, forcing them through rape destroys the household. However, women do not control their own sexuality; transferring the control of their sexuality makes a connection between households that has enduring social consequences of allegiance and alliance.

The Levite's telling of his story connects the worlds of household and nation by elevating his personal story to the status of national crisis; in so doing, he affirms that the intrusion of the public (i.e. the 'Lords of Gibeah', as a recognizable public entity) upon the private (him and his *pilegeš* – now an isolated couple) is an indicator of degeneracy in Israel. He does not represent the event as private violence by the men of Gibeah as individuals onto his private sphere; this is an attack by a publicly recognizable group onto the *whole* of Israel. What has transpired in Gibeah threatens the core identity of the people assembled there. In a society where the family is central to passing on land and covenant to the next generation, a disintegration of family, and the threat by what is deceivingly portrayed as a 'public' group to the family of the Levite (and, because it is a public group, the threat is to all families), the events in Gibeah threaten the very basis of Israel's transmission of national identity. In this sense, when Israel functions properly, the family is the locus of the articulation of the public and private. The picture of Judges 19—21 is that of a nation where family has fallen apart, so that both public and private realms disintegrate.

20.8–17: Challenging Benjamin

Israel does not stop to ascertain facts or question the Levite's account, or the bizarre link between events and dismemberment. The Levite has turned his private tragedy into a crisis of national identity, and the people respond 'as one' (20.11). A sense of broken national identity is evident as the story unfolds. For the first time in Judges the nation has gathered, yet it is to punish one of their own rather than settle the land. Despite the repeated mention of 'all Israel', Benjamin is clearly not present, and we find out later that neither was Jabesh-Gilead, which casts doubt on the unity portrayed. They gather at a significant site for national identity, Mizpah, a place of ritual, legal and political activity in Judges. Ritual language evokes the covenant (20.10), yet the gathering is only superficially centred on Yahweh. If Yahweh and the covenant are no longer the uniting centre of the nation, what is?

In 20—21 no new individual characters appear. All new actors are subsections of Israel, defined through group identity and relationships, characterized corporately. The move suggests a transition from the particular to the general, from localized behaviour to pervasive evil. Benjamin's place in 'all Israel' fluctuates between belonging and unbelonging, though the people of Benjamin are characterized much like the people of Israel, through their male warriors. The narrator had never implied that the men who attacked the Levite represented all Benjamin, yet Benjamin is accused. Initially there had seemed to be a resolve to punish Gibeah only (20.10), inviting Benjamin to participate in the punitive expedition; for a brief moment, the status of Benjamin hung in the balance. This 'evil' has been committed 'among you' (Benjamin): Benjamin is given an opportunity to distance itself from the crime. But tribal solidarity trumps national solidarity, and Benjamin refuses to hand over the guilty men, with no reason for their refusal. It may be misplaced loyalty, it may be lack of evidence, or the belief that judgement had already been passed. They do not seem to investigate or be prepared to apply their own justice. While the narrative begs sympathy for the grossly disproportionate punishment facing them, the narrator does not present them as guiltless, but as equally guilty of doing 'what was right in their own eyes'.

Israel and Benjamin each muster their troops, preparing for battle. In early chapters, Ehud the Benjaminite acted on behalf of all Israel, his left-handedness the unexpected gift that brought victory. In this closing tale, Benjamin is pitted against Israel, and its 700 left-handed fighters prepare not to deliver but to destroy. What is gift and what is curse is shaped by the tribe's own choices. The canonical setting of the story suggests further narratorial censure on Israel, with two parallels to legal texts: Deuteronomy 19 (laws regarding murder and false witness) and 13.13–16 (the apostate town). Deuteronomy 19 introduces the difference between manslaughter (accidental) and murder (following pre-existing enmity) and commands the death penalty for murderers. It prescribes the conditions under which judgements must be made: 'a single witness shall not suffice to convict a person of any crime' (19.15), 'the judges shall make a thorough enquiry' (19.18), and punishment of false witnesses (19.19); then follows, 'so you shall burn the evil in your midst'. The contrast is stark. The Levite is a single witness. His retelling distorts the story and implicates far more than the original men. Israel half-heartedly investigates, but when met with refusal from Benjamin, hastens to summary judgement. The men of Benjamin refuse to hand over culprits, contra Deuteronomy 19.12. When the people set out to 'burn the evil in their midst', their focus is much wider than just the guilty men, and recalls Deuteronomy 13.12–18, the only provision for *ḥērem* against Israel itself. When men of a town ('sons of Belial', as in Judg. 19.22) lead the whole town into idolatry, a thorough investigation is made and if proven guilty, the entire town is put to the sword, all spoils are burnt, and it should lie in ruins for ever. In Judges 20—21, Gibeah, all Benjamin and Jabesh-Gilead are subjected to *ḥērem*. None of them were guilty of leading others into apostasy, however horrendous their crimes, therefore the legal context does not apply. Judges 20—21 elevates the crimes of a band of 'worthless fellows' to the same level as idolatry, and the refusal of Jabesh-Gilead to participate in a questionable war to an act of treason that posits them as an 'enemy within', no longer part of 'Israel'. No thorough investigation is conducted. The judgement of Deuteronomy 13 on a *city* is widened to an entire *tribe*. In Jabesh-Gilead, a number of marriageable women are rescued, in direct contravention of the laws of *ḥērem*, just as 600 Benjaminite men are spared. Benjamin's cities are rebuilt, whereas Deuteronomy 13 proscribes it. The picture is that of a people who have gone their own way, carried out disproportionate and unlawful action against one of their own, and failed to abide by any of the foundational processes set out for the administration of justice. Israel is failing to uphold the very laws that undergird its identity.

The nation now descends into civil war. Israel does not look into the eyes of 'Benjamin their brother' and see a reflection of who they are, yet their behaviour towards Benjamin shows the same lack of brotherly solidarity that was shown to the Levite, and their treatment of women closely replicates the fate of the *pilegeš*. In response to Benjamin, Israel affirm their own identity by multiplying the otherness of the Benjaminites: they are cast as non-Israelites, ethnic Others, and, in chapter 21, deprived of the means of marrying and ensuring an inheritance through children (as the means to possess land), an act of symbolic castration, turning them into feminized Others. The very 'othering' of Benjamin and, later, Jabesh-Gilead makes it possible to mete out the punishment that Israel plans. When they are called 'brother' or 'kin', Israel wavers in its resolve (20.21; 20.28; 21.6). Killing another in war is never as easy as it seems, and war on kin rather than stranger places an increased psychological burden on warriors and needs more intense and elaborate justifications (Niditch, 1993, p. 21). The justification here is a process of othering that places Benjamin under the judgement normally visited on idolatrous people. Judges 19—21 is therefore a perceptive psychological tale that exposes the processes through which one group justifies the victimization of another through the differential construction of their identity. The fact that these processes are laid bare in a sacred text whose narrator is far from approving is highly significant: it bears witness to the victims, opening up a space for reflection and potential change for those whose sacred text it is.

Israel's struggles with affirming its identity show that merely coming out of Egypt and entering a covenant with Yahweh does not effect an immediate identity change; the story of Joshua and Judges is a story of how identity shifts and evolves – and struggles to do so – at a deeper level. In Judges, the underlying current is the failure of the reconfiguration of national identity: the people have not become the people of the covenant, which can be seen through their language and representations of themselves. Instead, there is a struggle between different pulls on their identity and self-representation. So, in the response recorded in 19.30 and the beginning of chapter 20, we have a simultaneous use of covenant language and concepts (purging the evil out of Israel) and a denial of the fundamental reality and basis of the covenant: 'since the sons of Israel came out of Egypt'. If identity is constructed relationally, then relationship with Yahweh is only one key relationship in the constitution of Israel's identity – one that is at times less significant than others.

20.18–28: Civil war

Israel prepares for war, in a parody of Joshua and the beginning of Judges. 20.18 repeats the question from 1.1, 'Who should go first?' The answer is identical: Judah. The parallel highlights an essential difference: in 1.1, Israel goes to *Yahweh*. In Judges 20.18, they ask 'God'. The difference is subtle yet crucial in marking out Israel's evolution over the course of the book, and introduces a note of uncertainty as to who they are speaking to, and on what basis. In contrast, it is Yahweh who answers. The different terminology creates space for Yahweh to be *other*, and highlights how the people have distorted the covenant and their own understanding of a God who is not subject to their manipulations but does have an independent identity. Israel has changed; Yahweh has not. The question they ask is one of tactics – they have not been sent into battle by Yahweh and do not seek the divine will. They seek victory and treat Yahweh as a divinatory tool and tribal god. Yahweh's response is unsurprising. Judah is the tribe of the *pilegeš*, therefore the one most aggrieved, who should take the lead in defending their own. The divine direction implicitly focuses the tribes on the woman, as well as reflecting a tradition of Judahite leadership. We never know whether Israel follows Yahweh's advice, only that *Israel* went out to battle (20.20).

Recounting Israel's *use* of God shows that God is used perfunctorily, as guarantor of Israel's tribal integrity, made in the image of the warrior male, a god who will not contest their decision to solve problems through force, who is expected to bless and legitimize their plans. When blessing fails to materialize, the people blame God for not preserving the integrity of the nation. The repeated rituals of 20 and 21 do not seek a dialogue with an Other who may have different views or counsel, but rather work to reinforce national identity and cohesion by bringing the men together. In 20.1 they assemble 'before Yahweh', yet do not involve Yahweh in discussion; when they finally speak to Yahweh, it is not to listen but to ensure victory. When they are defeated, their identity as a nation is rocked, because the God supposed to give them victory has not delivered. Yet the people do not question their initial judgement, which would have yielded dialogue and possibly repentance, but rather how to proceed from there on. Further encounters show that ritual and sacrifices largely take the place of dialogue with God – they are not expecting to meet Yahweh as subject, but see him as a totalitarian subject that can dictate the fortunes of the nation, much as the elders do in chapter 21. In an overall culture where men can assemble and decide on how to mete out punishment on those who fail to meet their standards, where the head of the household can summarily dispose of its women, God is imagined in like fashion: capricious and unpredictable, making decisions without consultation.

When battle does not go according to plan despite Israel's greater numbers, Israel cries out this time to Yahweh (20.23), and asks a more open question, a tentative acknowledgement that battle may not have been the right choice. Instead of the simple 'the sons of Benjamin' of the first question, which marked out their difference, this time they speak of 'the sons of Benjamin, my brother'. It is slowly dawning upon Israel that this is not a war against external enemies, but against their own. The answer is unexpected – Yahweh commands them to go into battle again. The purpose is unclear: is it because a terrible wrong needs to be recognized and avenged? Is it to 'purge the evil out of Israel'? Or is it a recognition that Israel will go back into battle regardless? Or a test of their obedience? Or a continuation of learning war on Yahweh's terms: unless Yahweh gives them victory, they will not get it; and they will learn that Yahweh cannot be manipulated, cajoled or bought, as they face a second defeat. The people of Israel had assumed that what was 'right in their own eyes' therefore must be right. Yahweh sends no prophet or angel now; as the people seek no advice on the righteousness of their action, he gives no advice, continuing the pattern of divine withdrawal in response to Israel's rejection of covenantal principles.

As a second day of battle brings another defeat (20.24–25), 'all the sons of Israel and all the people' (implying not everyone had participated before) now go back to Bethel; it is unclear whether this is warriors only, warriors and background support, or whether warriors, support and all the people, men, women and children. The effect, however, is to heighten the sense of common purpose of an entire nation weeping before Yahweh. The cultic indications in a parenthetical note indicate that the people are moving back towards covenantal forms of prayer. The oracular enquiry takes place in more legitimate fashion, under the ministry of a priest, Phinehas, son of Eleazar. Just like the Levite's filiation in 18.30, this may be a temporal marker, setting the episode early on in Israel's time in the land, or 'son of' may contain several generations; in either case, the note ties questionable events and practices back to ancestors that had been reliable. Israel's prayer is still simply about battle and whether they should persist (to win) or desist (and give up altogether); it is about ensuring victory, not discerning right from wrong. Saying 'should we desist' betrays their loss of confidence and the possibility that they may desist regardless. At this point, Yahweh assures them of victory, in a way that should re-establish his supremacy over battle.

20.29–48: The turning of the tide

Israel now changes tactics, and rather than simply going into battle with the confidence that Yahweh has assured them of victory, they set up ambushes. As with Ehud, there is a question mark as to whether the deception was needed and how far Yahweh approved of the tactics. The third day proceeds in parallel with the first two, yet readers know what the Benjaminites do not. From 20.29 onwards, the narrator draws out the irony with repeated clues that Benjamin really should have known better, yet expected everything to go just 'as before'; once the ambush takes place, the unsuspecting Benjaminites are slow to realize their demise; the split chronology serves to amplify the note of irony in the second telling of the ambush.

The convoluted battle account ends with the near-complete annihilation of Benjamin. The settled tribe flees from its cities back into the wilderness (20.42), yet all the civilians are killed and most of the warriors slaughtered. Many meet their death at the door of their own city, just as the concubine collapsed on the threshold and as Abimelech killed the people of Shechem. The decimation of the Benjaminite army in 20.40–48 is cast in individual, human terms: they are no longer 'sons/men of Benjamin', but simply 'Benjamin'. Once the tide of the battle turns, they become a victimized individual, like the concubine, harassed and ravaged to the point of exhaustion and collapsing on the threshold of shelter (Berman 2004, p. 55). Six hundred Benjaminites escape and hide in Rimmon (20.47). The four months at Rimmon echo the four months of 19.2. Just as the Levite went after his *pilegeš* after four months, so will Israel reach out to Benjamin. The echo sets up a parallel between Benjamin and the *pilegeš* as wayward partners, and Israel and the Levite as husbands seeking reconciliation. Yet the parallel also suggests that Israel's motives and behaviour are questionable, and may lead to disaster and dismemberment. 20.48 already makes the scale of the disaster clear, with a narratorial wrap up of the extermination of Gibeah: 'the city, the people, the animals, and all that remained'.

The disintegration of the nation is underlined with parallels to Joshua, as tribal cooperation reverts to civil war, leaders fail, and the covenant renewed at Schechem is broken. Beyond general antithetic parallels, the battle of Judges 20 echoes Joshua 8 and the battle against Ai in plot and vocabulary: the many people/men/Israel who form the army, Yahweh 'handing over', the counting of fighting men, lying in ambush, fleeing, the enemy thinking that the Israelites are fleeing/defeated 'as before', taking the city, setting the city on fire, drawing near the city, setting up camp, direction markers (east, west), fleeing towards the wilderness, pursuing, the smoke of the city rising to the sky, turning back, striking down, slaughter, counting those who fell, inhabitants, livestock ... Much of this is standard battle vocabulary, organized around a similar structure. Once again, the parallel enables the narrator to suggest what *should* have happened, in contrast to what *did* happen. Superficially, tactics are copied to ensure victory. At a deeper level, the Israelites show they have no understanding of the ethical, spiritual and covenantal dynamics that underlie Joshua 8 (Chisholm, 2013, p. 506; Wong, 2006, p. 64). In

Joshua, Yahweh is consulted first, and the ambush tactic is given directly by Yahweh; they do not enquire about tactics in Judges, but instead do to Gibeah, an Israelite city, exactly what they had done to Ai, a pagan city. The irony – and tragedy – is that Gibeah and the wider Benjaminite territory had been given to Israel as an inheritance in Joshua, and the trigger for the chain of events was the refusal to spend the night in 'foreign' Jebus. Benjamin is treated even more harshly than Ai, with far more dead, multiple cities burnt rather than the single Ai, and the cattle and all booty burnt in Gibeah, unlike in Ai. The cities of Benjamin, however, are rebuilt, unlike Ai, and therefore the ruins do not stand as a reminder of past tragedy for future generations to learn from. After Ai, the Israelites acknowledge Yahweh's hand in giving them victory and renew the covenant, whereas Judges 20 sees no celebration, no thanksgiving, and no acknowledgement of Yahweh's role (except to blame him for their mistakes). Once again, the intertextual echoes have served to underline the utter dereliction of Israel as a nation and how far it has fallen from covenantal life.

21: The dismembered body politic

21.1–7: More fateful vows

Chapter 21 opens with a flashback to Israel's pre-war vow not to intermarry with the Benjaminites. The men of Israel, who had had few scruples about intermarriage with Canaan, are now worrying about marrying their daughters to kinsmen, because of a rash vow whose consequences they could have easily foreseen. Just as Israel had asked, with respect to the concubine, how could such a thing happen, they now ask why Israel has been torn apart. At neither point do they reflect on their own responsibilities. Their next encounter with Yahweh therefore, in 21.3, is not one of celebration or renewal of covenant. They recriminate against Yahweh for allowing Benjamin to be cut off, and lay responsibility on 'Yahweh, the God of Israel' for the state of the nation. The choice of words for God suggests two things: they are trying to bring Yahweh back on their side, reminding him that he is their (tribal?) god and therefore the integrity of the people is his responsibility; they are also deflecting responsibility and blaming Yahweh for their own choices and actions. Unsurprisingly, there is no answer, and no indication that the people waited for one. They had a plan already, and the question was partly rhetorical, possibly to assuage collective feelings of guilt through scapegoating. Instead, they turn to another vow and another scapegoat: those who had not wholeheartedly participated in the very action that had led to the problem before them. Action in 21 proceeds mostly through speech, yet there is hardly any dialogue; speech is used for command rather than as a vehicle for increasing understanding. The subjectivity of the other is instead systematically ignored or quashed in the speeches of chapter 21. The 'congregation' deliberates in 21.6–7 in ways that show that they see the 'Benjaminite problem' as something for them to solve rather than something to work on *with* Benjamin. The congregation's words betray a lack of imagination as they phrase the present predicament as a logical inevitability: an oath was made. Nothing can be done, just as in the story of Jephthah. This is only their first conclusion, which will be undermined by their later plans for Shiloh. If it is possible to find two different solutions in chapter 21, it is not unreasonable to assume there could have been others to explore.

21.8–14: Jabesh-Gilead

The assembly of the people makes plans in 21.8–12: they will exterminate Jabesh-Gilead and take their young women. The instructions are self-contradictory; first warriors are told to put all to the sword, including 'women and children'; then the men and the 'women who have known a man by sleeping with him'. The instructions are precise, with use of a gloss to reinforce that the women to be put to death are the ones that are not virgins. Finding wives for Benjamin is not just about reproduction but about ensuring *right* reproduction whose filiation is beyond doubt. Israel is striving for purity through control of reproduction and wiping out undesirables. Meanwhile, they are oblivious to the increasingly absurd problems they are creating: striving for purity leads them to wipe out more and more Israelites who do not conform to the pure Israel of their imagined corporate identity. The inhabitants of Jabesh-Gilead have not been asked for an account of their choices. Just like Benjamin, and the *pilegeš*, they are silenced objects of speech and action.

The women of chapter 21 have no rights, status, power, voice or name. Neither do their prospective husbands, who are not the victors but the defeated Benjaminites. Nevertheless, commentators have often seen chapter 21 as a 'solution' to the Benjaminite problem, even if an 'imperfect solution to a complex problem' (Jones-Warsaw, 1993, p. 183), citing cultural norms for making peace and the normality of rape in war as a political rather than personal violation (Bach, 1998, p. 10). This, however, ignores the text and its structure. The exchange of women here is not practised to *achieve* peace, since the war has been won and no negotiations are needed. The Benjaminites are utterly defeated and hiding in a cave. The Israelites take the initiative; it is more akin to marriages in peace time to seal political alliances. The women of Jabesh-Gilead are not captives of war who happen to have been taken. Rather, they were the object of military action in the first place. One can hardly call it a war, given that it is presented not as a dispute but as unilateral punitive action. Nor does either episode conform to the pattern of bargaining between households, clans or political entities. The women are taken, not negotiated over. Given the circumstances, the captive bride law of Deuteronomy 21.10–14 does not apply, which makes the women's status even more precarious. Deuteronomy acknowledges the specific status of war brides, including the deeply humiliating effect of being forced into sex with a member of the opposing army. The law ensures some protection for these women with no male relatives to negotiate on their behalf. Provision is made to enable the woman to mourn her dead relatives (who could include her former husband and children). Virginity is not a concern here, and the stress is put on a woman's beauty and the desire it provokes. In Jabesh-Gilead no mention is made of a mourning period; virginity is key. The differences with Judges 21 highlight the even more vulnerable status of the women of Jabesh-Gilead. Why couldn't a different solution be found? If the men of Jabesh-Gilead had not come to Mizpah, they would not have taken the oath not to give their daughters in marriage and a deal could have been brokered? The logic of war and domination prevails, so that war tactics are used rather than peace-time negotiations.

And so a campaign, ostensibly to avenge one brutalized woman and possibly a man, now leads to the mass murder of men, women and children. The specific command to murder children is particularly chilling given that they, like women, would have had no part in the decision of whether to join the military campaign. Israel is ready to murder an entire city in order to repopulate another (Schneider, 1999, p. 280). The irony grates even more when we read, twice, of Israel's 'compassion' for Benjamin – a compassion so narrow it does not extend to Jabesh-Gilead. Was it compassion, or self-pity for their own broken sense of national identity? The men of Israel repeat Judges 19's story of sexual coercion and murder on a much larger scale – yet they are still short of their goal (21.14). Benjamin, meanwhile, are in hiding, traumatized, with no future unless they break the covenant and marry outside of Israel, or Israel takes pity on them. Israel proclaims peace in 21.13 – unilaterally, bringing a peace offering of war brides. No one had consulted with Benjamin, they are expected to accept. In a curious reversal, the men of Benjamin, who had tried to feminize the Levite through homosexual rape, are placed in a passive position of being 'done to' and having sexual partners imposed upon them. Benjamin may have survived, but whether it is still a tribe of equal standing in Israel is debatable.

Judges 21 picks up the theme of masculinity and its expression in Israel. The oath not to give wives to the Benjaminites was not anodyne. It was a calculated attack on Benjamin as a tribe, either to literally erase them through *ḥērem* ('purge the evil from Israel'), or to erase them from Israel by turning them into a separate nation. It was also an attack on the men's masculinity by preventing its normal social expression through bargaining for wives, marriage and reproduction – another way of feminizing the enemy in war. The crisis blooms when Israel wants to restore Benjamin but have cut off Benjamin's lineage, and the possibility of reintroducing them as men of the nation through normal processes of exchange. A conflict of identity ensues, between their image of themselves as men of their word who cannot break an oath, and men of Israel who must preserve the integrity of the nation. The decree against Jabesh-Gilead offers a way to save face while further humiliating others not considered 'man enough' to have gone to war. The campaign against the city therefore has a two-fold aim: to restore Israel's sense of wholeness by providing wives for Benjamin and to humiliate and eradicate the men who have not actualized male warrior identity in battle. The following episode, Shiloh, further strengthens the point that the search for wives is not solely about procreation. The elders aim to restore *every* Benjaminite warrior to full participation into the assembly of the *men* of Israel. The search for wives for Benjamin neatly ties issues of national identity (who is Israel, questions of land and inheritance) and male identity (the male as warrior, the male as potential head of the household).

Furthermore, the dilemma is rooted in the culturally-assumed inevitability of marriage and children; male genealogies are paramount, so Benjamin needs to reproduce. However, *all* the remaining Benjaminites *must* have wives (surely a few of them marrying would be enough to ensure the survival of the tribe). This is set as a primary, overarching principle to which all other become subsidiary or set aside – such as how to 'acquire' wives, the rights of other men (fathers and brothers), relationships between tribes. The juncture between family and society is powerfully exemplified: Benjamin can only be Benjamin if it reproduces through legitimate (Israelite) women, and Israel can only be Israel if a long-lived Benjamin is part of it. While possessions are not mentioned per se, the women of 21 are linked to Benjamin's ability to possess their inheritance. Women are used within the transactions with no voice or choice. An identical process, however, operates for the men of Benjamin: their wishes are not explored, their grief at the loss of existing partners and children not acknowledged. The social need for Israel to ensure the continuity of Benjamin overrides individual or familial concerns. They are subjugated to the idea of the family just as effectively as women are, and their new 'family' is constituted based on the need to reproduce. Males may have primacy, but they are not free to act independently. Working in tandem with the portrayal of masculinity, the brutalization of women emerges ever more clearly. The girls of Jabesh-Gilead are called 'young girls' (*na'ărāh*), like the *pilegeš*, linking the two stories. The link reframes the *pilegeš* as sharing in the sexual innocence of the girls, suggesting that the violence done to the girls of Jabesh-Gilead equals that done to the *pilegeš*. The link humanizes the women of 21, even though they are never individualized. Like the old man's daughter earlier, they do not exist in the text, only in the words of characters who plan their fate. Unlike her, however, their fate is actualized.

Sexuality and murder are consistently linked to gender violence in Judges: Jephthah's daughter, Samson's wife, the *pilegeš*. The language concerning the girls of Jabesh-Gilead is unusually emphatic about their sexual status: 'all the women who have ever known a male by sleeping with him, you will devote to the ban' (21.11), followed by 'out of the inhabitants of Jabesh-Gilead, they found 400 girls, virgins, who had never known a man, never slept with a male' (21.12). Not only are they looking for virgins, women of bodily integrity, but they actively put to death women who have been sexually active – women who have 'known' a man, rather than simply 'been known' by a man. This is a very rare instance of women being the subject of sexual activity and men the object; women are not allowed, in this story, to be active in their sexuality, even within legal relationships. One wonders how they ascertained virginity, and what happened to virgins too old or too young to bear children. Presumably, only women of childbearing age were chosen, so that virginity was allied with potential fertility as a necessary bodily characteristic for salvation. As a result, all the women mentioned in the text who have been sexually active are murdered in 19—21, while the only women mentioned in the text still alive by the end of 21 are those who have not 'known a man'.

21.15–24: Shiloh

The congregation has acted, yet the problem is not solved; it is now entrusted to a subgroup, the 'elders' (21.16). Their speech shows them as pragmatic, less concerned with overall purity than practical outcomes. They reiterate the congregation's concerns and authoritative stance towards Benjamin. While they locate responsibility for solving the problem with themselves, they externalize its cause through use of the passive: 'women were wiped out of Benjamin' (*šāmad* in the *Nifal*). In the same way, they state the problem as 'a tribe not to be blotted out', then see themselves as powerless to act positively, 'we cannot possibly give them wives from our daughters'. It is the narrator who points out, in a short aside reminding readers of the vow, that the problem is of their own making.

Leaders only appear properly here in 21.15–25. There they are called *zəqēnîm*, the elders. While the word normally describes legitimate leaders working together to protect the people, here it echoes the old man of chapter 19. No reason is offered for targeting Shiloh. The elders command the Benjaminites to interrupt a festival of Yahweh to abduct young women dancing outside the town. Not only is Yahweh irrelevant and not consulted, but a festival of thanks is interrupted, women are abducted (against the laws of Deut. 24), forcibly married, and their brothers and fathers enjoined not to seek revenge or help. The language parallels that of the ambush on Gibeah: 'lying in wait', directions at the crossroads, 'seizing'. The men treat the women like the enemy in Gibeah, and behaviour expected in war is now normalized in peace. Male relatives are expected to come and protest, not because they have not been included in the proper negotiation of bridal contracts, nor because the women have been mistreated, but because they may have incurred guilt through their daughters/sisters marrying the Benjaminites against their oath. What is at stake is how the men themselves relate to one another and whether they have preserved the men's status and moral standing. The instructions of the elders to Benjamin further strengthen the feel of the speech as an elaborate self-justification. In contrast to the episode with Jabesh-Gilead, they do not advocate battle and wholesale killing, but use the ghost of Jabesh-Gilead as a veiled threat to ensure the cooperation of the abducted women's families. The use of military vocabulary in describing the 'ambush' both highlights what could have happened (the women could have been captured through battle) and make the subterfuge more acceptable to Benjamin by painting them as warriors rather than men overpowering defenceless girls. The elaborate explanation to the fathers and brothers works to ensure the long-term cohesion of Israel by enabling all the men to feel they have done right and not broken vows. The elders, unlike the congregation, can portray themselves as having solved the problem peacefully, with no bloodshed and no further damage to the integrity of Israel.

The most tragic feature of the elders' speech is their planning of what to say to brothers and fathers who will come to protest, preventing them from acting as protectors. So just as the Levite put the woman under his protection out to be harmed, just as the old man was willing to throw out his daughter, the elders willingly sacrifice women; and as the Levite did not protect the concubine, out of choice the fathers and brothers of the women of Shiloh will not be able to protect their daughters. The elders have institutionalized the most brutal features of the rape and murder of the concubine. What was evil has now been officially sanctioned. What created the very crisis of identity in the first place has become a national act. What was particular is now general, and what was deemed abnormal and 'disgraceful' is shown to be rooted in attitudes and behaviour shared by the nation as a whole. The text therefore highlights that violence against women is endemic, socially acceptable, and a focused category, distinguishable from more widely-spread violence. Individual oppressive attitudes are replicated in all the men of Israel rather than belonging to the few. But the elders' intervention moves the story into the realm of institutional violence, by shifting from mob rule to a considered response by leaders, with justifications and a plan for a structural and legal answer to objections. The seeds and practice of oppression were there already of course – as we can see from study of legal texts – but this passage chronicles a specific moment in the public process of legitimization.

The treatment of Benjamin highlights the brutalization not just of women, but of all those who are not in positions of power in Israel. Women are slowly erased from both public and private spaces, so that as the book of Judges draws to its conclusion, they disappear from the text – with the final episode not narrated as it happened but existing only in the plans of the elders that the men of Benjamin are said to execute. Meanwhile, the men of Benjamin, who have lost entire families, friends, homes and possessions, are forcibly married to daughters of the people who killed those they loved. This background places the women in an even more vulnerable position, while both men and women are forced into unwanted sexual relations. As Benjamin regrows as a tribe, all its descendants will be products of sexual coercion, including Israel's future king, Saul.

The narrative therefore ends with a fragmented, broken and traumatized nation, yet eager to pretend that everything is fine. 21.24 parodies the end of Joshua, sending everyone back to their homes and inheritance. This time, instead of hope for a new future, the people carry with them deep wounds and trauma, and the nation is reshaped away from covenantal norms into what seemed good in the elders' eyes. In addition to individual, personal trauma, Israel is traumatized as a nation, by the realities of civil war. Civil war, an attack by the nation on the self, has different outcomes to war against external enemies. Rather than strengthening in-group solidarity and stabilizing identity (Niditch, 1993, p. 21), it leads to further disruption and uncertainty, while the normal processes associated with the transition from conflict to peace (ritualized celebrations, exchange of women) are jeopardized. 20—21 chronicles the unravelling of Israelite identity by the specific dilemmas of *civil* war. Despite their fight against 'this evil thing, not seen in Israel', the eleven tribes still experienced cognitive dissonance after the first round of fighting had concluded. The reality of Israel minus Benjamin was not a shift of identity that was either comfortable or acceptable. Reintegrating Benjamin therefore became the goal, to reach back to an ideal unity as a basis for communal identity. The tribes rejected the option of forming a new identity without Benjamin, but did not consider the possibility of forming a new identity based on dialogue and learning from the past. Instead, they considered ways to return to a pre-war state, having Benjamin back without questioning their motivations and responsibility in the quasi-extinction of a tribe. Israel reintegrates Benjamin through an act of force that re-victimizes those already in powerless positions. The power dynamics of the end of Judges are therefore radically different to those at the beginning, and set the scene for ongoing internecine conflict as the story of Israel progresses.

Consider, take counsel, speak out

Coming to the end of Judges is unsettling, with innumerable questions left open about the viability of the little nation as it continues to settle, each in their own inheritance. The downward spiral creates a sense of impending doom, dampening hope for the future. Yet Judges is followed either by Ruth (LXX), or Samuel and the story of Hannah (MT). Both stories focus on women at the time of the Judges, yet present positive stories proclaiming that there were still pockets of covenantal fidelity in Israel, even at the most desperate times – just as Manoah's wife challenged pervasive blindness to Yahweh in 13—16. These are pockets only, as the wider context of 1 Samuel shows – 'the word of the Lord was rare' (1 Sam. 3.1), and Eli and his sons symbolize continuing degeneration in religious leadership. Nevertheless, both stories correct the impression that Yahweh is completely silent: he may be silent in response to the *nation*, but he interacts with the prayers of those who seek him. Judges is therefore sandwiched between two more positive accounts of Israel, one before – Joshua – and one after. This positioning encourages readers to balance each text against the others and consider how the arc of Yahweh's compassion and faithfulness extends over the nation. Judges problematizes the entry into the 'Promised Land'. It reinterprets the conquest narrative of Joshua, systematically undermines achievements thought to be firmly acquired, and undermines the possibility of an easy transition into kingship. Both Judges and Samuel, together in MT, ask questions about power and the social management of conflict, and the conditions for the success of a monarchy. In LXX, the Judges–Ruth sequence creates an opposition between a negative monarchy (Saul the Benjaminite) and a positive one (Judean David), which then influences a reading of Samuel. The nature of Judges as sacred, canonical text is therefore key to understanding its underlying theology. However much the stories focus on human heroes, they are also part of God-talk, which enables the past to be given coherence and carry the seeds of a future becoming, forming an arc within which human identity can develop, constantly changing yet without endlessly reinventing itself. At its most basic, God-talk values events that must be remembered and integrated into the story of faith. Therefore, a book as controversial as Judges, with its violence and questionable characters, begs us to ask, what is it we remember, what kind of bridge is being built between past and future?

There is integrity in remembering not just the best but the worst of humanity. There is also deep integrity in not presenting an idealized version of the Yahweh–Israel relationship, but recognizing its challenges and sorrows. The brutal honesty of Judges about the reality of child abuse, of sexual violence, of abuses of power by leaders, gives space for today's stories to find themselves reflected in the canon. There would be little to say to a victim of abuse today if Scripture only told stories of miraculous deliverance. Judges offers a crucial counterpart to the stories of Isaac, or Lot and his daughters, by acknowledging apparent divine absence from places of deep pain and brokenness. Yet by being set within the canon, these stories are not the final word. Storytelling is not simply an act of remembrance or construction of a supposed past; it is about the coherence of memory that enables a different way of relating to the present and moving into the future. In this respect, telling the stories of violence and failure is both necessary and dangerous. Necessary lest we forget, and dangerous because we may look back and fail to see ourselves in the flaws of the past.

Focused God-talk in Judges is often one of absence. The God portrayed by the narrator resists rubber-stamping Israel's demands, resists being used, and does not impose compliance in totalitarian fashion. The silence of God forms an act of protest and self-limitation which makes space for the otherness of his human creatures, however destructive this otherness might be. God in the text is treated by the men of Israel in much the same way as women: done to, used, ignored, silenced. The narrative position that Yahweh occupies mirrors not that of the men, but of the women of the text, challenging Israel's understanding of the nature of Yahweh. As a sacred text, therefore, Judges offers a bridge between past and present that remembers the dis(re)membered, both women and traumatized nation, rather than simply echoing the cries of the victors. The gap between the god of the characters and the god presented by the narrator is crucial: if the two were identical, then the text would implicitly approve and theologize the gender and ethnic differences that lead to Israel's self-representation, legitimizing violence and oppression of the most vulnerable. In addition, it would theologize Yahweh as Israelite male warrior, using power unilaterally, a tribal god siding with one nation regardless of its actions, ethics and behaviour. Instead, the narrator challenges narratives of power, divine and human, and how power should be used.

The challenge to narratives of power fits within the wider portrayal of Yahweh as holding justice and mercy in creative tension, with complete freedom. The deteriorating spiral illustrates Israel's dependency upon Yahweh while demonstrating the non-predictive quality of Yahweh's actions, shaped by compassion. Human actions kindle anger and judgement; Yahweh's love and compassion motivate deliverance. Overall, the character of Yahweh weighs on the side of loving-kindness, patience and covenant-faithfulness. The covenantal framework is crucial in portraying the judgement–restoration cycles as more than the mechanistic workings of a remote deity. The language of accusation, judgement and confession can sound formulaic; in contrast, the divine speeches in Judges (2.1–3; 6.8–10; 10.10–16) are emotional and personal, closer to the relational framing of Yahweh's relationship with the patriarchs. It presents Yahweh as caught up in the events of the world, genuinely affected and anguished and impelled to take action – action that simultaneously preserves and threatens the ongoing existence of Israel. The cycle exemplifies the essential relationality of the covenant; what one partner does affects the other and changes the future. At a national level, Israel is the architect of its own pain: Yahweh gives Israel freedom to walk away from covenantal living, yet it is precisely this walking away that leads to wider social and ethical breakdown and the victimization of individuals. Yahweh cannot force Israel to repent, to act differently, without violating the freedom of his human partners. Conversely, the text highlights attempted misuse of Yahweh's presence, so that divine withdrawal and judgement can be seen as necessary to maintain his integrity as partner within the covenantal relationship.

Covenantal relationship holds within it the question of justice as equally central to Yahweh's being. The problematization of justice in Judges prompts micro- and macro-level questions. With each episode, violence mounts and human 'justice' becomes more disproportionate, with devastating impact on the wider community. The underlying thread of Judges suggests that justice is not found within revenge or severe violent action; the violence of the nation never yields long-lasting peace. Yet if we question human justice, should we then question divine justice too? Such questioning is consonant with lament material in the wider OT, which protests individual and communal suffering as either disproportionate or unjust. The placement of the text, just before the stories of Ruth and Hannah, reinforces the question: clearly not all Israel had deserted Yahweh; is punishment of the entire nation therefore fair, given it often impacts the most vulnerable Israelites who have little input into the shaping of national identity? How does national relationship with Yahweh relate to individual relationship? Different concepts of the individual–group relationship partly underlie the contemporary unease here; yet the text itself bears the seeds of the question and through Ruth and Hannah offers both a corrective to the sweeping statement of collective responsibility and a window onto Yahweh's relationship to individuals rather than just Yahweh–Israel. The divine response of compassion for suffering, even when this suffering is self-inflicted, prompts a redefinition of 'justice' as more than retribution or punishment, towards an account that includes a recognition of human frailty and the necessity of grace for true transformation and lasting change. A mechanistic framework on its own would have failed to engage with issues of social power, responsibility, oppression and victimization. Judges instead offers a stinging critique of the misuse of political power and its impact on the nation, while reconceptualizing divine power in ways that do not mimic hegemonic masculinity, but respect the freedom and integrity of the other and, crucially, highlight the vulnerability of Yahweh as a God who can be misused and grieved by his people, a picture that will bloom to its full extent in the Gospels. Biblical justice is deeply relational, embedded within social networks, and this prevents it from ever being reduced to individual accounts. Maintaining justice is therefore a product of joint human–divine deliberations and action. This moves humans away from being merely acted upon by a superior power to having a degree of reciprocity and influence, including the ability to question Yahweh's actions. The people of Judges, however, never embrace a true reciprocal covenantal relationship.

In the end, 'there was no king in Israel; everyone did what was right in their own eyes'. For some, 'right' was following Yahweh as king and seeking to live well; but this was an individual choice, rather than an attitude of the nation as a whole. Judges therefore shows the flaws of individualized religion: spirituality may be possible at a personal level, but for justice to be possible there needs to be a collective movement that shapes the life of the whole community. Justice is not something one person can achieve independently, but a shape of life for the community. The refrain draws attention to the recurrent problem Israel faces in seeking to be both a political nation and the people of Yahweh; as Israel's story progresses, and the OT moves into the New, the communal nature of faith remains and so does its political import, yet it becomes increasingly distinct from actual political structures. Even as early as the time of the Judges, the identity of the nation is problematized: what does it mean to be the people of Yahweh? How do human politics and covenantal identity relate? The subtext of the inclusion of Gentiles, and of Israel behaving as Canaan, makes clear that the two are not coterminous. Covenantal faith is inherently political because it sets a radically new vision that claims the whole life of a community, and acknowledges a king above any human ruler. Yet it does not prescribe a specific political system, even if it gives tools to assess the different configurations of national organization that Israel experiments with. What Judges makes abundantly clear is that the configuration of power per se does not guarantee flourishing, or covenantal faithfulness, and that all human authorities, however configured, are subject to Yahweh's judgement. Only the kingship of Yahweh has the power to transform frail and fallen human communities into ones where justice and mercy flourish. Yet this kingship is deeply challenging in setting out a completely alternative vision: one where human beings recognize and accept the kingship of Yahweh and its inherently radical claim to redefine power and human values. In this call to recognize the fallenness and limitations of humanity, held together with an offer of grace, Judges takes its place as a profoundly prophetic book, challenging its readers to read it as an account of the human condition, the nature of God, and the call to renewed partnership with Yahweh to be worked out in each time and place.

9

The Refrain (21.25)

Judges closes with the refrain, weaving together the meaning and main threads of the entire book: leadership and lack of leadership, the breakdown of the covenant that held Israel together by enabling them to see the world through the eyes of Yahweh, the individualization of choice, morality and life in the world. Israel, the body politic, is fragmented and dismembered by the people's actions. It is not merely fragmented into tribes, but every level of social belonging suffers from tears and dysfunction: the nation, the tribe, the clan, the town, the household, the couples. In a world where everyone does what is right in their own eyes, only individuals are left, amidst the ruins of community. Together with individualization comes the victimization of those with less power, while others stand by, because everyone's personal choices have become paramount. So the passivity of the community in chapter 19, when no one tries to defend, look for or tend to the *pilegeš*, is re-enacted by the entire congregation in chapter 21, as all accept the logic of the elders' plans. What was private in 19 becomes legitimized and public in 21. The chapters clearly work together to illustrate the relationship between the public and the private in the life of Israel, a relationship articulated forcefully in the refrain's conjunction of a comment on kingship and one on personal choice. By chapter 21, Yahweh is completely absent; referred to, but not interacted with. The Israelites do not want or seek his counsel or advice. They do not care about his laws. Even victims do not ask for his help. So Yahweh bows out, in response to their wishes, so that truly, 'in Israel there was no king and everyone did what seemed right in their own eyes'.

As Judges ends …

The people of Israel

Throughout Judges, who is part of Israel and who is not has shifted and reconfigured itself with each episode, non-Israelites and those on the margins weaving in and out of stories and different tribes representing 'all Israel'. An overall sense of national identity comes through with the frequent use of 'Israel', pan-Israelite expressions, the recurrent naming of the tribes that compose the nation, and Israel as '*the* people'. As the book progresses, tensions mount between tribes, with a number of intra-Israelite conflicts (Gideon–Ephraim, Jephthah–Ephraim, Samson–Judah) which culminate in all-out war in 20—21. Simultaneously, their shared covenantal identity crumbles, highlighting the difficulty of embodying the identity gifted by Yahweh on Sinai and making it a lived reality. Moving around Canaan, Israel's lived experience is one of struggle with local residents, or interweaving lives with an ethically less demanding culture.

By 19—21, characters reveal a sense of who Israel 'should' be, but this is divorced from Yahweh. The Levite's expectation of Israel is that people welcome their kin and respect a Levite by recognizing his public status. The tribes as a whole have expectations that 'such a thing' should not define Israel, but what 'such a thing' is remains ambiguous. The Levite accomplishes what has never happened since Joshua: bringing all the tribes together for one purpose. Except that it is the wrong purpose, and one tribe is excluded. The final three chapters, however, create a sense of all the people, the sojourners, the aliens, the disparate tribes, coming together and their separate, local identities merging into one as Israel acts 'as one man'. Local identities and filiation are no longer acknowledged, they are simply, 'the sons of Israel'. Identity is no longer defined over and against pagan nations, but over and against Benjamin. While the effect is to portray the whole of Israel assembled, this national identity only applies to some: women, children and non-warriors are not included. The construction of public identity is achieved by a sub-section of Israel and reflected back onto the whole. Only men who participate in active military decision-making and action have the power to define who 'Israel' should be – another aspect of hegemonic masculinity. This theoretical identity is then enforced in ways that take Israel further from covenantal identity, to punish one of their own instead of occupying the land.

That this identity is theoretical is shown in Israel's fragmentation – with the Benjaminites, with Jabesh-Gilead, with Shiloh. At every level a gap opens between Israel's concept of who it is and its performance of identity. At one level they see themselves as the people who came out of Egypt and whose allegiance is to their tribal god; the ideal narrative is enshrined in Exodus, yet it is not the narrative that shapes Judges 19—21. They refer little to Yahweh, often not by name, and seek no reciprocal relationship with Yahweh. Instead, they seek his reinforcing of their tribal/national identity, giving them victory because they are Israel, rather than because their cause is just. A large fissure looms between belief and ethics, and the question of who this God is they are praying to – Yahweh or idol. The Israelites find that identity is more complex than they had thought, and cannot be simply chosen or defined at will; choosing to cut off Benjamin seemed easy, yet provoked a deeper crisis. Regardless of Benjamin's actions, they are still 'our brothers' in 21.6. The identity of Israel is constituted relationally and therefore cannot be changed unilaterally – though the people ignore the fact and reproduce the pattern with Jabesh-Gilead. The repetition of the 'solution' suggests a gradual collapse of the notion of ethnicity and ethnic boundaries in the conscious mind of the Israelites, as it becomes difficult to distinguish between Israelite and non-Israelite, a distinction further blurred with mention of Shiloh (21.12), located 'in the land of Canaan'. Israel had a 'camp' there; it is deeply ironic that the locus of the 'solution' to restoring Israelite identity should be 'in the land of Canaan'.

By the end of 21, Israel papers over the cracks with an idealized view of perfect Israel, as the 12 tribes together as one nation each go back to their inheritance. The return to the inheritance marks another feature of identity – the identification with the land and its layout. Until chapter 19, the explicit threat that faces Israel is losing the land to external threat. In 19 the threat is internal; the threat from Leviticus lies under the surface: should they not obey the commandments, and the land be defiled, the land would 'vomit them out' (Lev. 18.25, 28; 20.22). The risk of losing the land that shapes their identity is both external and internal; chapters 19—21 reveal the sad irony that the people have failed all along to realize that external threats are let loose because they had departed from the covenant in the first place. In 19—21, on the surface, the people start to address the internal threat, the evil in their midst; yet their lack of repentance, their failure to turn to Yahweh and the re-enactment of 19 into 21 shows that their perception of what constitutes evil and how to address it is utterly mistaken. The people prove themselves to be more un-Israelite than ever, despite focusing on a perceived ideal of a pure national identity.

Individualism and victimization

One of the most salient themes in Judges is the exploration of justice and injustice. The further that the people move from the covenant, the more that vulnerable members are victimized: children suffer from dysfunctional family dynamics (Abimelech and Jephthah) and repeat the cycle of violence towards others; women suffer particular violence at the hand of men close to them (Jephthah's daughter, Samson's wife, the *pilegeš*). The stronger the sense of individual choice in matters of ethics, the less space there is for individuals to flourish. In a text that carefully depicts individuals, with a plethora of names, it is striking that individuals increasingly lose their names, in line with their status and power. By the final chapter, no one has a name.

Feminist critics have argued that the namelessness of women belies their apparent centrality in Judges (Brenner, 1993); however, the argument fails to account for the equal namelessness of male characters. Losing identity by losing one's name shows that dehumanization starts with the most vulnerable (young women like Jephthah's daughter), but progressively spreads to all because no one is safe when everyone does 'what is right in their own eyes'. The woman of Judges 19 is a nameless victim whose community has failed her twice: first by allowing her to be brutalized, second by failing to remember her. The men have been equally, though differently, failed, because namelessness allows them to hide and eschew responsibility; an entire community has failed to name them as perpetrators and is thereby complicit. The pervasive namelessness begs the reader to ask questions of the entire community, rather than locate responsibility on specific individuals, as well as ask how we today remember and bear witness to atrocious crimes. Anonymity in Judges functions as an indicator of the gradual loss of personhood and nationhood. In a world where everyone does 'what is right in their own eyes', there is no room for holding common values and processes that protect the rights of individuals and households. Paradoxically, the extreme individualism of the epilogue leads to a loss of the individual, symbolized by the descent into namelessness.

Sexual and gender violence

One of the greatest gifts of the book of Judges is that it enables us to speak of sexual and gender violence as a theological matter. It would be easy to dismiss this thread as to do with history, culture and sociology – and many have done so. However, gender and its link to violence is a sustained focus in Judges, made part of a sacred text that draws attention to the deterioration of gender relations as interwoven with socio-political matters, an approach which reflects the holistic nature of covenantal life. Sexual transgression is set as a theme in the opening verses of chapter 19, as the *pilegeš* commits *zānah*. Associating her with *zānah* creates a second level of transgression because Levites are forbidden to marry loose women/prostitutes (*'iššāh zōnāh*) or woman who have been defiled (Leviticus 21.7). By 'pimping' the *pilegeš* to the crowd and allowing her to be 'defiled' by others, the Levite effectively transgresses against his own identity. Other characters follow suit: the old man participates in the rape by offering her to the crowd, while the men of Gibeah rape another man's partner. The circle of responsibility and participation in the transgression widens as Benjamin sides with the culprits and the whole of Israel condones the use of force to find brides for Benjamin (who will then be doubly guilty). The entire nation is portrayed as one where sexuality has gone awry and the very fabric of society, the household, is threatened. Sexuality has become about appropriating the Other. When the Levite is Other in Gibeah, the men attempt to 'know' him, to possess him. As the *pilegeš* is doubly othered, as female and non-Benjaminite, she is known by the men and thrown even further into otherness, so that the Levite dismembers her dead body (dead, therefore impure, therefore quintessentially Other) and sends it out to Israel just as he had sent her out to the men of Gibeah. The dismemberment is intensely violent, intimate and sexualized. As the people of Jabesh-Gilead are declared traitors and put to the ban, their women's sexuality is pored over and either appropriated or erased; and the women of Shiloh are watched from a hidden place, appropriated visually before being seized physically. Sexuality and power over the Other are inseparable here.

The wider canon helps to assess and theologize the events of 19—21. Two other developed rape narratives are the rape of Dinah (Gen. 34) and the rape of Tamar (2 Sam. 13). Legal material is scant, and sits within the wider framework of sexuality as primarily a male experience (Aschkenasy, 1986, p. 124). Laws to do with what we would today consider to be rape focus primarily on men's rights and the proper re-ordering of households after a breach has occurred (Deut. 22.23–30).[1] Legal texts alone, however, open only a small window on attitudes to sexual violence. While there is not a single Hebrew word to translate rape, a nexus of terms consistently appears to mark out forcible sexual activity: the verb *'innāh* that denotes humiliation and defilement; terms to do with force; *nəbālāh*; and a reflection that such a thing should not happen. In form-

1 For a more detailed exploration of rape in the Hebrew Bible, see Gravett, 2004; Hamley, 2019, pp. 220–3; Scholz, 2010; Schroeder, 2007; van Wolde, 2002; Yamada, 2008.

ing a parallel between 19, where this nexus is present, and 21, where it is not, enables a widening of perspective that frames 21 as an incident of sexual violence. More widely, narratives of rape all lead to conflict and disproportionate violence, because the rape reveals much deeper tears within the social fabric of a world dominated by hegemonic masculinity. Within this wider framework, what are we to make of Yahweh's silence and withdrawal at the end of Judges? Yahweh's response may be a refusal to endorse masculinist responses: in a world dominated by violence and totalitarian aspirations, would a response of power be anything but replicating, and thereby identifying with, hegemonic masculinity? To some degree, Yahweh is caught in the web of the logic and grammar of the violent, hegemonic warrior discourse, so that the only response possible is a negative one: either enter this discourse or withdraw and be silent – thereby identifying with the other silent members of the story. Withdrawing when one has the power to change the course of events is problematic, yet identifying with victims may be less problematic than using the language and weapons of the oppressor. This withdrawal of divine presence then needs to be read canonically so that the apparent powerlessness and silence of Yahweh may be seen not as final, but as part of a pattern of relating to power differently, culminating in Jesus Christ, and bringing transformation through relationship and the choice of making himself vulnerable by walking alongside human beings, rather than overpowering them.

Bibliography

Abadie, P., 2011, *Des Héros Peu Ordinaires. Théologie et Histoire dans le Livre des Juges*, Paris: Les Editions du Cerf.

Amit, Y., 1989, 'The Story of Ehud (Judges 3.12–30): The Form and the Message', in C. J. Exum (ed.), *Signs and Wonders: Biblical Texts in Literary Focus*, Semeia Studies, Atlanta, GA: Scholars, pp. 97–121.

Amit, Y., 1999, *The Book of Judges: The Art of Editing*, Boston, MA: Brill.

Aschkenasy, N., 1986, *Eve's journey: Feminine Images in Hebraic Literary Tradition,* Philadelphia, PA: University of Pennsylvania Press.

Assis, E., 2005, *Self-Interest or Communal Interest: An Ideology of Leadership in the Gideon, Abimelech and Jephthah Narratives (Judg 6–12)*, Vetus Testamentum Supplements 106, Leiden: Brill.

Auld, A. G., 1984, *Joshua, Judges and Ruth*, Louisville, KY: Westminster John Knox Press.

Bach, A., 1998, 'Re-reading the Body Politic: Women and Violence in Judges 21', *Biblical Interpretation*, 6(1), pp. 1–19.

Bal, M., 1988a, *Death and Dissymmetry. The Politics of Coherence in the Book of Judges*, Chicago, IL: University of Chicago Press.

Bal, M., 1988b, 'The Rape of Narrative and the Narrative of Rape: Speech Acts and Body Language in Judges', in E. Scarry (ed.), *Selected Papers from the English Institute*, Baltimore, MD: Johns Hopkins University Press, pp. 1–32.

Beldman, D. J. H., 2020, *Judges, Two Horizons Old Testament Commentaries*, Grand Rapids, MI: Wm B. Eerdmans.

Berman, J., 2004, *Narrative Analogy in the Hebrew Bible: Battle Stories and their Equivalent Non-battle Narratives*, Vetus Testamentum Supplements 103, Leiden: Brill.

Berquist, J. L., 2002, *Controlling Corporeality: The Body and the Household in Ancient Israel*, Piscataway, NJ: Rutgers University Press.

Biddle, M. E., 2012, *Reading Judges. A Literary and Theological Commentary*, Macon, GA: Smith and Helwys.

Bird, P. A., 1997, *Mistaken Identities: Women and Gender in Ancient Israel*, Minneapolis, MN: Fortress Press.

Block, D. I., 1999, *Judges, Ruth. The New American Commentary. An Exegetical and Theological Exposition of Holy Scripture. Vol. 6*, Nashville, TN: B&H.

Bohmbach, K. G., 1999, 'Conventions/Contraventions: The Meanings of Public and Private for the Judges 19 Concubine', *Journal for the Study of the Old Testament* 83, pp. 83–98.

Boling, R. G., 1975, *Judges. Anchor Bible Commentaries*, New York: Doubleday.

Bonfiglio, R. P., 2013, 'Choosing Sides in Judges 4–5: Rethinking Representations of Jael', in A. Brenner and G. A. Yee (eds), *Joshua and Judges. Texts and Contexts*, Minneapolis, MN: Fortress Press, pp. 161–73.

Bowman, R. G., 1995, 'Narrative Criticism: Human Purpose in Conflict with Divine Presence', in G. A. Yee (ed.), *Judges and Method. New Approaches in Biblical Studies*, Minneapolis, MN: Fortress Press, pp. 17–44.

Brenner, A., 1993, 'A Triangle and a Rhombus in Narrative Structure: A Proposed Integrated Reading of Judges 4 and 5', in A. Brenner (ed.), *Judges. A Feminist Companion to the Bible (First Series)*, Sheffield: Sheffield Academic Press, pp. 98–109.

Brettler, M. Z., 2002, *The Book of Judges*, London: Routledge.

Brueggemann, W., 1994, *A Social Reading of the Old Testament: Prophetic Approaches to Israel's Common Life*, edited by Patrick D. Miller, Minneapolis, MN: Fortress.

Brueggemann, W., 2018, *The Prophetic Imagination, 40th Anniversary Edition*, Minneapolis, MN: Fortress.

Butler, T. C., 2009, *Judges, World Biblical Commentary*, Nashville/Dallas: Thomas Nelson.

Carman, J., 2019, 'Abimelech the Manly Man? Judges 9.1–57 and the Performance of Hegemonic Masculinity', *Journal for the Study of the Old Testament* 43.3, pp. 301–16.

Chisholm, R. B., 2010, 'The Ethical Challenge of Jephtha's Fulfilled Vow', *Bibliotheca Sacra* 167, pp. 402–22.

Chisholm, R. B., 2013, *A Commentary on Judges and Ruth. Kregel Exegetical Library*, Grand Rapids, MI: Kregel Publications.

Christianson, E. S., 2003, 'A Fistful of Shekels: Scrutinizing Ehud's Entertaining Violence (Judges 3:12–30)', *Biblical Interpretation* 11.1, pp. 53–78.

Conway, M. L., 2019, *Judging the Judges: A Narrative Appraisal Analysis*, Winona Lake, IN: Eisenbrauns.

Creach, J. F. D., 2013, *Violence in Scripture. Interpretation: Resources for the Use of Scripture in the Church*, Louisville, KY: Westminster John Knox.

DeMaris, R. E. and C. S. Leeb, 2005, 'Judges – (Dis)Honor and Ritual Enactment: the Jephthah Story: Judges 10:16–12:1', in P. Esler (ed.),

Ancient Israel: The Old Testament in Its Social Context, Minneapolis, MN: Fortress, pp. 177–90.

Edenburg, C., 2016, *Dismembering the Whole. Composition and Purposes of Judges 19–21*, Atlanta, GA: SBL Press.

Exum, J. C., 1993, 'On Judges 11', in A. Brenner (ed.), *Judges. A Feminist Companion to the Bible (First Series)*, Sheffield: Sheffield Academic Press, pp. 131–44.

Fewell, D. N., 1995, 'Deconstructive Criticism: Achsah and the (E)razed City of Writing', in Gale A. Yee (ed.), *Judges and Method. New Approaches in Biblical Studies*, Minneapolis, MN: Fortress Press, pp. 119–45.

Fewell, D. N. and D. M. Gunn, 1990, 'Controlling Perspectives. Women, Men, and the Authority of Violence in Judges 4 & 5', *Journal of the American Academy of Religion* 53 (3), pp. 389–411.

Fewell, D. N. and D. M. Gunn, 1993, *Gender, Power and Promise: The Subject of the Bible's First Story*, Nashville, TN: Abingdon.

Fokkelman, J. P., 1992, 'Structural Remarks on Judges 9 and Judges 19', in M. Fishbane, E. Tov and W. W. Fields (eds), *Sha'arei Talmon: Studies in the Bible, Qumran, and Ancient Near East Presented to Shemaryahu Talmon*, Winona Lake, IN: Eisenbrauns, pp. 33–45.

Frolov, S., 2012, *Judges*, Grand Rapids, MI: Eerdmans.

Frolov, S. and M. Stetckevich, 2019, 'Repentance in Judges: Assessing the Reassessment', *Hebrew Studies* 60, pp. 129–39.

Frymer-Kensky, T., 1998, 'Virginity in the Bible', in V. H. Matthews, B. M. Levinson, and T. Frymer-Kensky (eds), *Gender and Law in the Hebrew Bible and the Ancient Near East*, Sheffield: Sheffield Academic Press, pp. 79–96.

García Bachmann, M. L., 2013, *Women at Work in the Deuteronomistic History*, Atlanta, GA: SBL.

García Bachmann, M. L., 2018, *Judges, Wisdom Commentary*, Collegeville, MN: Liturgical Press.

Gillmayr-Bucher, S., 2009, 'Framework and Discourse in the Book of Judges', *Journal of Biblical Literature* 128(4), pp. 687–702.

Gravett, S., 2004, 'Reading "Rape" in the Hebrew Bible: A Consideration of Language', *Journal for the Study of the Old Testament* 28.3, pp. 279–99.

Greenspahn, F. E., 1986, 'The Theology of the Framework of Judges', *Vetus Testamentum* 36.4, pp. 385–96.

Greves, A. M., 2016, 'Daughter of Courage: Reading Judges 11 with a Feminist Pentecostal Hermeneutic', *Journal of Pentecostal Theology* 25, pp. 151–67.

Haddox, S. E., 2016, 'Masculinity Studies of the Hebrew Bible: The First Two Decades', *Currents in Biblical Research* 14.2, pp. 176–206.

Halpern, B., 1992, *The First Historians: The Hebrew Bible and History*, Philadelphia, PA: Pennsylvania State University Press.

Hamley, I., 2015, 'What's the Matter with "Playing the Harlot"? The Meaning of זנה in Judges 19.2', *Tyndale Bulletin* 66.1, pp. 41–61.

Hamley, I., 2017, 'Dis(re)membered and Unaccounted for: פילגש in the Hebrew Bible', *Journal for the Study of the Old Testament*, 42.4, pp. 415–34.

Hamley, I., 2019, *Unspeakable Things Unspoken: Otherness, Gender and Victimisation in Judges 19–21*, Eugene, OR: Wipf and Stock.

Hanselman, S. W., 1989, 'Narrative Theory, Ideology, and Transformation in Judges 4', in M. Bal (ed.), *Anti-Covenant: Counter-reading Women's Lives in the Hebrew Bible* (Bible and Literature, 22), Sheffield: Almond Press, pp. 95–111.

Havrelock, R., 2008, 'The Myth of Birthing the Hero: Heroic Barrenness in the Hebrew Bible', *Biblical Interpretation* 16, pp. 154–78.

Heller, R. L., 2011, *Conversations with Scripture: The Book of Judges*, New York/Harrisburg: Morehouse.

Hoffman, Y., 1999, 'The Deuteronomistic Concept of the *HEREM*', *Zeitschrift fur die Altestamenliche Wissenschafaft* 111, pp. 196–210.

Janzen, D., 2005, 'Why the Deuteronomist Told about the Sacrifice of Jephthah's Daughter', *Journal for the Study of the Old Testament* 29.3, pp. 339–57.

Johnson, B. J. M., 2010, 'What Type of Son is Samson? Reading Judges 13 as a Biblical Type-Scene', *Journal of the Evangelical Theological Society* 53.2, pp. 269–86.

Jones-Warsaw, K., 1993, 'Towards a Womanist Hermeneutic: A Reading of Judges 19–21', in A. Brenner (ed.), *Judges. A Feminist Companion to the Bible (First Series)*, Sheffield: Sheffield Academic Press, pp. 172–86.

Kamrada, D. G., 2010, '"Strangers to One Another": The Motif of Strangeness in the Jephthah-Cycle' in G. Xeravits and J. Dusek (eds), *The Stranger in Ancient and Mediaeval Jewish Tradition*, Berlin: Walter de Gruyter, pp. 16–35.

Kawashima, R., 2011, 'Could a Woman say "No" in Biblical Israel? On the Genealogy of Legal Status in Biblical Law and Literature', *Association for Jewish Studies Review* 35.1, pp. 1–22.

Kelle, B. E., 2020, *The Bible and Moral Injury: Reading Scripture alongside War's Unseen Wounds*, Nashville, TN: Abingdon.

Klein, L. R., 1989, *The Triumph of Irony in the Book of Judges*, Sheffield: Almond Press.

Klein, L. R., 1993, 'The Book of Judges: Paradigm and Deviation in images of Women', in A. Brenner (ed.), *Judges. A Feminist Companion to the Bible (First Series)*, Sheffield: Sheffield Academic Press, pp. 55–71.

Klein, L. R., 2003, *From Deborah to Esther: Sexual Politics in the Hebrew Bible*, Minneapolis, MN: Fortress Press.

Klingbeil, G. A., 1997 'מס' (#4989), in W. A. Van Gemeren (ed.), *New International Dictionary of Old Testament Theology and Exegesis* (5 vols.), Grand Rapids, MI: Zondervan, vol. 2, pp. 992–5.

Kruger, P. A., 1997, 'פלא' (#7098), in W. A. Van Gemeren (ed.), *New International Dictionary of Old Testament Theology and Exegesis* (5 vols.), Grand Rapids, MI: Zondervan, vol. 3, pp. 615–17.

Lapsley, J. E., 2005, *Whispering the Word: Hearing Women's Stories in the Old Testament*, Louisville, KY: Westminster John Knox.

Lemos, T. M., 2006, 'Shame and Mutilation of Enemies in the Hebrew Bible', *Journal of Biblical Literature* 125.2, pp. 225–41.

Lynch, M. J., 2020, *Portraying Violence in the Hebrew Bible. A Literary and Cultural Study*, Cambridge: Cambridge University Press.

Mandolfo, C., 2019, 'Women, Violence, and the Bible: The Story of Jael and Sisera as a Case Study', *Biblical Interpretation* 27, pp. 340–53.

McCann, J. C., 2002, *Judges. Interpretation Series*, Louisville, KY: John Knox Press.

Moore, G. F., 1985, *A Critical and Exegetical Commentary on Judges*, Edinburgh: T&T Clark (original edition pre-1923).

Morschauser, S., 2003, 'Hospitality, Hostiles and Hostages: On the Legal Background to Genesis 19:1–9', *Journal for the Study of the Old Testament* 27, pp. 461–85.

Mullen, E. T., 1982, 'The "Minor Judges": Some Literary and Historical Considerations', *Catholic Biblical Quarterly* 44, pp. 185–201.

Mullen, E. T., 1993, *Narrative History and Ethnic Boundaries: The Deuteronomistic Historian and the Creation of Israelite National Identity*, SBL Semeia Studies, Atlanta, GA: Scholars.

Niditch, S., 1993, *War in the Hebrew Bible. A Study in the Ethics of Violence*, Oxford: Oxford University Press.

Niditch, S., 2008, *Judges, A Commentary, The Old Testament Library*, Louisville, KY: Westminster John Knox Press.

O'Connell, R. H., 1995, *The Rhetoric of the Book of Judges*, Leiden: Brill.

Oeste, G., 2010, 'Butchered Brothers and Betrayed Families: Degenerating Kinship Structures in the Book of Judges', *Journal for the Study of the Old Testament* 35, pp. 295–316.

Oeste, G., 2011, *Legitimacy, Illegitimacy, and the Right to Rule: Windows on Abimelech's Rise and Demise in Judges 9* (LHBOTS 546), New York: T&T Clark.

Olyan, S. M., 2013, 'The Roles of Kin and Fictive Kin in Biblical Representations of Death Rituals', in A. Rainer (ed.), *Family and Household Religion: Towards a Synthesis of Old Testament Studies, Archaeology, Epigraphy, and Cultural Studies*, Winona Lake, IN: Eisenbrauns, pp. 251–63.

Park, S., 2015, 'Left-Handed Benjaminites and the Shadow of Saul', *Journal of Biblical Literature* 134.4, pp. 701–20.

Peels, H. G. L., 1997, 'נקם' (#5933), in W. A. Van Gemeren (ed.), *New International Dictionary of Old Testament Theology and Exegesis* (5 vols.), Grand Rapids, MI: Zondervan, vol. 3, pp. 152–4.

Penchansky, D., 1992, 'Staying the Night: Intertextuality in Genesis and Judges', in D. N. Fewell (ed.), *Reading Between Texts: Intertextuality and the Hebrew Bible*, Louisville, KY: Westminster/John Knox, pp. 77–88.

Polzin, R., 1980, *Moses and the Deuteronomist. A Literary Study of the Deuteronomistic History, Part 1: Deuteronomy, Joshua, Judges*, New York: The Seabury Press.

Rasmussen, R. C., 1989, 'Deborah the Woman Warrior', in M. Bal (ed.), *Anti-Covenant: Counter-reading Women's Lives in the Hebrew Bible*, Bible and Literature 22, Sheffield: Almond Press, pp. 79–93.

Reeder, C. A., 2012, *The Enemy in the Household: Family Violence in Deuteronomy and Beyond*, Grand Rapids, MI: Baker Academic.

Schneider, T. J., 1999, *Judges, Berit Olam*, Collegeville, MN: Liturgical Press.

Scholz, S., 2010, *Sacred Witness: Rape in the Hebrew Bible*, Minneapolis, MN: Fortress.

Schroeder, J. A., 2007, *Dinah's Lament: The Biblical Legacy of Sexual Violence in Christian Interpretation*, Minneapolis, MN: Augsburg Fortress.

Schultz, R., 1997, 'שפט' (#9149), in W. A. Van Gemeren (ed.), *New International Dictionary of Old Testament Theology and Exegesis* (5 vols.), Grand Rapids, MI: Zondervan, vol. 4, pp. 213–20.

Segal, A. F., 2012, *Sinning in the Hebrew Bible: How the Worst Stories Speak for its Truth*, New York, NY: Columbia University Press.

Smit, L. A., 2018, 'Judges', in L. A. Smit and S. E. Fowl, *Judges and Ruth, Brazos Theological Commentary on the Bible*, Grand Rapids, MI: Brazos Press, pp. 3–195.

Soggin, J. A., 1981, *Judges*, Old Testament Library, London: Westminster John Knox Press.

Stern, P. D., 1991, *The Biblical* Herem: *A Window on Israel's Religious Experience*, Atlanta, GA: Scholars' Press.

Stone, K., 1996, *Sex, Honor and Power in the Deuteronomistic History*, Sheffield: Sheffield Academic Press.

Thelle, R. I., 2019, 'Matrices of motherhood in Judges 5', *Journal for the Study of the Old Testament* 43.3, pp. 436–52.

Trible, P., 2002, *Texts of Terror. Literary-Feminist Readings of Biblical Narratives*, London: SCM Press.

van Wolde, E. J., 2002, Does '*innâ* Denote Rape? A Semantic Analysis of a Controversial Word, *Vetus Testamentum* 52.4, pp. 528–44.

Webb, B. G., 1987, *The Book of the Judges: An Integrated Reading*, Eugene, OR: Wipf & Stock.

Webb, B. G., 2012, *Judges, NICOT*, Grand Rapids, MI: Wm B. Eerdmans Publishing Company.

Wong, G. T. K., 2006, *Compositional Strategy of the Book of Judges: An Inductive, Rhetorical Study* (Vetus Testamentum Supplements), Leiden: Brill.

Wright, J. L., 2015, 'Urbicide: The Ritualized Killing of Cities in the Ancient Near East', in S. Olyan (ed.), *Ritual Violence in the Hebrew Bible: New Perspectives*, Oxford: Oxford University Press, pp. 147–66.

Yamada, F., 2008, *Configurations of Rape in the Hebrew Bible*, New York, NY: Peter Lang.

Index of Biblical References

Index of Names and Subjects

CPSIA information can be obtained
at www.ICGtesting.com
Printed in the USA
LVHW032059250821
696089LV00011B/1310